Contents

6   *Community Studies*

Australian Community Studies
and Beyond

Studies in Society

A series edited by Ronald Wild which sets out to cover the major topics in Australasian sociology. The books will not be 'readers', but original works —some will cover new ground and present original research, some will provide an overview and synthesis of source materials and existing research, all will be important reading for students of sociology.

Titles include:
  Cities Unlimited Kilmartin and Thorns
  The Migrant Presence Martin
  Social Stratification in Australia Wild
  Race, Class and Rebellion in the South Pacific Mamak and Ali
  Children and Families in Australia Burns and Goodnow
  Johnsonville Pearson

Studies in Society: 7
Series editor: Ronald Wild

Australian Community Studies and Beyond

R.A. WILD
Department of Sociology, La Trobe University, Melbourne

Sydney
George Allen & Unwin
London Boston

First published in 1981 by
George Allen & Unwin Australia Pty Ltd
8 Napier Street
North Sydney NSW 2060

This book is copyright under the Berne Convention. All rights
are reserved. Apart from any fair dealing for the purpose of
private study, research, criticism or review, as permitted under
the Copyright Act, 1956, no part of this publication may be
reproduced, stored in a retrieval system, or transmitted, in any
form or by any means, electronic, electrical, chemical,
mechanical, optical, photocopying, recording or otherwise,
without the prior permission of the copyright owner. Inquiries
should be addressed to the publishers.

© R.A. Wild 1981

National Library of Australia
Cataloguing-in-Publication entry:

Wild, R.A. (Ronald Arthur)
  Australian community studies and beyond.

  Bibliography.
  Includes indexes.
  ISBN 0 86861 219 7.
  ISBN 0 86861 227 8. (pbk.).

  1. Community. I. Title. (Series: studies in society (Sydney, N.S.W.);
no. 8).

307

QUEEN MARY
COLLEGE
LIBRARY

Printed in Singapore by Singapore National Printers Pte Ltd.

Preface

This book was conceived of, and is intended as, a textbook for
university students but it attempts to do more than present a series
of summaries of community studies. The book establishes three
basic models of community, argues for methodological pluralism in
the research process, interprets community studies from these perspectives, and, finally, indicates ways in which the study of community can be extended beyond traditional orientations.

Further, this book does not attempt to encompass everything
written on community in Australia, rather I have selected specific
studies that I consider important and of interest. The primary aim
is to provide the student with some in-depth examples and with new
ways of interpreting them in the hope that their new ideas and explorations in fieldwork will further advance our understanding of
Australian communities.

I wish to thank Patrick Gallagher for his constant encouragement both for this book and the series; Harry Oxley and David
Pearson for providing me with data on the background to their studies; and to the students of my first community studies class at La
Trobe University in 1980 who shared my enthusiasms for the usefulness of this most slippery of sociological concepts. My special
thanks go to the secretarial staff of the Department of Sociology at
La Trobe University who generously gave of their expertise, especially Julie Stayner who typed most of the manuscript.

R.A. Wild, Melbourne,
March, 1981.

For Nicolas, with love

1   Introduction

This book concerns the concept of community and those empirical investigations of particular places called community studies. More specifically it attempts to create closer, and therefore more fruitful, links between the theoretical concepts and empirical research in the field of community. First it is important to place community studies within the wider framework of sociology generally.

In the late 1960s, but more so in the 1970s, sociology experienced increasing fragmentation in basic theoretical orientations and methodological approaches. In the 1950s and early 1960s positivism held sway. By positivism I mean the assumption that the methodological procedures of natural science may be directly adapted to sociology and that the outcomes of sociological investigations can be formulated in terms parallel to natural science, that is, as law-like generalisations (Giddens, 1974: 3–4). Although community studies experienced a resurgence in the 1960s they were never fully accepted by the positivists who criticised them for resting on the observations of a single sociologist, not having systematic procedures, being unable to guarantee that another researcher would produce similar results, and not disentangling the observer's values from his or her data. In other words the positivists questioned the scientific validity of the community study method.

During the late 1960s and early 1970s positivism came under attack from both phenomenologists and neo-Marxists. The former followed Husserl's notion of phenomenology, an *a priori* investigation (rather than an empirical technique) of meanings which are seen as the objective logical elements in thought that are common to different minds. They concerned themselves with investigating the assumptions and meanings held and used by *individuals* in the process of going about everyday life. Those phenomenologists concerned with the sociology of knowledge emphasised the way in which commonsense knowledge about society feeds back, through social action, into the moulding of society. Others, called ethnomethodologists, concentrated on the unconscious routines by which people manage their interpersonal contacts in the trivial affairs of everyday life (see Schutz, 1967; Garfinkel, 1967).

Rex, in a brief paper called 'Threatening Theories', wrote,

> In Europe, phenomenology represents a revolt against not merely contemporary positivism, but more radically against the epistemology of Hume and Kant. Inevitably it shares with Hegel the rejection of Humean and Kantian skepticism and puts other forms of knowledge before science . . .
> So far as the American versions of phenomenological sociology are concerned, most of us suffer from a difficulty of a quite peculiar kind in understanding what they are saying, since the sentences which almost all ethnomethodologists use are cast in the reprehensible language and grammar of Harold Garfinkel. What they seem to be doing has its importance, for the construction of social reality — if it is to be completely understood — must involve understanding not only the major social structures based upon power, but also the social relations which are negotiated daily in simple contacts and the simple use of language. It is also useful, whenever the categories of sociology or of social practice become reified, to question them and to ask who is labeling who and how. But to consider *only* these questions and to imply that the more lasting structures are built up only from these fleeting ones is to misrepresent social reality and to trivialise it . . . Perhaps when phenomenologists begin to appreciate that what they are doing is part of a much larger whole they may be welcomed back into sociology and have their own important contribution to make. For the moment their influence is on the whole destructive. (1978: 49)

In a similar vein Giddens criticises phenomenologists for their 'crude voluntarism' and their 'retreat from institutional analysis' (1973: 15). In concentrating solely on trivial aspects of everyday life in which the individual supposedly shapes his or her phenomenal experience of social reality, phenomenologists have withdrawn from the basic issues involved in the study of macro-social structures and processes. Such an approach, as Giddens comments, 'simply abandon[s] the problems which have always been the major stimulus to the sociological imagination', (1973: 15) .

The second major attack on positivism came from the neo-Marxists, especially the critical theory of the Frankfurt School and the structural Marxism emanating from Louis Althusser in Paris (see Gouldner, 1980). Those of the Frankfurt School provided a critical theory of Marxism which opposed all forms of positivism, especially that variety stressing the possibility of value freedom in science. They exphasised Marx's early and more Hegelian writings concentrating on the more romantic and utopian elements. This approach led to a greater emphasis on existential rather than economic analysis, and consequently alienation rather than productivity became the central concept. Althusser and the French structuralists however took cognisance only of Marx's later writings. They argued that alienation was not a central concept for Marxism and contended that Marx had discarded the earlier Hegelian influences and had come to what Althusser calls a structuralist interpretation of society. Here deep structures centering on the mode of production, discoverable only by theoretical activity and not from empirical study, are believed to underlie, generate and thereby determine the phenomena that come under observation.

These two types of Marxism have pursued a different kind of activity to sociology. They are rather metaphysical sects which combine in complex and ambiguous ways metaphysics, science and politics. They are not as constrained as sociology must be by a sceptical distinction between propositions proven and understood and others not so proven and understood. Althusser's work has been described as doctrine, dogma or theology disguised as theory. (Thompson, 1978: 196) Further, it is a 'particularly obscure body of thought' (Bottomore, 1975: 72) whose 'development is described in a series of metaphysical assertions not themselves subject to test', (Rex, 1978: 48).The Frankfurt School in maintaining Lukác's notion of the inseparability of knowledge and political action argue that the sociologists cannot acquire knowledge from books or empirical data, for true knowledge is only revealed in the course of working class action to change society. In other words, only those who act politically find valid theories. As Rex comments, 'This view virtually rules the subject of sociology out of court' (1978: 48).

Neither phenomenology nor structural Marxism has much time for community studies. For the former, community sociologists are overly concerned with the institutional and organisational frameworks of localised social systems and do not pay sufficient attention to the perceptions held and meanings understood by individuals in their everyday interactions. For the latter, studying people with reference to specific localities is a fruitless exercise in 'abstracted empiricism' because the behaviour and beliefs of these people are determined by the 'laws of capital' which are found elsewhere.

Although community studies have always been on the margins of the major theoretical paradigms in sociology and are currently out of fashion 'the *genre* continues in fits and starts accompanied by, perhaps, a more realistic appraisal of their limits and possibilities',

(Newby, 1980: 78-9). The publishing dates of the studies described in this book, for example, span the years 1929-80. There are several reasons for the persistence of community studies. First, they allow the sociologist to get close to the data and to be able to observe situations first hand (Vidich, Bensman and Stein, 1964: x; Arensberg and Kimball, 1967: 30). They enable the sociologist to gain both an empathic understanding of relationships and situations and an intellectual level of explanation.

Second, there is often a personal quality in community studies. After all, the competent participant observer spends two years or more of his or her life living in the community. In this sense the research process is an important part of the sociologist's life and this is often reflected in the intimate connection between sociologists, their theories, methods and results and their intellectual development. This is a central theme in the later discussions of community studies in this book. These two points are part of the reason that community studies are relatively popular reading among undergraduate students and non-sociologists. They help to de-mystify part of the modern world for the educated layman and as Simpson remarks, 'the educated reading public outside the field accepts community studies as a contribution to social understanding in which sociologists excel in a distinctive way', (1965: 149).

Third, it is important to realise that community remains a reference point and source of social relationships for many people. Pearson is right when he suggests that, 'there has been a tendency for critics and defenders alike to treat "community" in a rather static manner. However defined, community is frequently depicted as an *object* which disappears with the passing of time — local becomes societal, communal becomes individual at a particular moment in history ...', but, 'strands of the community concept can be viewed as important processes which change in concert with the wider panorama of societal development' (1980: 148). Certainly for some, increasingly fewer social relationships are locality bound, nevertheless most people do not constantly move. In such situations there are patterns of locality-based relationships (as well as others) and they provide a source for interesting sociological questions. This, of course, does not mean that all sociological problems can be studied in a localised social system. Indeed it is one of the aims of this book to provide an assessment of the potentialities and limitations of community studies.

Fourth, community studies at their best are able to strike a valuable balance between specific content and generalisation, and between data and theoretical abstraction. In the social sciences, unlike the natural sciences, the more abstract and general the theory becomes the more devoid of content it appears. Sociology must always maintain a balance and an interaction between data and theory and community studies are able to fulfil this requirement (see Chapter 3).

Fifth, community studies are not either theoretically or methodologically exclusive. The positivists, phenomenologists and neo-Marxists all believe that they have discovered *the* method. 'No longer can there be only one style of social research with *one* method that is to be *the* method. Rather there are many', (Bell and Newby, 1977: 10). Reflections on community studies indicate that although participant observation is central, many different methods are used which include historical analysis, interviews, and random sample questionnaires, all of which allow for flexibility in interpreting the complex relationships between theory, method and data.

Finally, in the 1970s there has been a revival of the ideology of community. A desire to create a sense of belonging in the face of the impersonality generated by bureaucracy resulted in a revival of community values and contributed to the counter-culture and commune movements (see Chapter 8). Concerns with the environment, pollution and living simply contributed towards anti-urban, anti-industrial and anti-growth sentiments and led to a renewed desire to live in real (which usually means rural) communities. Community studies are in a good position to examine these developments both in terms of what they have managed to produce themselves and for what they are able to elucidate about wider societal structures and processes.

At this point I shall make my own theoretical position clear. The deterministic theories of phenomenology and neo-Marxism claim to explain a total reality. In my view a total reality cannot be objectively grasped by the human mind. Any view of the world must be limited and partial, and the meaning that it has is given to it in terms of the observer's values. This is especially clear in community studies and has been explored in such volumes as Vidich, Bensman's and Stein's *Reflections on Community Studies*; Hammond's *Sociologists at Work*: Bell's and Newby's *Doing Sociological Research*; and Bell's and Encel's *Inside the Whale*. This book continues this theme paying close attention to the background of, and the roles played by, the sociologists and the relationship of these matters to the substantive results. The sociologist's view of the world is, and can only be, formed and directed by what is of historical and cultural significance to him or her. This does not mean that sociologists impose their values on what they study, rather it calls attention to the relationship between those values and the patterns of relationships studied emphasising that sociologists must be aware of these connections and take them into account in the process of empirical investigation. It is for this reason that it is important to know what sociologists actually *do* in the process of fieldwork. Community studies are part of the empirical tradition of sociology and social anthropology. From this perspective theoretical models and propositions are examined and refined or rejected in terms of empirical data. Consequently, interpretations and explanations about social phenomena and their interrelations are necessarily limited and incomplete. Weber expressed this well when he argued that the social sciences have eternal youth:

> [for the] eternally onward flowing stream of culture brings new problems. . . . The history of the social sciences is and remains a continuous process passing from the attempt to order reality analytically through the construction of concepts — the dissolution of the analytical constructs so constructed through the expansion and shift of the scientific horizon — and the reformulation anew of concepts of the foundations thus transformed. It is not the error of the attempt to construct conceptual systems *in general* which is shown by this process — every science, every single descriptive history, operates with the conceptual stock-in-trade of its time. Rather, this process shows that in the cultural sciences concept-construction depends on the setting of the problem, and the latter varies with the content of culture itself. The relationship between concept and reality in the cultural sciences involves the transitoriness of all such syntheses. (1949: 104–6)

In Chapter 2 there are many attempts to define community. I shall not add to these definitional confusions. Instead I prefer to use various models of community in an attempt to develop some useful generalisations. There are four broad perspectives on community. First, community as geography or territory, that is, a finite and bounded physical location. Second, community as a local social system, that is as a locality based system of interrelated social institutions and relationships. Third, community as a particular kind of human association or relationship irrespective of location. For example, relationships of tradition may form the crucial tie that link together all Italians spread throughout Sydney. Fourth, community as ideology, that is, as an expression of what should be rather than what is or as Bell and Newby call it the good life (1974: xliii; see also 1976: 194; Pearson, 1980: 147–53). In any empirical situation all four expressions of community may well be complexly interrelated and any actual study may concentrate on one or more at the expense of the others. Towards the end of Chapter 2 I outline three models of community that encompass these major expressions of this concept.

Several themes run through this book. The first concerns the close but fluctuating relationship between theoretical constructs, methodological approaches and the substantive data. The ongoing interaction of these three areas describes the process of sociological research in community studies from the setting of the problems, through fieldwork, to the interpretation and explanation of the results. The second centres on the background to specific studies. Why they were done and from what perspectives gives us valuable insights into the whole *genre* of community studies. A third theme concentrates on what community sociologists actually *do* in the field and how they put their findings together. This sheds light on the actual process of research. Unfortunately the amount of information on these last two themes varies depending on what the authors have published about the background to their research although in some cases I have obtained extra material from personal communication. A fourth theme concerns recognising the limitations of the traditional community study and attempting to go beyond these by both comparative analysis and the development of broader models of community. This is pursued in recognition of the fact that community studies needs to be related more securely to some of the central problems of sociology as a whole, and thereby come into dialogue with a variety of theoretical debates.

It is always difficult when writing a book of this nature to decide which studies to discuss and which to leave out. My concentration on the anthropological tradition helped narrow my choice to one, albeit the major, branch of community studies. Those studies I have chosen I regard as the most important both theoretically and methodologically and they are the studies which have had the greatest impact on my thinking. Further, they represent a wide timespan and help to locate Australian community studies in terms of American and British developments.

In Chapter 2 I discuss theories and definitions of community and conclude with three models that are used to interpret some of the findings discussed later. Chapter 3 explores some of the major methodological issues surrounding community studies. The links established between theory, method and data are shown in operation in the discussions of specific studies. In Chapters 4, 5 and 6 I examine the empirical tradition of community studies in America, Britain and Australia. Here the emphasis is on the background to the studies, their substantive results and their relationships to the three models outlined in Chapter 2. Chapter 7 is concerned with extending community studies through comparative analysis in an attempt to establish wider level generalisations and to bring community issues into theoretical debates that are more central to sociology as a whole. Similarly in Chapter 8 I attempt to show the usefulness of broader models of community for interpreting issues on a wider scale than a localised social system. In the conclusion I discuss the limitations and potentialities of community studies and consider their role for the future. I emphasise that it remains the task of the community sociologist to describe, understand and analyse the community, and to generalise from the basis of the inter-relationship between empirical data and theoretical propositions.

2 Theories of Community

Community is one of the most notorious concepts in sociology. There is little agreement as to what is meant by the term. Some sociologists refuse to use it and refer to locality or village for the geographical aspect and to social system for the organisation of social relations. Others decline to define community and employ it in a deliberately vague way. Yet others carefully specify its meaning to suit their particular needs. Community has been applied to a wide range of social phenomena: it can refer to a geographically isolated small village, a dispersed ethnic group, a total institution such as a prison, those sharing such a common tie as residence or occupation, and to those who feel a sense of belonging together. Hillery (1955) compared 94 different definitions of community. He abstracted 16 attributes from these definitions which included territory, a sense of belonging, social interaction and common norms. He then isolated 22 combinations of the 16 attributes. For example, some stressed geographic locality, others locality and kinship, and still others locality, kinship and common norms. Hillery concluded that 70 out of the 94 definitions included territory, social interaction and common ties as important elements of community, but that all the definitions had only one factor in common — people.

Most of the definitions Hillery examined combined two or more variables and concluded with a composite view of community such as 'a collectivity of people who occupy a geographical area, who are engaged together in economic and political activities, who essentially constitute a self-governing social unit with some common values, and who experience feelings of belonging to one another'. It sounds an ideal state of affairs. It represents what Bell and Newby have called the 'good life'. Sociologists' 'definitions of community have ... incorporated their ideas of the good life. The result has been a confusion between what community *is* (empirical description) and what the sociologists have felt it *should be* (normative prescription)' (1974: xliv). This process has been an easy one for sociologists to slip into, first because community is an abstract concept and not an empirically observable entity such as a nuclear family or Aborigines, and second, because community has no unfavourable connotations.

Notions of community representing the good life have a long sociological pedigree and many contemporary composite definitions are directly related to the nineteenth century founding fathers of sociology. There is a long tradition which views social change as a gradual evolutionary movement from traditional community to modern society. Community and society, in this sense, are ideal types, that is, they are hypothetical constructs developed from empirically or historically recognisable components with the aim of making comparisons and developing theoretical explanations. Community and society are not descriptions of the real world. No permanent human association can be found which contains all the attributes of community and none of society, and vice versa. Reality is too diffuse, fluctuating and ambiguous to be grasped as a meaningful whole. Ideal types provide us with a way of talking and thinking about actual events, processes and experiences in a general and comparative manner. Perhaps the major problem concerning the ideal types of community and society is that sociologists put into them what they feel should be the case rather than what is the case.

Traditionalists such as Henry Maine, Emile Durkheim and Ferdinand Tonnies showed nostaglia for the old and disgust for the new. The coming of the new rational society meant the destruction of a stable environment and traditional patterns of authority. They mourned the impending decline of neighbourhood, family and kinship. For Maine it was a movement from the laws of status to the laws of contract; for Durkheim from mechanical solidarity to organic solidarity; and for Tonnies from *gemeinschaft* (community) to *gesellschaft* (society).

Maine argued that society had evolved from an ancient condition in which the family was dominant to a modern situation where the individual predominated. Using the legal system as an index of change he called the laws governing family norms *status* laws and those governing relations between individuals *contracts*. In traditional communities people's relationships were determined by status within the family, whereas in modern societies they were determined by individually agreed contracts (Maine, 1861).

One of Durkheim's primary concerns was to understand the conditions that produced social solidarity or settled community in society. He was concerned about the growth of anomie or normlessness in modern societies which he saw as destroying solidarity. He argued that in traditional societies with a simple division of labour and technology, a small population sharing a sense of belonging and with norms based on repressive laws, which both punished offenders and reinforced traditional morality, there was *mechanical solidarity*. For Durkheim modern society was characterised by a considerably larger population and, therefore, a greater density of relationships among its members, an increase in reciprocal demands centred on mutually agreed contracts and a much more specialised division of labour. The complexity of the modern situation was further enhanced by the growing preponderance of restitutive law whose aim was to make restitution for injuries done, and consequently reinforce the role of contract and undermine any overarching morality. Durkheim characterised the modern order by the term *organic solidarity* attempting to indicate the intricate nature of interdependence within it (1960).

Tonnies classified his evolutionary model in terms of social action. Humans acted either naturally in community or rationally in society. For Tonnies community centred on blood/kinship, land/ neighbourhood and mind/friendship. Together they constitute 'the home of all virtue and morality' (Bell and Newby, 1971: 25) and gradually give rise to common sentiments and a common will involving close and enduring loyalties to the place and people. Gesellschaft or societal relationships were largely the opposite of those attributed to community. Here people are bound together by one thing only: a specific contract which delineates a mutually rationally calculated association. As Tonnies (1957: 192) comments 'all its activities are restricted to a definite end and a definite means of obtaining it'.

Other nineteenth century writers, notably Karl Marx but also someone as different as Herbert Spencer, welcomed the destruction of the old coercive and narrow traditional world. Increasing contractual relations between individuals were to wipe out the tyranny of custom and replace it with the new order of individualism, and eventually, for Marx, socialism.

Spencer attempted to construct a genealogy of types of social structures on the basis of increasing differentiation (specialisation of functions through the division of labour) and integration (the mutual interdependence of the structurally differentiated parts and the coordination of their functions) resulting in a general trend to greater complexity. This evolutionary progression was from the simple to the complex, the homogeneous to the heterogeneous, and the indefinite to the definite. Spencer thought and hoped that with the emergence of large, complex industrial societies war would decline and that an extension of the laissez faire system to all spheres of life would produce a more responsible society and help fight the growth of bureaucracy and centralisation (Spencer, 1896; Andreski, 1971).

Along with other nineteenth century writers Marx and Engels

conceived several stages in the development of human society. Their typology was also based on tracing the progressive differentiation of the division of labour. As they wrote in *The German Ideology*, 'The various stages of development in the division of labour are just so many different forms of ownership, i.e. the existing stage in the division of labour determines also the relations of individuals to one another with reference to the material, instrument, and product of labour' (1965: 33).

For Marx, human society was at first wholly communal. Individualism developed through history from an increasingly complex division of labour. Marx emphasised the growth of urbanism as representing the sharpest index of differentiation within the division of labour. 'The opposition between town and country begins with the transition from barbarism to civilisation, from tribe to state, from locality to nation, and runs through the whole history of civilisation up to the present day' (1965: 65). The division between city and country provided the historical conditions for capital accumulation for as Marx commented, in the cities we find the 'beginning of property having its basis only in labour and exchange' (1965: 66). Consequently, capitalist society replaced the relatively autonomous local communities characteristic of earlier types of social orders by a division of labour which draws different cultural groupings into the same social and economic system. The myths and traditions with which people have lived for generations are swept away with the spread of bourgeois society. Marx welcomed this state of affairs for it meant, under his evolutionary schema, the coming of socialism. As Giddens (1971: 63) rightly comments, 'the abolition of the division of labour is both the prerequisite to and the expression of the transcendence of alienation ... in this most basic aspect as in others, socialist society is predicted upon the historical development of capitalism'.

The Rural-Urban Continuum

Although the traditionalists and the modernists had these differences of opinion, they all agreed that group loyalties and emotional attachments were declining as the rationalistic ties of utilitarian interests and uniform law were gaining predominance. Traditional privileges and inequalities were being swept away as a more egalitarian order took its place, just as the common beliefs of religion were undermined by the onslaught of secular and scientific argument.

Variations of the community-society ideal type dichotomy continued to be influential in the twentieth century, especially as a theoretical framework for field research. Its widespread use gave rise to the rural-urban continuum debate but before I discuss this dispute it is important to examine the events which led up to this debate.

In his studies of Mexican communities the social anthropologist Robert Redfield (1941, 1947) postulated an ideal type of folk society at one end of an unilineal continuum and an ideal type of urban society at the other. The folk society 'is small, isolated, non-literate and homogeneous, with a strong sense of group solidarity ... Behaviour is traditional, spontaneous, uncritical and personal ... Kinship, its relations and institutions, are the type categories of experience and the familial group is the unit of action. The sacred prevails over the secular; the economy is one of status rather than the market' (Redfield, 1947: 293). The members of a folk society remain within their small territory and experience little social change. Urban society, for Redfield, is the opposite. It is large, non-isolated, heterogeneous and lacks group solidarity; it is impersonal and rational and undergoes rapid processes of social change. Redfield placed the towns and villages he studied in Yucatan at various points along his folk-urban continuum. Consequently, the village of Tepoztlan came close to the ideal type of folk society. Redfield described it as a smoothly functioning and well-integrated social system that was isolated and homogeneous. He emphasises the cooperative nature of the society. Almost twenty years later Oscar Lewis re-studied the same village and emphasised 'the underlying individualism of Tepoztlan institutions and character, the lack of cooperation, the tensions between villages within the municipio, the schisms within the village, the pervading quality of fear, envy, and distrust in interpersonal relations' (Lewis, 1953: 123).

Many reasons can be evinced to explain these different interpretations: changes must have occurred in the intervening period, Lewis had the advantage of Redfield's pioneering work, Lewis had more resources, personnel, field-work time and informants but perhaps the most important factor is what Bell and Newby (1971: 77) have referred to as 'the blinker-like nature of theory in fieldwork'. The rather simplistic and value oriented folk-urban dichotomy directed Redfield to particular facts and interpretations. He concentrated on the process of change from the folk to the urban rather than on the complexities and paradoxes of both village and city life. As well as writing a fuller ethnography, Lewis was also arguing against the folk-urban continuum and consequently he concentrated on those aspects of life Redfield ignored. The question here is not the truth of the matter but which viewpoint helps us to come to grips with the complexities of reality.

In this case Lewis showed Redfield's model and data to be inadequate. Folk villages may be characterised by individualism and distrust and cities by stability and success. Lewis' later work in Mexico City clearly showed that peasants could easily adapt to urban life and at the same time retain much of their traditional culture (Lewis 1964). Similarly, as Avila (1969) indicated in his re-study of two of Redfield's villages, peasants of the folk society are often very much interested in social change to better their existence and consequently are they quite prepared to respond to market forces.

A more crucial difficulty with Redfield's approach is that he misused Tonnies' twin concepts. Tonnies characterised *gemeinschaft* and *gesellschaft* as types of relationships rather than as actual social systems. The former included relations of emotion, continuity and fulfilment whereas the latter referred to the impersonal, contractual and rational aspects of human relationships. As such, these concepts remain useful ideal types but Redfield among others took them much further, for as Newby points out:

> First, the concepts became reified—that is, *gemeinschaft* and *gesellschaft* soon ceased to be tools of analysis and became instead to be viewed as actual social structures which could be observed and enumerated. Secondly, and consequent upon this, they became identified with particular settlement patterns (1980: 25).

Although the community-society approach was now coming under increasing criticism for its inability to explain the burgeoning data from community studies, it continued to exert considerable influence, especially in its attempts to synthesise the results of several studies.

As McGee points out:

> The main problem is that once the model of the rural-urban continuum, with its fallacious assumptions of the nature of rural and urban society, is created, it becomes rather like an institution—self-perpetuating and not to be criticised (1971: 43).

Frankenberg's (1966) *Communities in Britain* is a good example. He called his polar ideal types 'rural' and 'urban' and drawing from almost every writer on the topic he subdivided these into 25 opposing dichotomies which represented rural and urban criteria. For example, little division of labour, mechanical solidarity, close-knit networks and integration typified ruralness whereas extreme specialisations of labour, organic solidarity, loose-knit networks and alienation characterised urbanness, and so forth (1966: 286–92). According to Frankenberg, 'Towns and cities make more sense if they are seen as part of an evolutionary process in which the progression from a simple to a diversified technology is accompanied by certain sociological changes' (1966: 12). Two of the changes he emphasised are differences in the nature of social networks and in the roles people play. 'In truly rural society the network may be close-knit; everybody knows and interacts with everyone else. In urban society individuals may have few friends in common. ... The pattern of change in roles from rural to urban is one of increasing role differentiation' (1966: 19–20). With this framework Frankenberg proceeded to place British studies of 'truly rural hamlets', villages, small towns and urban housing estates along the continuum.

The same rural-urban continuum was being used in Europe by such rural sociologists as Lupri (1965: 57–76; 1968: 298–300) and in America by the neo-ecologists Duncan (1957) and Schnore (1966). The position of Lupri, echoed by Schnore, 'is that rural-urban differences, while clearly diminishing, still remain crucial, even in highly industrialised nations ... These different environments still tend to produce different behaviours and attitudes' (1966: 131). Schnore goes on to say that the rural-urban continuum is 'a conceptual framework within which *certain* rural-urban differences may be meaningfully interpreted' (1966: 131, emphasis added). As a neo-ecologist Schnore's 'certain differences' concern such demographic and ecological data as the size, density and age of settlement patterns. The rural-urban continuum may be of some value for correlating this type of distributive data but as Schnore (1967) admits elsewhere social structures and social relationships are much more complex and cannot be as easily described and understood in terms of the rather simple evolutionary view that is a crucial part of the rural-urban continuum.

In an attempt to explain patterns of migration Richmond (1969) expanded the continuum at the urban-industrial end to include the so-called post-industrial society. This, he argues, is characterised by 'forms of social interaction [that] take place through networks of communication maintained by means of telephone, teleprinter, television and high-speed aircraft and space-craft' (1969: 278). In other words, we have moved from the rural to the urban to the automated society where relationships are no longer territorially based but rather are determined by 'networks of interdependent communications systems'. Perhaps fortunately our society is not as mobile as this suggests and as Bell and Newby (1971: 47) aptly comment 'people still live and breed somewhere'.

All of these views are open to the same criticisms made of Redfield's model. Notions of unilinear evolution, encompassing increasing alienation, individualism, rationalism, achievement and decreasing solidarity, multiple roles, integration and regionalism while containing some valuable insights are just not sophisticated enough to explain the available data. Further, these ideal-types were riddled with value judgements about what makes the good life, and for that matter the bad life and remained but 'a thinly veiled expression of very common nineteenth century cultural perspectives on rural life in academic sociological theory' (Newby, 1980: 25). According to Gans, cities are complex, heterogeneous structures containing such groups as urban and ethnic villagers, cosmopolites, suburbanites and others, and the urban process is unable to exert a common influence on such diverse ways of life. He argues 'that no single urban, or suburban, way of life can be identified', that 'differences in ways of life between the big city and the suburb can be explained more adequately by class and life-cycle variations' (1968: 95), and that ecological and typological approaches are not sensitive enough to explain the many different life styles encountered. Ways of life in modern societies do not correspond with settlement types.

Other researchers have reached essentially similar conclusions. Pahl, for example, criticises vulgar Tonnieism; he finds little evidence for the rural-urban continuum, doubts its usefulness as a classificatory tool and maintains that there are multiple non-overlapping continua with sharp discontinuities, especially 'the confrontation between the *local* and the *national* and between the *small scale* and the *large scale* (1968: 285–6). He concludes, 'Any attempt to tie particular patterns of social relationships to specific geographical milieux is a singularly fruitless exercise' (1968: 293).

In a comparison of five Australian community studies (see Chapter 7) I conclude 'the rural-urban continuum has ceased to have much relevance for the explanation of social processes and relationships in Australia. It is ravaged by marked discontinuities and is not sufficient to explain, or even classify, the range of similarities and differences established by the five studies' (see also Wild, 1978a: 88). Sociologists should be primarily concerned with the nature of changing social relationships rather than with plotting demographic and geographic indices.

What is 'Community'?

It should be clear from the above discussion how the development and variations of the community-society dichotomy gave rise to the definitional dispute over the concept of community which I referred to at the start of this chapter. Community became everybody's ideal notion of the good life and consequently ended up as a ragbag into which was put whatever each sociologist thought constituted the good life. Some sociologists, however, attempted to overcome this difficulty and apply rather more stringent criteria in their attempts at defining community. Most have been concerned with one or more of the following and, where relevant, their interrelationships: locality, systems of social relations and a sense of belonging.

Taking a broad view Martindale (1964: 69) defined community as a collectivity which forms a total system of social life capable of bringing its members through the ordinary problems of a single year or a single life. In other words Martindale has removed the geography from the concept of community and has equated it with a social system incorporating a total way of life. Given this definition a community may be an isolated village, a prison, a city, a group of immigrants or a nation state. Why then do we need the term community?

Stein (1964: 100–1) takes a slightly narrower perspective and attempts to retain the geography in community. He defines the concept as 'an organised system standing in a determinate relation to its environment which has a local basis but not necessarily a rigid boundary'. In other words he accepts that large parts of the social system lie outside the community which must have some locality relevance. Consequently, community for Stein may be anything from a rural hamlet to a sprawling metropolis. His definition, moreover, does not exactly fit with the argument in his book *The Eclipse of Community*. Here he argues that the increasing processes of industrialisation, urbanisation and bureaucratisation are decreasing levels of local autonomy, fragmenting primary groups and bringing the community into eclipse. But if community can be used to refer to cities as well as villages then there is an inconsistency in the argument. As Martindale (1964: 66) points out 'urbanisation is inconsistently treated as one of the processes which bring the community into eclipse. If the city is a community and if urbanisation represents the extension of patterns typical of a city, urbanisation ought more logically to represent a peculiar kind of community formation rather than community destruction'. This is a good example of the confusion between what community is (empirical description) and what this sociologist thinks it should be (normative prescription) (see Bell and Newby; 1974: xliv and pp. 17–18).

Warren (1963: 9) emphasises locality more than Stein. He defines community as 'that combination of social units and systems which perform the major social functions having locality relevance ... we mean the organisation of social activities to afford people daily local access to those broad areas of activity which are necessary in day-to-day living'. Warren isolates production/distribution/consumption, socialisation, social control, social participation, and mutual support as the social functions having locality relevance. It is clear that the locality relevance of such functions has declined especially during this century. Multinational corporations and nation states now control production; the mass media has affected socialisation; social control has passed from family to peer group, from commercial constraints to societal agencies; social participation has suffered from privatisation; and mutual support has been partially replaced by state support. This is, of course, a simplistic view but it should be sufficient to show us that Warren's approach to community leads us straight back into the simplicities and confusions of the community-society continuum where we again become blinkered by, in this case, a multi-lineal continuum which visualises a weakening of local autonomy, psychological identification with locality, and integration of localised social units and a strengthening of their opposites (Warren, 1963: 14). I shall return to this point shortly.

In the views considered so far the relationship between geography and people — or more accurately, between territory and social relationships — has not been at all clear. As sociologists we are concerned with *social* life and as Martindale (1958: 29) bluntly pointed out, social life is a 'structure of interaction, not a structure of stone, steel, cement and asphalt, etc.' Nevertheless, social life takes place somewhere and without some type of territorial reference it is difficult to distinguish social interaction within a family, a commune, a village or a city. In his paper 'The Principal Structures of Community' Parsons (1959) attempts to come to grips with this difficulty. He defines community as:

> that aspect of the structure of social systems which is referable to the territorial location of persons (i.e. human individuals as organisms) and their activities. When I say 'referable to' I do not mean determined exclusively or predominantly by, but rather observable and analysable with reference to location as a focus of attention (and of course a partial determinant). (1959: 250)

For Parsons, therefore, community must have a territorial aspect but the sociologists emphasis should be with 'persons acting in territorial locations' (1959: 250). Further, as the stress is on social relations, 'persons acting in relation to other persons in respect to the territorial location of both parties . . . The *population*, then, is just as much a focus of the study of community as is the territorial location' (1959: 250 original emphasis).

Bell and Newby (1971: 31–2) go along with Parsons' general notion of community. Although they do not add a further exhaustive definition to the long list, preferring to 'merely treat community as what community studies analyse' (1971: 32), they do comment at one point that, 'Communities can be understood as ongoing systems of interaction, usually within a locality, that have some degree of permanence' (1971: 55).

Some sociologists would not even accept Bell's and Newby's careful position and argue that community is a non-concept. Hillery (1963: 779) refuses to use the word because it 'embraces a motley assortment of concepts and qualitatively different phenomena'. Stacey (1969: 134) agrees and comments, 'It is doubtful whether the concept "community" refers to a useful abstraction'. In the same paper Stacey asks the most extreme question of those who incorporate territory in their definition of community when she writes, 'What system of social relations can one say has any geographic boundary except a global one?' (1969: 136). Nevertheless, as I have previously mentioned, people live and interact somewhere and are therefore involved in systems of social relations that are located in time and space. Further, many people have notions and feelings of belonging to a particular geographical area regardless of what else accompanies that attachment albeit feelings that change with the social context.

Stacey makes a stronger point when she writes, 'What then is the point of studying social relations in a particular locality? Would it not be better to concentrate upon an analysis of particular social institutions, e.g. the sociology of industry, religion, politics, family?' (1969: 136–7). Community is not an institution. It is not a relatively easily identifiable entity such as a nuclear family, the working class or Anglicans. Community is a more abstract concept containing several dimensions, hence its ambiguity. For Stacey community is a non-concept, and consequently not of interest for sociological analysis, but she contends that if there is a system of interrelated social institutions (like politics, religion, family and law) covering most aspects of life and the associated belief systems of each within a geographically defined area then there are sociological problems worth analysing within that locality. I shall outline Stacey's view of a localised social system in more detail below. Before I do this I shall examine three attempts to retain dichotomous notions of community structure.

Hillery (1968) approches community by comparing and contrasting three types of social systems — the folk village, the city and the total, all encompassing institution. 'The folk village is a relatively homogeneous grouping in space of families engaged in mutual aid, the city is a relatively heterogeneous grouping in space of individuals, with their families engaged in contracts' (1968: 65) and the total institution is 'a social system that not only tended to regulate the total lives of its inmates but which also set barriers to social interaction with the outside' (1968: 14). The folk village is assumed to contain community (1968: 12) but, he adds, it may be possible to find community in the other social systems. In order to determine this he lists the traits of the folk village which are brought together by the concepts of locality, cooperation and the family. In applying these components to the city and the total institution he concludes that the differences between the folk village and the city are 'best to be viewed as varying from each other in degree, that is, existing on continua' (1968: 61). Total institutions however, are a qualitatively different kind of entity from both the city and the folk village (1968: 142) and consequently do not contain community. For Hillery, then, community exists in varying degrees along a range of continua from folk village to city. As he comments, 'localised groupings range from more to less homogeneous; the organisation of the members ranges from virtual complete dominance of the family to the presence of the family among other institutions; and the mode of cooperation varies from mutual aid to contract' (1968: 65). In other words, Hillery ends up with a slightly more sophisticated version of the rural-urban continuum.

Perhaps Hillery's major difficulty is that there is no satisfactory taxonomy of community, consequently he assumes it exists in the folk village on the grounds that, 'no definition could be found which clearly stated that the phenomenon of community was *not* to be found in such a social system' (1968: 12). In doing this he implicitly accepts all the problems inherent in the earlier notions of community. His stress on cooperation and down-playing of conflict, for example, brings him close to Redfield's position but takes him away from the warnings sounded by Lewis. What we have here is a complex delineation of rural-urban criteria covering all implicit notions of community which has not changed from earlier formulations and consequently adds little to our understanding of social relationships and social change.

Another attempt to come to grips with the changing nature of community through a dichotomous model is Warren's distinction between the horizontal and vertical, or local and national, dimensions of localised social systems. For Warren a community's horizontal pattern is 'the structural and functional relation of its various social units and sub-systems to each other' (1963: 162) whereas its vertical pattern represents 'the structural and functional relation of its various social units and sub-systems to extra-community systems' (1963: 151). Warren argues that in America there has been a 'great change' involving the increasing orientation of local community units towards national-level systems. The vertical has largely superseded the horizontal and in the process reoriented the American community towards extra-community, especially national, systems. Warren bases his argument on changes, particularly increasing complexity, occurring in seven criteria: the division of labour, differentiation of interests and associations, increasing systematic relationships to a larger society, bureaucratisation and impersonalisation, transfer of functions to profit enterprise and government, urbanisation and suburbanisation, and changing values (1963: 54). He then matches up the impact of these changes on his four dimensions of community, *viz.* local autonomy, coincidence of service areas, psychological identification with locality, and strength of the horizontal pattern and concludes that 'the great change involves a movement through time from independence to dependence on the autonomy dimension; from coinciding service areas to differing service areas; from strong psychological identification with the locality to weak identification; and from a strong horizontal pattern for communities to a weak one' (1963: 44) Once again we have a sophisticated version of the simplistic rural-urban continuum but even this does not satisfy Pahl (1968) and Gan's (1968) criticisms that relationships of most types are found in the same localised social system whether that be a village, town or city, 'that it is not so much *communities* that are acted upon as groups and individuals at particular places in the social structure' (Pahl, 1968: 293), and that the local and the national confront each other in conurbations, cities, towns and villages and the same methods and concepts can be used to examine social processes and relationships in all these situations. Warren has failed to come to terms with the changing nature of community because of the limitations inherent in the dichotomous model.

More recently Gusfield (1975) has written 'a critical response' to ideas of community. The framework of the study centres on the community-society dichotomy which Gusfield treats in a critical yet sympathetic manner. He identifies three dimensions to community (1975: 21). First, it describes a specific form of human association, that is the feelings of the actors that they belong together. Second, it is part of a theory of change through social evolution. Third, it forms a segment of an ideological debate over the value of the present compared to the past and to possible alternative futures. I shall briefly summarise his main conclusions within these three dimensions.

First, he emphasises community as a relational concept rather than a territorial one: the former defined as the existence or absence of bonds of similarity and sympathy, the latter as particular physical location and territorial boundaries. Gusfield (1975: 33) writes 'community is part of a system of accounts used ... as a way of explaining or justifying ... behaviour ... it is the behaviour governed by criteria of common belonging rather than mutual interest'. He stresses that community is an important component of modern life which places limits on the principles of rational individual goals as the main cornerstone in the organisation and conflicts of contemporary life. One of the problems of this view is that it ignores the bonds produced by the persistence of groups over time, and often in one place. One of the central reinforcements of a common identity between people has been through long association and sheer survival as a group through periods of crisis, situations which concern complex relationships between locality, human association and ideology. Further, even in his analysis of the relational view Gusfield does not take into account the important distinction between relationships of tradition and those of sentiment (see pp. 39–41).

Second, Gusfield sees the linear evolution theory from community to society as far too simplistic. He argues that the processes supposed to weaken communal systems and strengthen societal ones do not do so 'in fact, they are just as likely to strengthen them; to support both communal and societal groups; or to appear in conflict. In the analysis of specific and concrete events, the concepts become blurred and their co-existence and mutual interaction more important than their clash and conflict' (1975: 79–80). He concludes, that rather than a movement from community to society the complexities relating them in specific cases makes the general theory unacceptable as a description of how social change occurs. Gusfield prefers to see community and society as points of reference brought into play in particular situations or arenas. The individual brings to every social situation a plurality of groups, associations and networks on which he or she can draw to define behaviour. Consequently, the individual can stress one community rather than another or can focus attention on the associational or societal interests binding him or her to otherwise conflicting communities. The difficulty with this approach is that in only examining the connections between community and society in specific situations any notions of processes of social change over a period of time are downplayed, if not altogether ignored.

Third, in his examination of community as ideology Gusfield discusses the utopian commune movement, and following Weber, argues that this development represents a self-conscious rejection of a society seen as 'too organised, too calculating and too much devoted to consumption, ambition and egotistic struggle' (1975: 99). The debate over the value of the rationalisation of life is, of course, not new. The concept of community, as a contrast to contemporary rational industrial society, has its basis in the resistance to industrialisation in the nineteenth century. Nisbet (1966: 6) referred to such dichotomies as community-society as the unit ideas of the sociological tradition. They are, he continued, 'the rich themes in nineteenth century thought. Considered as linked antitheses, they form the very warp of the sociological tradition. Quite apart from their conceptual significance in sociology, they may be regarded as epitomisations of the conflict between tradition and modernism, between the old order made moribund by the industrial and democratic revolutions, and the new order, its outlines still unclear and as often the cause of anxiety as of elation and hope'. Bell and Newby (1971: 25) have indicated that these ideas have a longer history but that the nineteenth century orientations are 'the most relevant theoretical inheritance for modern community studies, and must be the starting place for more recent conceptualisations ...' As Gusfield correctly points out, a revulsion against rational thought, scientific growth and the secularisation of spiritual life 'is a corollary of the centralising and organising character of life in the industrial societies of Europe, Japan and America' (1975: 100). Nevertheless, Gusfield does not fully explain how or why this occurs and what the results are. In following Gusfield's view we can again see his concern with the interconnections between community and society but unfortunately his analysis of these situations remains static since he has removed the processes of social change inherent in the traditional use of the dichotomy and not replaced it with any explanation of how communities and societies change.

Perhaps the major problem with Gusfield's work is that it remains within the confines of the dichotomous model. He has explained its history, analysed its shortcomings, indicated how much more complex things really are by stressing those events, processes and relationships that bring community and society together in the same situation, but he has ignored the source and directions of social change. Further, his confined view has resulted in little attention being paid to ideas that have been generated by the community studies tradition—by researchers grappling with data in communities. This particularly means that the notion of community as a localised social system is not to be found. Yet this conception is widely held at the present time and has shown to be useful in research since Stacey formalised the concept. It is to this I shall now turn.

The Localised Social System

According to Stacey 'it is doubtful whether the concept "community" refers to a useful abstraction' (1969: 134) consequently she avoids the term and argues that such institutions as the family, education and religion 'may, or may not, be locality based. They may, or may not, be interrelated. If they are locality based and interrelated then there may well be a *local social system* worth studying' (1969: 135). For Stacey the arguments about community involve difficult conceptual and philosophical problems which cannot be easily resolved, therefore sociologists should concentrate on social institutions and their interrelations in specific localities. Stacey isolates two kinds of locality studies. The first is concerned with examining particular institutions as they are manifested in a locality — a study of the family in a specific suburb or town for example. The second type examines the interrelations of institutions in a locality, that is, the more traditional community studies. Stacey limits her interest to the latter where the sociologist studies locally-based institutions and their connections and examines whether or not this is an aspect of society which can be isolated and is worth studying.

As well as providing a context for the detailed study of any one institution or social process the locality also provides a situation where the sociologist can explore for hypotheses about the interrelations of institutions. For this purpose it does not matter whether the locality is isolated or not for as Stacey comments 'the consequences for the social relations within a locality of changes introduced from outside have all produced some interesting studies' (1969: 139). Further social relations and their interconnections must be interpreted within time and space. Where local social systems have been identified they have usually developed in a relatively confined locality for some considerable time. At the very least sociologists should be able to analyse:

(i) the establishment and maintenance of a local social system; (ii) local conditions where no such system could be expected; (iii) some circumstances under which an existing system might be modified or destroyed; (iv) certain interrelations between systems and their parts; (v) the interaction of local and national systems (1969: 139).

Stacey's formulation is a rigorous model where she defines terms and isolates 31 interrelated propositions about local social systems. A social system is 'a set of interrelated social institutions covering all aspects of social life, familial, religious, juridicial etc. and the associated belief systems of each. ... A local social system occurs when such a set of interrelations exists in a geographically defined locality. ... The set of interrelations which compose the social system may be more or less complete' (1969: 140). Stacey uses Ginsberg's (1934: 42) definition of a social institution — 'recognised and established usages governing the relations between individuals and groups'. In practice, of course, all social systems are partial because not all sub-systems and institutions are present and not all are connected. A complete social system is an ideal type. Such a formulation allows the sociologist to examine the extent of system integration in any particular locality and to determine its basis and the conditions for its continued maintenance. As Stacey comments, 'empirically, in any one geographically defined locality, the likelihood is that there will either be no local social system, or some kind of partial local social system' (1969: 140). In her list of 31 propositions Stacey is moving towards a systematic model of the institutions which might be present and all the interconnections. If such a model can be developed she suggests the presence or absence of institutions and connections could be plotted and compared for different localities. All the propositions cannot be listed here but numbers 18 and 20 are important ones that relate to Stacey's conclusion. They are as follows:

18. In localities where there is a local social system, there will also be elements of other social systems present in the locality, i.e. the local social system will not totally encompass all institutions and relationships present, e.g. migrants bring with them *nationally legitimated* rights to vote for *local* political bodies'.
20. Where there is a local social system elements of it will be connected with systems outside the locality, that is, not that the local system as a whole is part of a wider system, but that its parts are parts of wider systems. Thus, while a local social system will have its own associated beliefs and cultural systems, the local system of beliefs and culture will share elements of the beliefs and cultural systems of the wider society. (1969: 143–4)

Stacey concludes that localised social systems are partial, that in any particular study the sociologist must, probably increasingly, consider social processes which take him or her outside the locality and that the 'eclipse' of local systems is unlikely. Further, she emphasises that locality studies must be compared with each other and with data gathered in other ways, such as, national statistical generalisations and macro studies of institutions.

Stacey's basic idea of the localised social system has gained widespread acceptance among many sociologists working in specific localities. It has proved to be a useful framework for research directing sociologists to significant theoretical problems within a territorial situation. Nevertheless the question must be asked why has this model not been extended and refined at a theoretical level? There are several reasons. First, during the 1970s there was a sharp movement away from the empirical and theoretical concerns of community and locality which had tended to concentrate on uniqueness, ideosyncracies and microprocesses to an interest in the general macroprocesses and structures of capitalist societies that largely created, some would say determined, the features of localised social systems. Instead of collecting data from localities within a rigorous framework and attempting to compare this material with similar studies in order to arrive at some comprehensive generalisation, as Stacey suggested, the aim now was to generate new forms of grand theory, usually centred on some aspect of Marx's work, which would then be imposed on social situations to show how they meshed with the total design of capitalist development (see Castells, 1976; Pickvance, 1976; Kilmartin and Thorns, 1978).

Second, Stacey's framework was developed from an amalgam of small-scale generalisations from many studies and consequently it suffers from some of the same limitations of those studies even though it went much further in a more rigorous manner. The method and model remain more suitable, and are more easily put into operation, in clearly bounded localised situations. Virtually all of Stacey's references and examples in the 31 propositions refer to the small town type of study. Despite her implications to the contrary it remains a model more suited for research in villages, towns and small cities for it is extremely difficult to isolate the characteristics of a localised social system within an urban metropolitan environment.

Third, Stacey calls for comparative work not only between different localised social systems but also with such types of data as national statistical studies. Very often the distance between national statistical data on class which usually refers to either attitudes or occupational distribution (that is the attributes of individuals), and community type of material on class (which usually refers to systems of social relationships) is so great as to almost defy comparison. Further, the theoretical assumptions and methodologies underlying such diverse studies are often directly opposed hence making any comparison or attempted accumulation of knowledge a dubious enterprise.

For these reasons some of those sociologists involved in community-type studies have accepted in principle the localised social system model; they have increasingly taken into account the impact of outside forces on local systems but have found little need or benefit in attempting to further develop the framework (Oxley, 1973; Wild, 1974; Pearson, 1980). Other sociologists have taken a more micro perspective within the localised social system approach and concentrated on the type and intensity of networks of familial and communal relationships in different types of localities (Martin, 1970). Others less happy with the locality approach have moved to studying relationships on a wider regional level, often concentrating on one institutional area (Newby, 1977; Newby et. al., 1978). Still others have given up the field altogether for macro-level theory and analysis (Frankenberg, 1976).

Weber's Model of Community

Weber's view of community which was outlined and expanded by Gertrude Neuwirth (1969) is at once more universal and more closely tied to general sociological theory than is Stacey's localised social system. Community is 'based on a subjective feeling of the parties ... that they belong together' (Weber, 1947: 136). The essence of community — belonging together — implies that members share a common set of interests, values and attitudes, and these in turn, define the boundaries of social interaction. The source of community formation, communal relationships and the sentiment of belonging is seen in competition for economic, political and social interests. Common interests — economic, political and social — are seen to underpin communal solidarity, which, in turn, is instrinsic to this shared orientation and the concomitant processes of status equalisation within the community. Communal relationships are treated as 'social relationships which enable these interests to be monopolised and usurped' (Neuwirth, 1969: 148). Communities then, are defined in terms of the solidarity shared by their members and this forms the basis of their mutual orientation to social action. Solidarity is not a function of common residence, rather it is a response to external pressures that are attempting to usurp the groups' interests. Territory, therefore, is not a defining attribute of community in this model. Territory assumes importance only if the choice of residential area by community members is an expression of their social power. In other words competition for economic, political and social interests is seen as the source of community formation and solidarity and communal relationships enable these interests to be monopolised by the group.

Four main processes are involved in this view of community. The first is community formation. Competition for economic interests, political power and prestige eventuates when there are more contenders than available opportunities to obtain them. Consequently, it pays the contenders for power to limit their numbers. One way of doing this is for a segment of the competitors to use an easily ascertainable characteristic of the other contenders, such as skin colour, the lack of education, religion and so forth, as a pretext for excluding them from competition. The processes of exclusion constitute communal action. At the same time the community's awareness of their own attributes, such as ethnic descent or the type of education, strengthens the basis of their solidarity. Such matters eventually become a focus of pride and positive identification for members of the community. It is exactly these processes of competition and exclusion that enable communities to be formed.

The second process is community closure. Once communal relationships have been formed the members attempt to maintain this situation by monopolising their economic, political and social advantages. This process of monopolisation is called closure and may range from total exclusion of others to admittance on special grounds. Economic closure, for example, may mean the monopolisation of business opportunities already possessed by the group. On a political level it may mean an attempt to usurp political offices for community members.

Third there are associative relationships which enable communities to consolidate their interests. Processes of community closure are often concomitant with the rational pursuit of interests, consequently communal relationships may be closely tied to associative or contractual relationships. In such cases members tend to form interest associations usually with qualifications for membership. Responsibilities for communal interests may be delegated to the officers of the association. Such associations help to enforce community norms by setting standards and having sanctions against people who break them.

Fourth, there are processes of consensus and conflict. Compliance to community norms does not necessarily rest on voluntary consent. Weber does not envisage community members as being engaged only in harmonious relations as is implicit in many formulations of community. This view of community allows for the possibility of power struggles, for the use of coercion and for the dominance of the weaker by the stronger. A community elite, for example, may attempt to effect closure against other community sub-groups. Consequently, communities may be internally stratified where subgroups are in conflict.

This formulation of community has a great utility in helping to explain communal relationships in many different social situations. Neuwirth (1969) uses this model to examine processes of community formation and closure among American blacks in 'The Dark Ghetto'. The blacks are excluded from economic, political and social privileges by the whites and are therefore unable to influence the imposition and application of rules which define their participation in the larger white dominated society. Consequently, the blacks are unable to effect their own community closure and, in fact, are prevented from achieving such closure by the representatives of the white community. In these terms such movements as Black Power which uses such slogans as 'Black is Beautiful' may be seen as trying to instil some social honour into being black thereby attempting to establish communal solidarity and, in turn, force community closure.

Both Stacey and Neuwirth are concerned with the nature of the connections between types of relationships and social groups and with the ties between behaviour and ideology. The concept of social network was introduced to attempt to analyse and explain some of these connections. As it has turned out the idea of social network has been of more use at the descriptive-analytical level than at the explanatory level.

In a now well-known paper John Barnes (1954) first used the network concept when he wrote, 'the image I have is of a set of points some of which are joined by lines. The points of the image are people, or sometimes groups, and the lines indicate which people interact with each other' (1954: 43). Barnes' terminology distinguishes 'total network', 'partial network', 'portion' of network and 'set'. The total network refers to a model of the linkages which connect each individual (or social unit) to other individuals (or social units) within a field of interaction. The partial network is 'any extract of the total network based on some criterion applicable throughout the whole network' (Barnes, 1968: 111). A political network is an example of a partial network. The set is the part of the total or partial network containing all the people linked, directly or indirectly, to an individual person. In other words the set is an egocentric model whereas the network has no central point. Elizabeth Bott's (1957) study of 20 families conceptualised their relationships in terms of types of networks. Bott recommended that 'the immediate social environment of urban families is best considered not as the local area in which they live, but rather as the network of actual social relationships they maintain, regardless of whether these are confined to the local area or run beyond its boundaries' (1957: 99). Different localities and different individuals exhibit varying types of networks. Some may be dispersed and loose-knit whereas others are clustered and close-knit. Martin's Adelaide study illustrates the general point. She focused on the social networks of families living in three different kinds of suburban environment: a prestigious residential district ('Eastville'); a government housing trust area ('Northville'); and a long-established but heterogeneous suburb

('Westville'). Overall she found many Westville families embedded in a localised, close-knit, community-type network. Here 'the number of units in the field is large enough for them to be linked together in a variety of ways — kin, occupational, religious and political ties criss-cross one another; relationships between members are dense, either over the whole portion or in multi-linked clusters; and links exist — not necessarily directly, but not so circuitously as to be irrelevant — between each member and all other members' (1970: 337). From data on associational membership and informal contacts Martin concludes that Eastville families came close to a clustered type of network. Here 'the individual's set contains people whose only links with one another are through him. Relationships between members in some areas of the individuals set may still, nevertheless, be dense, reflecting the fact that the individual belongs to one or more clusters or groups which are themselves close-knit' (1970: 337). The Northville network, however, was loose-knit. Here the individual's set consists largely of people who have few or no relationships with one another. Martin notes that even kin ties in Northville were less dense with 'each family selecting a few contacts — themselves not necessarily in contact with one another — from the large number of kin available' (1970: 337).

In this context Martin sees community as refering to those who share a sense of belonging and are characterised by a locality bound close-knit network. I shall explore the connection between community and network in more detail below; here I shall briefly mention two difficulties with the network concept which was heralded in the late 1960s and early '70s as 'a powerful analytical tool' (Bell and Newby, 1971: 53). First, it is limited in the scope of its application. Studies of groups of families, socialisation in communes and so forth lend themselves to network analysis even though recording and mathematical problems become immense with more than a handful of people. The solving of some of these difficulties with the aid of computers, however, does not help the second issue which concerns levels of analysis and explanation. The nature of class in a large-scale capitalist society is not especially illuminated by network analysis for class structure is concerned with categories of types of relationships, such as those between employees and employers, rather than with networks of individual actual relationships. Further a concept like class is tied into a more general theory which attempts to explain the formation, maintenance and development of relationships. From this point of view network analysis is largely a descriptive methodology which only becomes analytical and explanatory when it is related to other higher-level concepts which themselves are part of a broader theoretical framework. Although there has been considerable technical advance in the measurement of networks with the aid of computers, theoretical advance lies in its relationship to more abstract concepts. Because there has been little progress in the latter area, network analysis has largely remained at the descriptive level and hence it has not fulfilled the lavish claims made for it on the basis of the early studies. Nevertheless the concept of social network is of crucial importance for the student of community for it is one of the few, along with such others such as status group and social closure, that attempts to relate empirical community study data to theories of community.

Community, Communion and Society

After all this we are still left with the question of how valuable is the concept of community in helping us to explain the changing nature of social relationships? Should we follow Hillery and Stacey who refuse to use the term? I do not think so because community is a key word (see Williams, 1976: 65) that is of considerable importance in our society, and a word that has figured prominently in discussions of the very nature of our society. For these reasons alone community demands the sociologists' attention. Although Stacey's localised social system and Weber's notions of community formation and closure are useful and rigorous frameworks for examining differing aspects of community, they are not sufficiently connected to broad processes of societal change over a long period of time — a central relationship for understanding some types of community activity and structure and how they change. Consequently, I shall now suggest a different way of viewing community; one that attempts to explain changing patterns of social relationships over time, avoids the confusions of mixing up locality, tradition and sentiment and connects processes of social change to the nature of domination.

Community and society are competing modes for the organisation of social relationships. Community is a social order developed on the basis of natural interdependence through traditional relationships. Society's character lies in the priority of the individual over social or collective existence. It is a type of relationship that presupposes the unrelatedness and separateness of individuals. The confusing aspect of this dichotomy is that community is invoked to explain not only relationships of tradition but also relationships of emotion developed through common experience and emphasising a sense of belonging. It is essential to separate these and I shall refer to relationships of tradition as *community* and relationships of emotion as *communion* (see Schmalenbach, 1961; Bell and Newby, 1976).

I have moved, then, to a trichotomous model: there is community, communion and society. Now community, as I have mentioned, is a social order developed on the basis of natural interdependence through traditional relationships. This includes consanguinity, locality (as social space), time (as temporal contiguity), tradition and custom. 'Community implies the recognition of something taken for granted and an assertion of the self-evident' (Schmalenbach, 1961: 334). People are not usually aware of the communities to which they belong because community is *given*: communities simply *exist*. Community circles, of which we are a part, cover connections of all kinds but it is only through conflict that a community becomes an object of attention for its members. 'The reality and basis of community do not consist in feeling' (Schmalenbach, 1961: 335) because a feeling of communal belonging always presupposes a conscious recognition of community. Feelings of community always point to something that pre-existed. They are products of community.

Communion concerns feelings or sentiment and is carried by emotion. If community is *given* then communion is *experience*. 'Emotional experiences are the very stuff of the relationship' and it 'arises only through the actual experienced recognition of a mutual sense of belonging' (Schmalenbach, 1961: 335, 337). Relationships of communion tend to be unstable, precarious and oriented to change. They are short-lived because they are easily routinised and, therefore, they are transformed into community, or society-type, relationships in an attempt to create an enduring arrangement.

Society, as I have mentioned, is characterised by individualism. Individuals in society bridge their mutual distances with such visible and rational connections as contracts and laws formulated by thoughts and actions which are conscious in accord with the rules of logic and empirical knowledge (see Wild, 1978a: 26).

Thus far I have outlined three analytical ideal-types but in actual empirical situations they are closely intertwined. For example, one can be a member of a community but also sustain relationships of communion with selected members of that community. But also every experience of communion has the effect of moving towards community bonds in an attempt to make the ties permanent. It is possible to combine relations of community and communion. This may involve strain or even conflict, for those who are part of community usually distrust others whose relations involve elements of communion. In Bradstow, for example, the town's businessmen and the local gentry are proud of the fact that they belong to the community of Bradstow—that is a statement of tradition that is given. But the businessmen often resent the communion shared by the gentry which is symbolised by the exclusive golf club from which the businessmen are banned, albeit a communion which has become a routine (Wild, 1974). At other times society comes closer to communion than community. This is because both society and communion are more concerned with the individual and his or her experiences, whereas community is primarily concerned with an interdependent social group. It is in these complex interactions that community, communion and society are linked to broader processes of social change and the structures of domination and it is to these I shall now turn.

The three ideal-types are linked together by processes of social change more complex than the simple evolution from traditional community to modern society. Here we have a more cyclical or spiral view of social change where the differential interaction of the three provides a range of explanatory typologies for different empirical situations. For example, the increasing rational demands of *society* emphasising impersonality create reactions which centre on the emotional experience of *communion* and result in, say, a dropout movement into communes. As the division of labour develops and children are socialised, the sentiments of communion are routinised into patterns of settled community. As the community creates more complex forms of social organisation, distributes its produce in the marketplace and loses its young generation through outward migration, the ties of rational-legal *society* take over in a more pervasive way than previously. Social change, then, can be conceived partly as developmental and partly as cyclical. Some social forms of antiquity form the basis for later developments, and, therefore, lie along a unique linear sequence. Others are repeated again, albeit at different levels of development. (For more detailed examples see Chapter 8.)

The trichotomous model of community, communion and society recalls Weber's tripartite division of charisma, tradition and rational-legality as archetypes of human experience (Weber, 1968), and before that Pascal's and Goethe's distinctions among faith, custom and reason as the three sources of belief (Winkelmann, 1952). One of the reasons for Gusfield's inability to go beyond the dichotomous model is his limited interpretation of Weber. He regards Weber as an evolutionary theorist along with Tonnies, Durkheim, Spencer and others. According to Gusfield, 'Weber used the concepts of traditional authority and rational-legal authority to express the great changes he saw in the modern period' (1975: 4), hence implying that Weber conceptualised a unilinear movement from traditional to rational in the same way that Tonnies saw a development from community to society. Weber's typology of authority, or what I prefer to call domination, was of course, a trichotomy. For Weber there was *traditional domination* where the legitimacy of a social order arose from time-honoured custom and habit; *charismatic domination* where the legitimacy of a social order arose from a belief in the extraordinary qualities of a leader; and *rational-legal domination* where the legitimacy of a social order arose from a belief in a rational system of rules which are based on logic and scientific knowledge. Although Weber was an evolutionary theorist in that he believed the process of increasing rationalisation was the predominant process in Western history, he also held a cyclical view of change which recognised that rationalisation was regularly interrupted by irrational forces such as a charismatic leader, a call to traditional forms of behaviour or a religious ideology. A summary of the relationship between the two trichotomous models is shown in diagram one.

Diagram 1

Mode of organisation	Community	Communion	Society
Basis of relationships	tradition	emotion/ sentiment	associations determined by contract
Form of social action	irrational/ substantively rational	irrational	substantively rational-formally rational
Type of domination	traditional authority relations	charismatic authority relations	rational-legal authority relations

Unlike Marx, Weber was not primarily concerned with the internal crises of capitalism. He emphasises its rational nature. He wrote, 'the development of economic activity must be conceived before all else as a special manifestation of the universal rationalisation of life' (1914: 7). Capitalism was, for Weber, the highest form of rational operation yet experienced. The increasing complexity of the capitalist enterprise and the rapidly developing role of the State in the economy aided the growth of bureaucracy; that is, administration in the hands of appointed officials with specialist qualifications who possess the necessary technical knowledge. Similarly, the modern concept of a legitimate legal order developed gradually through the history of Western civilisation as a specific product of human deliberation rather than from the charismatic hero or a sacred tradition. A system of legal domination (rather than charismatic or tradition) 'exists only where the rules of a legal order are implemented and obeyed in the belief that they are legitimate because they conform with the statutes of a government that monopolises their enactment and the legitimate use of physical force' (Bendix, 1960: 390).

The structures of capitalism, bureaucracy and legal domination are united in the historical process through rationalisation; that is, thoughts and actions which are conscious according to the rules of logic and empirical knowledge, and which result in growing precision, explicitness and formalism in the principles governing social organisation. The extension of exact calculation in the economy, the subjection of work and social life to precise regulation, and the codification of norms into formal laws are examples of this process. For Weber the general process of rationalisation entailed the spread of modern capitalism and it was this very rationality that separated it from more traditional forms.

As may be seen in Diagram 1, Weber distinguished between formal and substantive rationality. Formal rationality concerns the increasing procedures of calculability and predictability in organisation based on scientific methods. Albrow comments:

At the heart of Weber's idea of formal rationality was the idea of correct calculations, in either numerical terms, as with the accountant, or in logical terms, as with the lawyer. This was normally a necessary though not sufficient condition for the attainment of goals. (1970: 65)

Consequently, formal rationality is characteristic of the societal situation and not community or communion. Substantive rationality is *purposive* action concerned with the selection of specific means to obtain desired ends or goals. Substantive rationality, then, may be found in both communal and societal situations. Matters of communion are characterised by irrational action, that is, irrational in the sense that it is not either formally rational or substantively rational as defined above.

The ideal-types of community, society and communion and their relationships to traditional, rational-legal and charismatic domination are of basic importance for the systematic development of the concept of community and the empirical analysis involved in community studies. Community, society and communion do not represent types of concrete structures, such as the family, the working class or youthful peer groups. Rather they are forms of ideal-typical relationships — modes of organisation that may or may not be assumed by such concrete structures. It is the job of the sociologist to determine where and why they exist at particular times and how and why relationships change from one to the other. In my view this conceptual framework helps us to understand the nature of changing relationships and later chapters elaborate on its value for providing us with some insights into the characteristics of community in the modern world.

The idea of the localised social system, the notions of community formation and closure and the trichotomous model of community, communion and society all provide valuable theoretical orientations for understanding different aspects of community life and between them they virtually encompass most of the sociologically significant perspectives on this most slippery and abstract concept. Later in this book I examine a range of community studies from within the guidelines of these three theoretical formulations, but before doing this, it is essential to first consider some central aspects of methodology.

3 Community as Method and the Methods of Community Studies

Introduction: Some comments on sociological methods

The Rise of Methodological Pluralism is the sub-title of Bell and Newby's 'Introduction' to *Doing Sociological Research* (1977). It expresses what has become a central problem for sociology: is there something that can be called *the* sociological method? The attacks on positivism—which based its explanation on the experimental model of the natural sciences—since the early 1960s have led to methodological exclusivism, as in Cicourel's *Method and Measurement in Sociology* (ethnomethodology), Moser's and Kalton's *Survey Methods of Social Investigation* (positivism), Althusser's *For Marx* (structural Marxism), Wolff's *Surrender and Catch* (sociology of knowledge). These attacks have also led to methodological pluralism as in Bell's and Newby's *Doing Sociological Research*, Bell and Encel's *Inside The Whale*, Hammond's *Sociologists at Work* and Vidich, Bensman and Stein's *Reflections on Community Studies*. There is no longer one sociological method (if indeed there ever was) rather, there are many and there are no clear ways of choosing between them. It has become increasingly impossible to share the certainties of the methodological exclusivists for none provides discipline-wide paradigms and all over-emphasise the amount and certainty of sociological knowledge and explanation. Methodological pluralism emphasises the use of different methods in collecting data, constructive scepticism and ethical scrupulousness in describing how the work was done.

Bell and Newby pay considerable attention to Gouldner's distinction between *epistēmē*, 'which embodies awareness of the known, of the knower and of knowing' and *technē*, 'which consists of the lessons of experience of trial and error, of clever skills refined through diligent practice' (Gouldner, 1967: 268). As Bell and Newby comment, 'Much of the assault on positivism is an assault on *technē* from *epistēmē*' (1977: 18–9). Both intuitive insight and disciplined method have some difficulties. For Gouldner, '*technē* tends towards

narrowness. Its characteristic product is the brief and direct technical article capable of being understood only by a few other specialists
... It is intolerant of intellectual ambiguities and builds intellectual
structures into which all things can be fitted neatly' (1967: 272).
Epistēmē, on the other hand, 'has a tendency towards mystification
... things are felt to be much more complex than they seem ...
Enjoying the mystery of life, it seeks to protect it, and it can therefore become the enemy, not only of science, but of reason as well'
(1967: 274). Bell and Newby argue that some of these difficulties are
solved if *technē* and *epistēmē* are maintained 'in some form of tension or even in some sort of dialectical relationship' (1977: 19).
They point out that if sociologists describe what they actually do
when they are conducting research, rather than pay lip-service to
what they ought to do as described by the official methodology textbooks, then 'it is possible *both* to illustrate the relationships between *epistēmē* and *technē and* to show how these tensions can be
creative in the doing of sociological research' (1977: 19).

It is not sufficient however, just to say that intuitive insight and
disciplined method must be combined. We must be able to explain
how this can be done. This is not easy for as Gouldner warns us
epistēmē cannot be taught in a straightforward manner and that
when *technē* is taught it becomes sterile because it is divorced from
actual sociological practice. *Sociologists at Work, Reflections on
Community Studies, Doing Sociological Research* and *Inside the
Whale* have all in varying ways attempted to come to grips with this
problem by carefully describing exactly how sociological work was
done. Such enterprises are extremely important and I follow their
lead in this book by delving into the unofficial background of the
community studies selected in an attempt to see how they were
actually carried out. This is a difficult task because of the varying
amount and quality of the background data available. Bell and
Newby suggest 'that a close examination of actual sociological practice ... will probably show a wide variety of incommensurate procedures' (1977: 28). This may well be the case with respect to specific
methods for studying particular problems, but at the more general
level of, say, the relationship between theory and data in sociology
might there not be an approach that is more general across a wide
scope of the discipline? Baldamus (1972, 1976) has moved tentative-
ly in this direction and part of his argument is worth considering
here because it has enormous relevance for establishing common
patterns in 'reflections' on community studies and in other descriptions of how sociological work was actually done.

Because of the nature of the sociological enterprise the sociologist
is always sandwiched between systematically controlled inquiry and

the experience of uninterrupted reality. Unlike the natural scientist the sociologist cannot arrange controlled experiments. The sociologist can only observe and ask questions. But the sociologist's presence is part of an ongoing reality which he or she is experiencing as a process through time and it may produce changes in the data being observed. Controlled inquiry and experience are related by 'the universe of pragmatic knowledge' (Baldamus, 1972: 280) because all the sociologist's observations — all that comes from interviews and goes into codified responses — are already the results of typical conceptualisations in everyday life. In other words, sociological data are derived observations based on secondary sources. The aim in a questionnaire or an interview is not to obtain the objective truth, rather it is to gather honest and sincere answers whether or not they are true in their own right. Sociological data in these terms is knowledge which may be more or less valid or true. This data — that is, our observations on elements of pragmatic knowledge — have a validity *of their own* which is centred in the contexts of everyday life, and consequently, they have their own power to assert themselves. These data themselves constantly generate *theoretical* interpretations of the world that compete with the sociologist's own theories and analyses.

If the sociologist's observed facts can generate knowledge by themselves then the undirectional procedural rules of scientific method — axiomatic theory, hypothesis formation, *observation*, testing and conclusion — are dissolved and the method seems irrelevant. What do sociologists do in practice? Do they follow the procedural rules found in official methodology textbooks or is there an underground reservoir of unofficial, non-formalised techniques of inquiry? Exactly how important are personal experiences, hunches, guesses and unexpected insights in the research process? To answer this we must examine how sociologists work in some considerable detail as a type of lengthy and variable activity, that is, as a social process through time. This is not an easy task, partly because there are no clear dividing lines between formal and informal methods, between fieldnotes and drafts and the published document, and between the perceived and the real processes of social research. As I have already mentioned, we do have some insights into this process from those few books where sociologists have written about what they actually did (Hammond, 1964; Vidich, Bensman and Stein, 1964; Bell and Newby, 1977; Bell and Encel, 1978) None of the work described in these volumes, be it theoretical or empirical, easily fits into any established categories of conventional methodology and the explanatory bases of these studies cannot be delineated by any of the many types of social science theory pres ent, for example, in Brown's *Explanation in Social Science* (1963). Theory, for example, is used as a lax informal term to refer to 'a sort of continuous speculation without a definitive purpose' (Baldamus, 1972: 290). It certainly does not yield a significant end product that can be used to design a set of hypotheses that in turn might be tested by observation or experiment. Further, it is clear that informal theorising of this type is a highly personal process and experience. It happens by organising general ideas around a central theme or a conceptual model or framework. In other words during the process of sociological work the investigation is steered in a particular direction. The research projects described in these volumes were not preceded by consciously elaborated hypotheses. Rather they tended to grow gradually out of hunches and dissatisfactions with other work, that is, a sort of implicit hypothesising that gives thought a free rein.

It should be pointed out that none of the contributors to these books are solely theoreticians. All are primarily concerned with empirical research. What is clear from their reports is that any preoccupation with theory takes place during the process of empirical research. Theorising, then, is an integral part of the data collection process. Clearly such an approach contradicts the idea of scientific testing. Here the sociologist pursues a selected central theme, looks around for observational data that fit the theme and then constructs a hypothesis or a model that fits the facts. The reason for this brings us back to the nature of the sociological enterprise and the character of sociological data. There is such an abundance of questions to ask, of correlations to pursue and of meanings to interpret — how is the sociologist to decide between them? As there is an infinite number of ways of classifying human action, how does the sociologist decide which one to pursue? With such a wide range of choice of facts to select from and lines of argument to follow and with the inability of sociology to find a meaningful, total reality informal theorising becomes central. The process of informal theorising is crucial because it is necessary constantly to reinterpret the accumulating new findings until they appear 'strategically relevant' to some central problems of the discipline. Theorising, in this sense, is 'a trial and error process by which conceptual frameworks become progressively more articulate' (Baldamus, 1972: 294).

There is, therefore, in much sociology a constant dialectical relationship between theory and data. Baldamus calls this 'double-fitting' and gives the example of 'a carpenter alternately altering the shape of a door *and* the shape of the doorframe to obtain a better fit' (1972: 295). In strict scientific terms such a technique is deliberate falsification. What then is the rationale for this procedure? This is not easy to pinpoint but first it should be noted that the direction of the procedure is itself uncertain. Emphasis, for example, may be placed on problems of theory and conceptualisation or on empirical observations. In other words, double-fitting can be predominantly theoretical or empirical. Baldamus calls the first 'theorising' (1972: 296). Here a vague notion of some puzzling phenomenon is gradually articulated by trying to fit it into a succession of combined criteria usually chosen from already acceptable concepts. It is the new combination that might provide new insights and meanings which in turn illuminates the puzzling phenomenon. This search for conceptual frameworks by double-fitting theorising is, according to Baldamus, a result of the trivial and eclectic nature of sociological 'discoveries' made by the scientific model, if indeed there is anything worth calling a 'discovery' in sociology.

The second approach, that is, from the empirical side Baldamus calls 'hypothesising'. The arbitrary starting point is a more or less articulate theoretical statement. This statement is a means to finding the existence of some regularity among factual observations, that is, some causal connections between types of events may be found to exist to a greater or lesser degree usually based on what seem to be the most promising possibilities or on the findings of comparable cases. Both theorising and hypothesising therefore, are based on an informal, trial and error process.

If theorising and hypothesising are at root part of the same informal process, this procedure points to some of the goals and satisfactions of sociological work rather than to the logical structure of the enterprise. In theorising there is some satisfaction in the ability to perceive some order in the mass of eclectic data by relating them to major problems, core social structures or central values. This type of satisfaction is centred on value-commitments. Hypothesising stems from the striving for detachment and scientific certainty and relies on the assertive power of facts. Both processes occur to a greater or lesser degree in any given piece of sociological work. The 'reflections' on community studies described later in this book, as well as the volumes listed above, enable us to see some of these processes in action.

The two processes of hypothesising and theorising are not separated in time or application. In an actual study the sociologist cannot spend one month theorising and the next hypothesising. Both go together, albeit in different degrees at different times. There is a constant and ongoing relationship between theory and data that is progressing in a particular direction largely determined by the results of trial and error actions. From theorising comes an increasingly higher level of abstraction and from hypothesising comes increasingly complex relationships between variables. In any particular study both occur simultaneously and in the end product they look considerably more established and structured than they did initially.

Theorising and hypothesising as types of double-fitting interact and materialise as an ongoing process through time, consequently it cannot be seen by looking at the final published version of a particular study. That this process exists in sociological work is clearly established from existing accounts. How it is possible and how it is done are the real questions and as yet we do not have the answers. Baldamus suggests that sociology's preoccupation with discoveries of the experimental sciences type has 'blocked the view to the *sui generis* features of our methods ... [for] ... an increasing amount of evidence is accumulating that suggests that the procedures used in the praxis of social research and theory may well turn out to be a unique, unprecedented type' (1972: 300, 1976: 40). This argument is in many respects tentative; nevertheless it points towards a basic process common to a wide range of sociological work. It is especially relevant for community studies for this is one area where the contradictory pressures of intuitive insight and controlled, technical inquiry have been the subject of considerable dispute. I have attempted to incorporate in this book (especially in the Australian studies section) as much material as possible on the informal and unofficial methods that played such a large part in determining the final results. In my view these accounts of sociological research, sketchy as some of them are, are at least as valuable to both students and sociologists as are the prescriptive outlines in methodology textbooks. By reading accounts of how work was actually done students may gain insights into sociological research as process and experience. By using this approach I hope to convey some aspects of the special relationship between theory and data, not only in community studies, but in sociology generally.

Participant Observation

Although there is a grain of truth in Bell and Newby's comment, 'there seem to be as many community study methods as there have been community studies' (1971: 54), it is possible to establish some generalisations, especially concerning participant observation. As later examples indicate, community studies are characterised by methodological pluralism. The methods employed to obtain data include the examination of historical records, journals and newspapers, oral history, participant observation, structured and unstructured interviews, random sample questionnaires, case study analysis, and reputational surveys. All of these methods are later discussed in the context of particular studies: here I shall briefly comment on the approach that characterises community studies — that is, participant observation. Although community studies are eclectic in their methodology participant observation is the central method and characterises all the studies discussed in this book.

Becker and Geer define participant observation as 'that method in which the observer participates in the daily life of the people under study, either openly in the role of researcher or covertly in some disguised role, observing things that happen, listening to what is said, and questioning people, over some length of time' (1970: 133). Further, they argue that participant observation is a central or core approach because 'an observation of some social event, the events which precede and follow it, and explanations of its meaning by participants and spectators, before, during, and after its occurrence . . . gives us more information about the event under study than data gathered by any other sociological method' (1970: 133). Participant observation allows the researcher to obtain firsthand knowledge about the empirical social world in question. The researcher is close to the data and thereby able to develop some concepts to aid explanation and understanding from the data. Some sociologists, such as Garfinkel (1967) and his sect of ethnomethodologists, have taken this to extremes. Ethnomethodology concerns the study of everyday activities, however trivial, concentrating on the methods individuals use to report their 'commonsense' practical actions to others in acceptable rational terms. In other words, it is concerned only with how the *individual* experiences and makes sense of social interaction (Turner, 1974). Consequently, this approach is opposed to the sociological theories of Marx and Weber that concentrate on how such social structures as class and bureaucracy constrain individual beliefs and behaviour. Participant observation in community studies allows the researcher to collect material on groups and institutions as well as to collect the trivialities of an individual's everyday life. The competent studies then place and interpret this data within the broader social structures of the society in question. Here there is a dialectical tension and relationship between the individual and social structure, between, on a broader canvas, methodological individualism and structural determinism. Community studies, then, should display a balance between empathic understanding of individuals and situations through participation and an ability to relate these with, and explain them with reference to, the logic of the wider social system.

Having placed participant observation within a wider theoretical context let us now return to examine some of the more specific problems, advantages and disadvantages of this approach. Participant observation is a social process through time that is sequential and cumulative. Each succeeding stage of observation depends on some analysis in the preceding stage. In other words analysis is being made during the collection of data. It is here where the 'double-fit' relationship between theory and data occurs. Consequently the final comprehensive analysis is not possible until the fieldwork is completed.

Much of the success of participant observation often depends on how the fieldworker entered the situation. Entry largely determines the initial position into which the fieldworker is placed. Once 'placed' it is difficult for the sociologist to change this position, especially in a locality with a small population. Further, the position filled places either greater or lesser restrictions on what will be observed. As I later note Whyte's success in his participant observations of gang social structure partly depended on his initial acceptance by 'Doc', the gang leader. When I moved to Bradstow there were two houses for rent in the town, one close to an exclusive residential area and the other near the railway line in a working-class district. I took the former. As a general rule it is to the sociologist's advantage to enter with the acceptance of the powerful for it is easier to filter downwards than it is to work one's way up.

A further difficulty concerning entry to the field is whether the research process is to be open or covert. Most covert research has taken place in specific organisations such as factories or hospitals. An Australian example is Kreigler's *Working for the Company*, a study of Broken Hill Proprietary Company's (BHP's) Whyalla shipyard. As with most other covert studies, Kreigler argues that being hired by BHP and covertly collecting data was the only way he could obtain the material required. He comments, 'there was no other way of gathering such detailed, intimate, biographical information on the workers, even if I had wished to use other techniques. It was very much a case of the situation dictating the procedure, because Whyalla shipyard workers exhibit an unmistakable suspicion and distaste for academics ...' (1980: viii). Apart from the ethics of sociologists which are later discussed (see pp. 113, 147 −8) it is questionable how far the legitimate desire to be unobtrusive makes recompense for misleading the people studied and probably making it impossible for other sociologists to work within that company. If it is decided to work openly in such a situation then some sponsorship or permission is required and often this may only be granted with special conditions which could include the right to censor the results. Vidich and Bensman found themselves in such a position when the University and the community influentials, attempted to suppress their findings (see below pp. 75–6). In such closed systems as factories and rigidly programmed and directed studies, covert research depends on guile and open research on sponsorship. Both involve important restrictions on scholarship and major ethical issues for which there are no absolute answers (see Bell, 1969: 417; Barnes, 1970, 1979; Erickson, 1970; Roth, 1970).

The localised social systems described in this book are open systems but the sociologist must still decide whether to work overtly or covertly. Most do the former for sponsorship is not necessary and the restrictions are the sociologists own from his or her ethical position. But the real situation is more complex than this because the overt-covert dichotomy is rather simplistic. As Roth has pointed out 'all research is secret in some ways and to some degree' (1970: 278). There are several reasons for this. First, research areas and interests often change through time during the process of fieldwork consequently what the sociologist tells everyone he or she is starting out to study may end up as something different. Second, the sociologist does not want to influence respondents' behaviour by telling them everything you are interested in. Third, the terms of the research are not always easily understandable. I agree with Roth's conclusion that:

> Secrecy in research is not something to be avoided or that can be avoided. It is rather a problem to be faced as an integral part of one's work. We are more likely to develop a useful and satisfying work ethic by analysing *the research process of the sociologist himself* than by drawing up written codes of ethics which merely perpetuate current moral biases and restrict rather than aid further ethical development. (1970: 280; emphasis added)

Once entry has been secured, or even during the process of entry, the sociologist will be socially 'placed' by the residents. As Vidich remarked, 'in a broad sense the social position of the observer determines what he is likely to see' (1970: 164). Those being studied attempt to fit the research worker into a plausible role within a context meaningful to them. The anthropologist studying a tribal society may be initially identified as a trader, a missionary or a spy but gradually this identification may change and the anthropologist may even be incorporated into the kinship system. Similarly in modern communities sociologists have to find a basis on which respondents can react towards them. In a highly stratified localised social system such as Bradstow this entails playing different roles for different classes and status groups (see pp. 140–5). The wearing of different clothes, the varying of language and accent and the knowledge of, and ability to act out, different behavioural expectations are all important in establishing close relationships with members of divergent status groups. In a small group situation as with Whyte in Cornerville, it is almost impossible to significantly change one's assigned place but in stratified localised social systems it is possible, if sometimes difficult, to maintain different places at varying levels in the hierarchy. Vidich is right when he concludes, 'Perspectives and perceptions of social reality are shaped by the social position and interests of both the observed and the observer as they live through a passing present. The participant observer who is committed to relatively long periods of residence in the field experiences a continuous redefinition of his position' (1970: 172). As the sociologist's position changes, he or she has access to new types of data. The interpretation of this data will be largely conditioned by theoretical preconceptions. Here we have the complex interplay of theory, method and data each interacting with and affecting the other through time. This process is one of the 'triple-fitting' and continues throughout the fieldwork period.

The types of informants available or selected may be related to entry and placement. Whyte's acceptance by 'Doc' meant that he had an informant who was central in the social structure of Cornerville's gangs. Vidich and Bensman, however, suggest seeking out such marginal people as newspapermen who are likely to be somewhat detached from the local social structure and are thereby able to describe it for the fieldworker. This raises a general problem for participant observation studies — whose view of the social structure is the sociologist reproducing? Warner, for example, was justly criticised for adopting his upper middle class informant's views of the social structure of Yankee City (see pp. 65–8). In Bradstow I attempted to use both central and marginal respondents, people placed at different levels in the social hierarchy, informants at different stages of the life-cycles and both males and females. Further, the type of in-depth data gathered from such informants must be examined and supported or questioned with reference to material obtained from random sample surveys carried out after intensive participant observation. In order to establish the validity and generalisability of participant observation data we must know exactly what sociologists *do* in the fieldwork period.

Many community sociologists in the past have been loath to use surveys and have depended almost wholly on participant observation and a few close informants. Bell and Newby, for example, rightly criticise Frankenberg's study of Pentrediwaith for 'totally lacking in sociographic data, even an accurate figure for the population' (1971: 140). But Bell and Newby are also aware of the limitations of the survey:

> The sample survey as normally carried out by sociologists is a wonderful instrument for collecting facts about individuals. It facilitates the collection of these facts by bureaucratically convenient categories and allows them to be statistically described. This is obviously worthwhile and valuable ... yet the survey is arguably of marginal relevance for studying the community. Despite there being little agreement on what community is, most sociologists include within their definition of community, and for that matter *their subject*, something about interaction. Interaction implies that there are groups, persistently patterned interaction implies social institutions and their interrelation implies social systems. This is the subject matter of sociologists, not individuals. (1971: 61).

Nevertheless, surveys carried out on the basis of a thorough knowledge of the historical and socio-cultural context of a localised social system can provide valuable, if somewhat limited, data as an aid to further description and careful analysis and as a check on certain corollaries of more qualitative propositions. Runciman wrote that the survey 'may, like an aerial photograph, enable us for the first time to see clearly the outline of the woods and fields; but this only increases our curiosity to look under the trees' (1966: 7). I prefer to turn this around. There is little point in surveying the forests if the types of trees are unknown. First, we must look under the trees and then take an overview which may assure us that what seems to be a forest actually exists and extensively so. It is important in community studies to strike a balance between the objective and subjective, between hard and soft data, for although participant observation is the core method of community studies it must always be supplemented with surveys of various types in order to support qualitative propositions, establish representativeness and provide a basis for comparative analysis. Weber made clear this point in a more general way when he wrote:

> All interpretation of meaning, like all scientific observation, strives for clarity and verifiable accuracy of insight and comprehension. The basis for certainty in understanding can be either rational, which can be further subdivided into logical and mathematical, or it can be of an emotionally empathic or artistically appreciative quality. In the sphere of action things are rationally evident chiefly when we attain a completely clear intellectual grasp of the action—elements, in their intended context of mean-

ing. Empathic or appreciative accuracy is attained when, through sympathetic participation, we can adequately grasp the emotional context in which the action took place. (1947: 90–1)

If participant observation cannot provide adequate quantitative data neither can it supply the sociologist with the historical development of a localised social system except the beliefs held by respondents about the history of their community. Warner was criticised for accepting residents' myths about the history of Yankee City as representing the actual course of events. It is important for community sociologists to be aware of both and to be able to explain the differences. Local traditions, ideologies and forms of action, although undergoing changes in the present, are always rooted in the past and community studies are never complete until the contemporary data have been placed within an historical context.

The final issue about participant observation concerns the validity of the material collected. How can this data be checked? Ultimately it cannot but some precautions can be taken. First, the data can be checked with other observed phenomena to establish internal consistency. Second, team research can be used to control the possible idiosyncracies of the single investigator but as Vidich found in Springdale, and Stacey and her colleagues in the Banbury re-study, team research can bring other problems which are explored below. Third, observed data can be checked against material collected in other ways such as surveys or structured interviews. Fourth, the localised social system can be re-studied but again, as we shall see with the Banbury re-study, this also brings new problems. Fifth, and very generally, the more time spent in the place, the closer one can get to the people, the more varied the social contexts experienced; and the more methods used to gather information the more accurate the data collected. Finally, and perhaps most important of all, sociologists should provide 'a description of the natural history of our conclusions, presenting the evidence as it came to the attention of the observer during the successive stages of his conceptualisation of the problem ... In this way, evidence is assessed as the substantive analysis is presented. The reader would be able, if this method were used, to follow the details of the analysis and to see how and on what basis any conclusion was reached' (Becker, 1970: 199–200). Accounts of doing sociological research are at least as valuable as the general prescriptions for research found in methodology texts and it is for this reason that this chapter is brief in comparison to the accounts of community studies which follow.

Given all its difficulties participant observation remains a central and crucial approach both for community studies and sociology generally. It is the only method that allows us to explore the important differences between what people say they do and what they actually do. It provides a rich experiential context that constantly confronts the sociologist with unexplained facts. It makes the fieldworker sensitive to a wide range of implications and connections with other observed phenomena. Most importantly it pushes the sociologist to continually revise and adapt theoretical ideas and methods of gathering data in the direction of greater relevance to the problems under scrutiny and in this process indicates the difficulties inherent in those arbitrary attempts to discuss theory, method and data in isolation from each other. The strengths of participant observation have perhaps been best put by Herbert Gans when he described his book *The Urban Villagers* as follows:

> This, then, is not a scientific study, for it does not provide what Merton has called compelling evidence for a series of hypotheses. It is, rather, an attempt by a trained social scientist to describe and explain, using his methodological and theoretical training, to sift the observations, and to report only those generalisations which are justified by the data. The validity of my findings thus rests ultimately on my judgements about the data, and of course, on my theoretical and personal biases in deciding what to study, what to see, what to ignore and how to analyse the products. Properly speaking the study is a *reconnaissance*, an exploration of a community to provide an overview, guided by the canons of sociological theory, and method, but not attempting to offer documentation for all the findings. I do not mean to cast doubt on the conclusions I reached (I stand behind them all) or on the methods I used. Participant observation is the only method I know that enables the researcher to get close to the realities of social life. Its deficiencies in producing quantitative data are more than made up by its ability to minimise the distance between the researcher and his subject of study. (1962: 349–50)

Community as object and community as method

Arensberg and Kimball were the first to draw attention to the differences between those studies that treated the community as an object in itself to be found, itemised and analysed and those that saw community studies primarily as a method of getting at some data to examine more general sociological problems. According to Arensberg and Kimball, 'The traditional community study has as its goal the enumeration of the attributes that distinguish it' (1967: 30). But they saw community studies as a way of 'getting to grips with social and psychological facts in the raw' (1967: 8) and with these facts building models to help explain differing patterns of social relationships. Havighurst and Jansen in their trend report on community research supported the latter approach: 'A community study is not a branch of sociology, such as ecology, demography and social psychology. Rather it is a form of sociological research that is useful for a variety of research purposes' (1967: 7). Bell and Newby made considerable use of the object-method dichotomy and argued that there was a crucial distinction 'between those studies which treat communities as objects, that is to say, those that tend to go in for classifying communities as different sorts of communities (and then ... hint at what is a good or bad community), and those empirical studies of a sociological problem in a locality, that, to put it rather crudely use the community as a laboratory to get at social facts in the raw and are primarily interested in saying something about this problem rather than about the locality' (1971: 252). They strongly support the 'community as method' approach and contend 'that communities, unlike organisations, such as factories and schools, or institutions, such as the family, should not and cannot be objects of study for social scientists' (1971: 54). More recently Newby commented that there has 'been a notable movement away from exploring communities as objects of study in their own right towards using a community study as a methodology to study broader social processes' (1980: 79). Newby attributes the decline of community as object research to 'the general disenchantment with the "abstracted empiricism" manifested by such studies' (1980: 79).

The major criticisms of object studies are that they are concerned with uniqueness rather than representativeness, consequently they tend to be idiosyncratic, non-comparable and non-cumulative. Method studies, because they are concerned with theoretical issues arising from sociology generally, are capable of being representative, comparable and cumulative and are able to contribute to such substantive areas as the family, social stratification, political sociology and so forth. The problem with this formulation is that by viewing object and method as a dichotomy little attention is given to the relationships between them. Rather, it is better to view them as ideal-types, each study representing either more or less one than the other. Bradstow, for example, is primarily a method study oriented towards theoretical issues concerning social stratification. But at the same time that study tells us a lot about the localised social system that is Bradstow. We learn a lot about the history and growth of the town and the changing nature of its social structure. Although there are some aspects of uniqueness in this process it is also possible to see such general processes as bureaucratisation in operation—a process that affected all Australians during the period under discussion. In other words community studies should always strive to show and explain the relationships between the unique and the representative. One of the strengths of community studies has been their ability to vividly portray how people live their everyday lives, to explore the paradoxes of altruism versus egoism, of democratic ideology versus political manipulation. To treat the community study as just another method would, I believe, in the end lead to a routinisation, and consequently, a loss of fresh, spontaneous insights. It is perhaps for this reason, as I discuss later, that the Banbury re-study does not have the spontaneity, freshness or completeness of *Tradition and Change*.

This issue raises a question of more general concern for sociology, which is: given the intertwined nature of the relationship between theory and data how abstract can our explanations become? The aim of community as method studies is to produce more comparable and generalisable data and explanations by emphasising representativeness. Object studies have remained much closer to what is seen as unique data in seeking their explanations. I have argued for a balance between the two that emphasises special content and general trends and addresses itself to the relationship between them. Weber's comments on this theme, although at a more general level, are well worth considering.

Laws are important and valuable in the exact natural sciences, in the measure that those sciences are universally valid. For the knowledge of historical phenomena in their concreteness, the most general laws, because they are most devoid of content are also the least valuable. The more comprehensive the validity—or scope —of a term, the more it leads us away from the richness of reality since in order to include the common elements of the largest number of phenomena, it must necessarily be as abstract as possible and hence devoid of content. In the cultural sciences the knowledge of the universal or general is never valuable in itself. (1949: 80)

4   The Empirical Tradition of Community Studies: The American Case

The history of modern community studies started with the functionalist, empirically descriptive and wholistic traditions of social anthropology. Sociologists wanting to study communities in their own countries borrowed the method used by social anthropologists studying primitive societies, that is, living with a group of people for a considerable period in order to understand their way of life. Both major branches of community studies (the American and the British) started from this perspective.

In this chapter I discuss five American community studies, each of which has made a major contribution to the field and has been influential in determining the direction of later community studies. The studies are the Lynds' *Middletown* and *Middletown in Transition*; Warner's *Yankee City* series; Whyte's *Street Corner Society*; and Gans' *The Levittowners*. The discussions have three major emphases. First, I examine the background of the projects, concentrating on what these sociologists actually did during their fieldwork. Second, I review their major substantive findings. Third, I attempt to interpret their approach to community in terms of the three models—localised social system; community formation and closure; community communion and society (see Chapter 2). Finally, the following vignettes are not intended as summaries, rather, they highlight the three aspects just mentioned. There is never any substitute for reading a community study in the original.

Middletown and the Lynds

The book *Middletown* by Robert and Helen Lynd is generally regarded as the first community study. It also remains one of the best for the Lynds established a model for future studies and their approach, techniques and analysis have been closely followed to the present day. In 1923 the Lynds were working for an institute of social and religious research. The research programme of the institute included a 'survey of religious provision and practice in a typical small American town'. The town selected was Muncie, Indiana which was later given the pseudonym 'Middletown'. In preparing for this project the Lynds were influenced by the work of Clark Wissler and W.H.R. Rivers—anthropologists who had worked on the religious practices of North American Indians. The Lynds were attracted by the functionalist-wholistic view that primitive religion could not be wholly understood unless it was seen as a functioning part of the total society. Consequently, the Lynds argued that to understand religion in an American town it was essential to examine its interrelations with other institutions. With this in mind, Robert and Helen Lynd adopted W.H.R. Rivers' six-fold classification under which the activities of any 'culture' could be described: getting a living, making a home, training the young, using leisure, engaging in religious practices and engaging in community activities. This anthropological frame of reference provided their framework for the selection, organisation and interpretation of data.

The Lynds eventually decided to study the effects of industrialisation on Middletown by tracing these effects through the six major areas of life. They assumed, as do most functionalists, that changes in any one area would reverberate in others to a greater or lesser degree and that 'getting a living' would have most impact because it encompassed many of the changes set in motion by industrialisation. The two main groups differentially affected by industrialisation were the working class who 'dealt primarily with things', and the business class who 'dealt primarily with people'. In the Lynds analysis, this cleavage became the most significant division in Middletown's social structure.

Such general orientations as these placed within the descriptive anthropological framework are useful for obtaining and organising field data but they do not provide a theoretical framework. The whole process is descriptive rather than analytical. As the Lynds wrote in their first paragraph, 'Neither fieldwork nor report has attempted to prove any thesis. The aim has been, rather, to *record* observed phenomena, thereby raising questions and suggesting fresh points of departure in the study of group behaviour' (1929: 3). It was systematic description and not theoretical propositions or external judgement that was the objective of Middletown. They set about collecting facts in order to convey impressions and they do this thoroughly and well.

It was with these ideas in mind that the Lynds, with two assistants, set up a small office in Muncie in early 1924 and proceeded to collect data. The basic method used at the beginning was to explore in as detached a manner as possible the activities of Middletowners.

The Lynds started to get to know people, worked towards an impressionistic feel of the town, gradually established ways of systematically observing typical behaivour and avoided impersonal questionnaires. They gradually entrenched themselves into the social structure of the town.

The Lynds wanted to view Middletown in a thoroughly historical perspective. Historical analysis is crucial to the understanding of what goes on in the present and many later community studies have ignored this ending with a static description which is somewhat like viewing a still from a moving picture. Originally the Lynds intended to study in detail the period from 1880 to 1924 but in order to simplify this complex and time-consuming task, they decided to take two key dates: 1890 and 1924. Much of the book is organised around the changes experienced by Middletowners during those 34 years.

In an appendix to Middletown the Lynds categorise their formal methodology into five parts. The first is called 'participation in local life' which I have already mentioned. Throughout the research period they attended meetings of clubs, went to churches, schools, court sessions, political rallies, trade union meetings, rotary dinners, card parties, weddings, funerals and so forth. In most places they took extensive notes. Where this was impossible, a record of the event was made immediately afterward from memory.

The second method was the examination of documentary material — another matter often ignored by later studies. The Lynds went through census data, court files, school records, meeting minutes and so forth. The two leading daily newspapers were read in detail for 1890 and 1891 and the following years were covered by sampling. They used such private documents as family records and diaries and gradually built up a picture of the town in 1890 and acquired some insights into the major processes of change.

Third was the collection and compilation of statistics from both official sources and their own surveys. Fourth came the interview, of which they describe four types — casual conversations with anyone willing to provide information; planned interviews with such community leaders as churchmen and politicians; a sample of interviews with 'working-class wives' (because the interviews were done during the day working wives were excluded); and interviews with businessmens' wives (called 'just good substantial folks') who were willing to cooperate. Such samples as these do not fit today's strict scientific samples but at every point the Lynds treat their data with complete fairness and always indicate their sources and type of interviews.

Finally, the Lynds used questionnaires which were given to community leaders, voluntary associations and high school children to ascertain club membership patterns, values and social attitudes.

The fieldwork took about 18 months and was completed in late 1925. There was then a period of gestation before the book was published in 1929. In the preface the Lynds wrote, 'No-one can be more aware than the writers of the shortcomings of the report — the lack of adequate data at certain points and frequent unevenness of method. Furthermore, the fieldwork was completed in 1925; the point of view of the investigators has developed during the subsequent years, and the treatment would be at many points more adequate were the investigation to be undertaken now.' There was, however, no justification for their slight lack of confidence — the book was an instantaneous success and in 1929 alone there were six printings. *Middletown* had succeeded in its attempt to set down the facts about a small American town.

This was not the end of the Middletown story. In 1935 the Lynds returned to re-study Middletown in order to find out how the town had managed during the depression and in what ways the community had changed. But in the intervening years the Lynds themselves had changed. At Columbia University they had been exposed to European sociological theory including the work of Marx and Engels and they realised that fieldwork should be conducted from an informed theoretical position. Consequently the Lynds began to revise their thinking about the American community especially in terms of its class structure and the distribution of power. This new perspective is clear in their second book *Middletown in Transition*. The first volume concerned systematic description through collections of facts but the second is a hard-hitting exposé of power and privilege founded on theoretical propositions and firm judgement.

In *Middletown* there is little reference to politics and power but in *Middletown in Transition* these topics run throughout the analysis. The simple division between workers and businessmen becomes a stratification system with six classes or status groups and the X family, not mentioned in the first book, reign supreme. Some commentators have questioned whether the Lynds overlooked the X family's power in 1925 and others have suggested that their powerful position was not sufficiently significant at that time to justify separating them from the rest of the business class. In my view it was the former reason, combined with their growing interest in theory, that led them to identify this ruling family in 1935 when they were very much concerned with showing how the wealthy and powerful families, using every agency at their command, protect their class interests.

This issue raises an important question for community studies concerning what Bell and Newby (1971: 77) have called 'the blinker-like nature of theory in fieldwork'. A rigid theoretical orientation can determine the selection and organisation of facts, consequently other facts which may contradict those chosen are ignored. The opposite weakness — conducting fieldwork without any theoretical direction — is just as bad. All and sundry data are gathered and interpretations are made later. In this case facts and observations are subject to retrospective selection and sometimes to falsification. Community studies are not just collections of facts, for facts do not speak for themselves. They have meaning only from the way they are bound together with theory. Facts, of course, may be gathered in accordance with an unconscious preference (as in many 'official' histories of small towns) or in terms of some descriptive theme (as in the cultural framework used for *Middletown*) or in line with an explanatory scheme (as in the political and class analysis in *Middletown in Transition*). Since it is impossible for anyone to observe a 'total reality', theory narrows the range of observation, aids the selection of relevant material and helps to systematise empirical findings. It is of utmost importance, however, that there should be some interplay — a dialectical process — between the levels of fact and theory. In other words theory must be flexible enough to be refined and re-directed by the empirical data and the most significant theory is that which explains the widest range of factual material. If this can be achieved then community studies which are always primarily empirical can also make a theoretical contribution.

The Lynds' two studies illustrate this general point. They started research in a condition of almost total theoretical naiveté, organised their facts around a current anthropological framework, recognised a need for theory, and finally adopted a stratification model centering on power. In summary, the Lynds provide us with a sociological history of Middletown from 1890 to 1936. The first volume clearly shows the influence of industrialisation on the social structure by detailed and rigorous reporting of the different areas of life and by analysing the changes in the relative statuses of the two main classes. The second volume established a model to interpret the effects of the depression and to explain the influence of the X family in determining the two classes' responses to this episode. Finally, the Lynds saw developing a modified social structure, something much more complex than the basic divisions they recognised in 1924.

The Lynds do not specifically discuss the concept of community and they tend to use it in a general way. Nevertheles, their usage of the term partly coincides with Stacey's approach, (see pp. 31–5). They approached Middletown as a localised social system, but at the same time they did not treat it as an isolated unit. They were intensely concerned with the impact of such outside forces as industrialisation and the depression. Consequently they saw Middletown as a partially localised social system — a social system which in a whole range of activities was often autonomous but also one where national social processes affected local decisions and relationships. Further, they traced the increasing importance of the vertical relationships (see pp. 28–9) and the decreasing importance of the horizontal over a period of some 46 years. In the process the Lynds fulfilled many of the requirements outlined by Stacey. They examined the establishment, maintenance and historical development of the town; they detailed the conditions under which the social structure changed; they analysed the interrelationships between the major institutional areas of life; and they outlined the impact of outside forces on Middletown. Further, they did not assume (at least in the second volume) that Middletown was completely harmonious, sharing a common value system and an intensive sense of belonging. Instead they showed us the conflicts in politics and ideology between the major groups but they also explained how they were held together within the local order. If we look deeply enough Middletown provides us with many of the basic building blocks for the development of the concept of community as a localised social system.

Yankee City and Lloyd Warner

Lloyd Warner was entrenched in the anthropological tradition. Before he started research on American communities, Warner had completed a field investigation into a group of Australian Aborigines which resulted in the book *A Black Civilisation*. He returned to America to apply his anthropological techniques to the study of American society. The place selected was the small New England town of Newburyport for which Yankee City is the pseudonym. The initial idea was to work in one of the sub-communities of Chicago to enable the research to be coordinated with Elton Mayo's well-known Hawthorne experiments but Warner was not attracted to this prospect because Chicago 'seemed to be disorganised'. He argued, 'If we were to compare easily the other societies of the world with one of our own civilisation, and if we were readily to accommodate our techniques, developed by the study of primitive society, to modern groups, it seemed wise to choose a community with a social organisation which had developed over a long period of time under the domination of a single group with a coherent tradition' (1941: 4).

Warner's framework for the research and analysis was wholistic, functionalist and ahistorical. He approached Yankee City as if it were an isolated, primitive village and paid little attention to written records and relationships between the town and the rest of American society. He regarded the community as a 'working whole in which each part had definite *functions* which *had* to be performed or substitutes acquired, if the whole society were to maintain itself' (1941: 14 emphasis added). Further, he saw Yankee City 'as a microscopic whole representing the total American community' (1952: 33).

Warner's main concern was to describe the system of social stratification and to indicate its importance in determining the composition and distribution of families, club memberships, residential areas, church attendance, occupations, educational levels and so forth. He began with the assumption that people were placed in ranking order on the basis of economic factors but his research showed these were not the only ones used. According to Warner, 'Great wealth did not guarantee the highest social position. Something more was necessary' (1941: 82). Consequently, Warner formulated his definition of social stratification to encompass the effects of whatever factors the members of a society use to rank each other in an overall hierarchy. This was 'two or more orders of people who are believed to be, and are accordingly ranked by all the members of the community, in socially superior and inferior positions' (1941: 82). In this scheme the layer of equally-ranked statuses which comprised a class cut across the entire community.

Warner's method was to live with a community, interview all its occupants on such topics as occupation, family history, association membership, and the ranking of people they know, collate this date, and from it identify several social strata consisting of those who were in the same prestige position. Warner and his 30 assistants collected data on 16 785 individuals and punched this material onto machine-readable cards. According to Warner this technique was used to prevent the analyst from imposing his ranking on the people. In other words, events set their own framework while the analyst remained a passive but sensitive recorder. Warner clearly believes that a community has a neat and tidy social structure with 'classes' being 'real things' (rather than conceptual categories) into which all inhabitants can be unambiguously placed, that people use their local community as a reference group and that people agree on their criteria of ranking and can classify each other by them.

Warner's voluminous writings (there are five volumes on Yankee City and several more on Jonesville and American society generally) have been subjected to wide ranging criticisms on almost every aspect. Pfautz and Duncan attacked Warner's techniques and argued that class placement through interviewing a core of informants was impossible to use in a large city, that no procedure was specified for equating the social levels named by several informants and that there was no satisfactory way of dealing with cases where informants disagreed about the social class placement of an individual. They concluded 'their conceptual formulations are inadequate to account even for their own findings, [they] are theoretically uninformed in relation to the existing literature on social stratification, and further are ideologically suspect' (1950: 216).

C. Wright Mills attacked Warner's definition and concept of social stratification. Warner's concept 'indiscriminately absorbs at least three items which . . . [class, status and power] it is very important to separate analytically' (1942: 264–5). Mills, following Weber, argues that the amalgamation of all three into one 'sponge' word 'class' prevents the investigation from examining the relationships existing among them. According to Mills, most of the confusions and inadequacies of Warner's study flow from this basic difficulty.

Chinoy takes issue with Warner's claim that class is what he 'found' it to be in Yankee City and argues that Warner's class structure 'is actually a composite version of the prestige hierarchy which is built from the varied perspectives of the local residents. It is basically a construction of the researcher rather than the consensus of the community' (1950: 259). Lipset and Bendix went even further and claimed that Warner's studies 'reveal the perspective of the social climbers just below the upper crust of small town society . . . If this is the view of the upper middle class then the question arises whether other social groups in the community look at class in the same way. A careful reading reveals that the subjective definition of class is by no means the same for all residents' (1951: 162). Warner, then, has not fully described even the status structure of a small town; rather, he examined the prestige hierarchy as seen through the eyes of its middle class residents.

Merton, Handlin and Thernstrom all criticise Warner's lack of attention to historical data. Merton wrote, 'Little is said of the dynamics of the class system. Forces which make not only for mobility of personnel within the structure but also for change in the structure itself are virtually ignored . . . As a result we are given a picture of a basically stable and practically unchanging system' (1942: 438). Warner's conception of a stable unchanging community, which was largely pre-determined by his dependence on the anthropological functional-equilibrium model of society, was invalidated by Handlin's historical research. He pointed out, 'When one realises that in 1930 about 40 per cent of the native born [of Yankee City] had foreign parents, that the foreign birthrate was never lower than the native, and that a constant stream of Yankees was leaving the city throughout the last century, it is clear that the vast majority of the city's residents in 1930 were foreigners or the descendants of those who had immigrated in the previous nine decades' (1942: 555–6). Warner's rationale for not using the historical record and depending solely on the acts and opinions of living members of the community was to prevent ethnocentric bias (1941: 40) but exactly this procedure led them to accept uncritically the town's legends about itself which is, as Thernstrom remarked, 'surely the most ethnocentric of all possible views' (1964: 230).

As Bell and Newby commented, 'never in the history of community studies has so much effort been expended by so many people with such wrongheaded assumptions and with such inappropriate concepts and techniques' (1971: 110). Essentially Warner's ahistorical, wholistic, functionalist assumptions of the equilibrium school of anthropology provided a totally inadequate framework for studying a modern complex community in a capitalist society. Nevertheless Warner's work made an enormous impact. He opened up the debate about social stratification in the United States both academically and publicly. Many of his ideas and techniques were used by others. In America, Davis and Gardener's project *Deep South* was directed by Warner. Arensberg worked with Warner on the Yankee City project and together they planned a study of County Clare, Ireland, which resulted in the famous book *Family and Community in Ireland* by Arensberg and Kimball. Williams' study of the village of Gosforth in Cumberland carried out from 1949 to 1951 utilises some of Warner's methods and his class terminology. More recently in Australia Oxley, who sees Warner's work as 'one of the notable foundation stones of modern sociology' (1974: 31–2), has used Warner's framework to analyse the 'ideology of status ranking and status striving' (1974: 36) in Rylstone and Kandos. Clearly, the 'Warner approach' to community studies is not yet dead.

William Foote Whyte and *Street Corner Society*

Whyte, whose father was a college professor, came from a long-established upper middle-class family. At university his studies centred on economics with a leaning towards social reform. On graduation Whyte was granted a three-year research fellowship at Harvard where he planned to study the economics of rackets and racketeering. He decided to work in a slum area because it was there that racketeering was supposedly to be found. He strolled around Boston and found the section of the city that he calls Cornerville.

As he worked on his plan for the study he found himself moving away from economics and closer to sociology and social anthropology. During this period he was partly influenced by the Middletown studies but he found their orientation to the impact of industrialisation and the depression on a small town too broad. Whyte was more interested in what held the small-scale mechanics of a social system together. Arensberg, who had just returned from fieldwork in Ireland, had an important effect on Whyte especially in introducing him to the fieldwork techniques of social anthropology and the theoretical writings of Durkheim and Pareto. In other words, in the planning stages of his research Whyte was exposed to the functionalist-equilibrium model of social anthropology and its research methods. The focus of his research outline changed as he moved away from strictly economic considerations and towards examining the relationships between friendship patterns, factions and gangs.

Feeling he should know something about the social welfare problems he would encounter in Cornerville, Whyte took a course on 'Slums and Housing'. Part of this involved a survey aimed at locating housing problems. Whyte was sent to ring doorbells and ask the prescribed questions. He was unhappy with this procedure because he had little confidence in the answers. He found that people tended to say anything to get rid of you or say what they thought you wanted to hear. These are basic points applicable to much survey sociology done today. To obtain data on what people actually do, not just what they say they do (and this often differs) the researcher must undertake participant observation to observe and interpret social relationships (see Wild 1978a: 68–75). It was now clear to Whyte that the survey approach was of little use in answering his questions as he was concerned with the varying networks of social relationships.

Whyte had several false starts in his attempts to gain entry to Cornerville society. Eventually, a social worker told him to speak to a man called 'Doc' who was a native of Cornerville and who knew everybody. The two men took a liking to each other and because Doc was a local leader or influential, Whyte was immediately accepted by others. Whyte's acceptance into Cornerville society depended far more on the personal relationships he was able to develop than on any rational or logical explanation of what he was doing. As long as he had the support of key individuals he was fairly sure to be able to obtain what he wanted from others. Doc was able to help Whyte so much because he was leader of his gang and a central figure in the local social structure. But, as Bell and Newby (1971: 59) point out what if Whyte had been adopted by a marginal member of the gang? He would have clearly been provided with a different view of the gang structure and might not have had access to the leader. The point is that people who are placed in different positions in the social structure will have varying perspectives on how the system works and it is important to obtain data on these differing perspectives.

Participant observation, as Whyte soon discovered, was a valuable way of comprehending the many sides of life in Cornerville but he also found it had some drawbacks. First, it was enormously time consuming and filled up all his life during the research period. Second, it was unsuited for collecting quantitative data. Third, the participant observer often affects the social situation. One day Doc said to Whyte, 'You've slowed me up plenty since you've been down here. Now when I do something, I have to think what Bill Whyte would want to know about it and how I can explain it. Before, I used to do things by instinct' (Whyte, 1955: 301). This comment indicates the influence a participant observer can exert on the ideas and actions of those being studied and the investigator must always be aware of such possibilities. Fourth, Whyte found that the role of the participant observer entails many delicate dilemmas. It is one thing to be accepted but the investigator does not have to pretend to be exactly like his or her subjects. One day Whyte thought he would act like the gang members and enter the spirit of the small talk by letting forth a stream of profanities. He wrote, 'The talk came to a momentary halt as they all stopped to look at me in surprise. Doc shook his head and said, "Bill, you're not supposed to talk like that. That doesn't sound like you"' (Whyte, 1955: 304).

Much of *Street Corner Society* concerns the description and analysis of two gangs — the corner boys and the college boys. As Whyte's research was conducted during the depression there were many gangs of unemployed youths in American cities. Whyte describes the two gangs as follows:

> Corner boys are groups of men who centre their social activities upon particular street corners, with their adjoining barber shops, lunch rooms, pool rooms or club rooms. They constitute the bottom level of society within their age group and at the same time make up the great majority of young men of Cornerville . . . The college boys are a small group of young men who have risen above the corner boy level through higher education. As they try to make plans for themselves as professional men, they are still moving socially upward. (1955: xx)

Both corner boys and college boys were the 'little guys' of Cornerville. Behind them lay the 'big shots', the racketeers and politicians who dominated local activities. Whyte came to the conclusion that to fully understand Cornerville it was necessary to observe the 'little guys', the 'big shots' and their interrelationships.

Through a detailed examination of both gangs, a careful analysis of biographies and the description of such everyday situations as ten pin bowling, Whyte paints a rich picture of gang social structure. He then places this in the wider context of Cornerville by examining the roles of the racketeers, politicians and police. As outlined in Diagram 2 the 'little guys' and the 'big shots' form a functioning social system which is held in equilibrium by carefully maintained relationships. The racketeers provide protection and votes and their success partly depends on good relations with the corner boys who fill in as prospective customers as well as employees. Some of the more capable corner boys graduate into the rackets. The Cornerville police, instead of being an impersonal agency of social control, are willing collaborators of the racketeers. The extent of their cooperation depends on the amount of graft they can extract. The politicians serve as intermediaries between the racketeers and the police. The interests of all these groups are satisfied when gambling operations are kept smooth. Whyte carefully describes the reciprocal relations that maintain this system.

Diagram 2

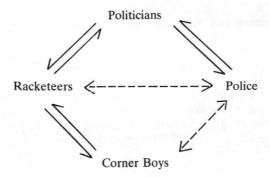

Politicians

Racketeers ← - - - - - - - - → Police

Corner Boys

Clearly Cornerville is a different type of unit altogether from Middletown, yet both may be referred to as communities. Middletown is a partial localised social system containing a whole range of institutions, classes, status, religious and ethnic groups and so forth. Cornerville is a small and relatively homogeneous neighbourhood — most residents are Italian, most are Catholic, most are at the bottom end of the social hierarchy and so on. It seems that Cornerville is much more a community in Max Weber's sense as outlined by

Neuwirth (see pp. 35–7). According to Weber communities are defined in terms of the solidarity shared by their members on the basis of their common economic, political and social interests. Community solidarity and a sense of belonging are a response to outside pressures attempting to obtain their economic, political and social advantages. Such a process can be seen operating in Cornerville. The relationships between the cornerboys, politicians and racketeers enable them to monopolise their economic and political interests and keep others out. The four aspects of community detailed by Neuwirth are visible in Cornerville. A community is *formed* or created through their awareness of their own common characteristics (e.g. immigrant, Italian, Catholic, low status etc.), their attempts to maintain these, and their efforts at keeping others out. Community *closure* occurs through the resident's monopolisation of their advantages, especially in racketeering, gambling and business opportunities. Cornerville consolidates its interests in *associations*, such as the Community Club and the Social and Athletic Club. These associations enforce Cornerville norms and help control the community's monopolies. Both *harmonious* and *conflictual* relationships occur in Cornerville: the former between the corner boys, politicians, racketeers and police and the latter between the gangs. Cornerville is internally stratified but the top groups eventually reject Cornerville norms and move out into the middle-class world.

Vidich, Bensman and *Small Town in Mass Society*

As the title implies, one of Vidich and Bensman's main concerns in *Small Town in Mass Society* was to view the community within the framework of a large-scale bureaucratic mass society rather than as a rural isolate opposed to urbanism. Vidich and Bensman write, 'This study views the community as a limited and finite universe in which one can examine in detail some of the major issues of modern American society ... [it] is an attempt to explore the foundations of social life in a community which lacks the power to control the institutions that regulate and determine its existence. It is in this sense that the community is viewed as a stage on which major issues and problems typical of the society are played out' (1960: ix–x).

This study was a by-product of Studies in Social Growth, a large programmed research project established by Cornell University. One part of this project was to study community activity in a rural area. Vidich was the resident field director and it was his job to observe and participate in community life, maintain liaison between the community and the research organisation based in the university, and provide background data for the formal study of community participation and leadership.

Through participant observation Vidich gathered considerable material that was not encompassed by the formal project but the research directors tended to regard as data only that information collected in structured interviews by the 60 or so interviewers employed by the project. Vidich's insights were regarded as peripheral by the project hierarchy. Bensman, a friend of Vidich and not connected with the project, helped the field director explore his ideas and observations on Springdale (a pseudonym for a small town of 2 500 people in rural upstate New York). The extension of these explorations over two years led to a view of Springdale independent from the project and with its own theoretical focus. At this stage Vidich left the project and he and Bensman asked for permission to do their own study of Springdale. Permission was granted on the understanding that the manuscript be submitted to the project directors before publication and that any information collected be made available to the project staff if required.

Vidich was unhappy with the rigidity enforced on the research by the organisation of the project and he noticed several tensions that arose from the basic conflict between free-ranging research and bureaucratic demands. First, because the project staff had specialised interests they ended up with a narrow view of informants and the community. This resulted in meetings which reduced the community to a single bureaucratically acceptable image to enable the staff to work with this fictional definition while playing their separate project roles. Second, because of the uneven standard of staff, all the data was rigidly standardised and formalised. Third, once the project bureaucracy was committed to accepting only formal data it was almost impossible for it to acknowledge material that might undermine that commitment. Consequently the research perspective of an individual who is independently pursuing knowledge is different from the one that prevails in bureaucratically organised projects. The perspective of the independent investigator, as described in Whyte's case (see pp. 68–72) is based on the theoretical background and experience the researcher brings to the field and on the discovery of problems and issues in the midst of the field experience. In a formalised project the investigator must work within the preordained design and avoid the pursuit of interesting insights. As Vidich and Bensman conclude:

> Bureaucratic constraints make it all but impossible for the individual to follow the insights he otherwise would because such constraints are central to the plans and obligations that are the

heart of large-scale organisation. As a result large-scale research organisations are most effective at gathering and processing data along the lines of sharply defined hypotheses which have standardised variables, dimensions, and methods of analysis. The work of the individual scholar, no matter where he is located, and no matter how he is financed, organised, constrained, or aided, is perhaps the sole source of creativity. (1964: 349)

Vidich and Bensman pursued several areas of Springdale life that did not fit the formal project design, first because they found these areas interesting, and second, because they related to significant theoretical issues. The most important of these areas were the relationship of Springdale to the wider society; the analysis of social and economic class as central features of the social structure; an examination of politics and power; and reporting on the 'negative' aspects of community life as necessary for an understanding of the social basis of community participation. It was largely their analysis of class and politics, including critical comments about Springdale's middle-class leaders with whom the project had established a close liaison, that made the publication of *Small Town in Mass Society* a *cause célèbre* in American sociology.

Vidich's and Bensman's analysis follows in the Middletown tradition. Their main concern is the localised system of social relationships and its connections to the wider social systems of New York State and the American nation. Their historical analysis of the growth of Springdale since 1793 shows the town's increasing dependence on forces originating in the wider society, such as business competition, the price system, extensive bureaucracies, and both State and national political systems. A consequence of such processes is the central conflict detailed by the authors between the traditional image of Springdale as a stronghold of opposition to urbanism, industry and their associated ills, and social reality. According to Vidich and Bensman, Springdale takes great pride in its neighbourliness, equality, grass-roots democracy, rugged independence and rural stability. The dominant ideology is summed up as 'equality, industriousness, improvement and optimism, all of which gain meaning and substance through the pursuit of hard work' (1960: 49). The authors' research however, found that only 25 per cent were actually born in the town; that Springdale contained a set of 'socio-economic classes' with clearly differentiated lifestyles; that judgements of personal worth were based almost entirely on economic achievement and success; that no cultural life in the popular sense existed; that political affairs were dominated by a single top leader who used three associates to control elected political offices and made most of the crucial policy decisions; and finally, that this political elite served as a mediator between Springdale and the wider political authorities of the State and the nation.

Time and time again Vidich and Bensman do what all efficient community studies do and that is penetrate the facade of social life. They constantly show the great disparity between public imagery and social reality. Despite the ethos of democracy, for example, Vidich and Bensman clearly document the existence and activities of what they call an 'invisible government' which Springdalers refuse to recognise and when specifically pointed out, they vigorously deny its existence. If it was recognised it would represent a threat to local social integration and make a mockery of their belief in 'grass-roots democracy'. Recognition is prevented by what the authors call 'particularisation'. Events and processes are seen in isolation, consequently general patterns of behaviour are ignored. As Vidich and Bensman conclude:

> Objectively, the community members live in a world which they do not control. They come to this world, however, with a belief in their ability to shape their own destinies. In fact, in almost every sphere of their lives they find their inherited beliefs and traditions at odds with their institutions and social environment. But the people of Springdale are unwilling to recognise the defeat of their values, their personal impotence in the face of larger events and any failure in their way of life. By techniques of self-avoidance and self-deception, they strive to avoid facing issues which, if recognised, would threaten the total fabric of their personal and social existence. (1960: 319—20)

For this very reason *Small Town in Mass Society* created a furore on publication. Springdaler's were faced with many facts and situations which opposed their cherished beliefs. Vidich and Bensman had previously submitted their manuscript to the project organisers who immediately demanded that it be completely reviewed. From the project's point of view, the manuscript included material that 'although it may represent public knowledge is, in our judgement, highly questionable from the point of view of professional ethics and possible injury to the persons involved' (1964: 332). The project organisers took a protective attitude to Springdale's middle-class leaders on the basis of personal attachments and their cooperation with the formal project. They demanded that the manuscript be read by Springdale's leaders: a demand that suggests censorship on non-academic grounds. After considering these matters and others, and after making some alterations to the manuscript, Vidich and Bensman went ahead and published *Small Town in Mass Society*.

This immediately evoked a public apology from the project organisers which was published on the front page of the *Springdale Courier* in an attempt to placate Springdale's leaders. The town came to its own defence in reviews also published in the *Courier*. Springdale's political leaders rode down the main street for the Fourth of July celebrations wearing hoods with their fictitious names on the back followed by an effigy of 'The Author' bending over a manure-spreader full of rich barnyard fertiliser. Springdale's middle class had now called it even and returned to their former comfortable self-image as if the book had never been published.

Vidich and Bensman do not specifically discuss the concept of community, rather, they use it in a general way to refer to the system of social relationships in Springdale. As with the Middletown studies their usage is close to Stacey's view of community as a partial localised social system. In *Small Town in Mass Society* the authors examine a wide range of relatively autonomous local activities, detail the increasing impact of external structures and processes and analyse the relationship between the two while indicating the town's almost complete dependence on the latter. Springdale is a much more partial social system than Middletown; nevertheless, both studies provide us with rich bodies of data along with some of the basic concepts that are necessary for viewing community in this way.

Herbert Gans and the Levittowners

Gans' study of the first two years in the life of a new suburb on the outskirts of Philadelphia was directed towards destroying what Bennett Berger had earlier called 'the myth of suburbia' (1960: 5). Such popular (and grossly exaggerated) writing as William Whyte's *The Organisation Man* had led to a widespread view of suburbia as consisting of mass produced houses and people driven into a never-ending round of group activity ruled by the strictest conformity. According to this view 'surbanites were incapable of real friendships; they were bored and lonely, alienated, atomised and de-personalised' (Gans 1967: xvi). Domineering wives, absent husbands and spoiled children gradually emerged and with them rising marital friction, adultery, divorce, drunkenness and mental illness. For supporters of this view (see for example Spectorsky, 1955; Riesman, 1957) individualism was dying, surbanites were miserable and the fault lay with the homogeneous suburban landscape and its population. For Gans this was an inaccurate picture and as it was being swallowed by planners who were changing their recommendations accordingly, he felt that it was time to do a sociological study of a new suburb.

Levittown is a dormitory suburb of some 12000 houses developed by a single builder for working-and middle-class families. The houses are divided into ten neighbourhoods, each with its own primary school and swimming pool and community-wide facilities include a large shopping centre, high school, library and parks. On the first day Levittown was opened to potential purchasers Gans bought a house and a few months later moved in with the very first residents. His main technique was participant observation. He supplemented this with a small sample of formal interviews and a mailed questionnaire sent to Levittowners before they arrived in the new community.

Levittowners were primarily young families who had arrived to raise their children and almost half said they had come to settle permanently. Occupationally 26 per cent were manual workers, 56 per cent lower white collar and 18 per cent lower professional. Gans distinguished three 'class cultures'—working, lower middle and upper middle—by their 'styles of life'. Working-class families in Levittown were typically Catholic; their parent-child relationships were adult centred; male and female roles were segregated; they rarely entertained; they were highly suspicious of strangers, government officials and private organisations; and they stayed 'close to home and make the house a haven against a hostile outside world' (1967: 27). The lower middle-class families were characterised by a higher education; less role segregation; child centred parent-child relationships; considerable activities in church and voluntary associations; little interest in government; and a marked concern with respectability. The upper middle-class families are part of 'the culture of the college educated, cosmopolitan population, trained to be interested in and to participate in the larger world' (1967: 30). There was little role segregation; family life was child-centred but adult-directed; participation was high in both voluntary associations and community-wide activities, such as working for better schools and race relations as well as attending concerts, plays and art exhibitions; and finally, they were intensely involved in government and politics. Consequently, Levittown was in no sense the totally homogeneous community of the suburban myth.

Gans found that these families came to Levittown for modern comfortable housing and that they did not especially want to change their old way of life. Their initial concerns were for their family life. Gradually wider patterns of social relations developed as they made friends on the basis of shared interests and not on the grounds of who happened to live close by. The next stage was the sorting of the community into informal clubs and cliques—what Gans calls 'the community stratification process' (1967: 49). Formal voluntary associations followed with the working-class clubs being primarily 'social' centred and the middle-class clubs 'activity' or 'community' oriented. Gans described these organisations as 'sorting groups which divided and segregated people by their interests and ultimately, of course, by socio-economic, educational, and religious differences' (1967: 61) Gans' analysis of the origin of formal organisations, the founding of churches, the establishment of the new school system and the growth of political parties clearly demonstrated the cultural diversity of Levittown.

Gans argued that because Levittown was not a place of employment its power structure was determined more by the local class system. Following his stratification model he commented that because of the builder's influence, the existence of a considerable Catholic, Democratic working-class bloc and the Democratic party leader's ability to control the machine there was 'a somewhat more monolithic local power structure, less varied from issue to issue than in most American communities' (1967: 135). Unfortunately his political analysis suffers from the lack of broad survey data on voting and political attitudes which would have facilitated more useful generalisations.

Gans did not find hyperactive neighbouring, overt conformity, or deliberately changed behaviour to copy neighbours as postulated by the 'myth of suburbia'. Of course Levittown is not a microcosm of American society. It has no drop-outs or upper class, for example, and the three class cultures identified are at times similar. Almost all, for example, were raising children. As Gans comments, what is seen by the critics of suburbia 'as blandness and apathy is really a result of the invisibility and home-centredness of lower middle class culture' (1967: 186). Levittowners are not organisation men, exurbanites or transients but neither do they have the 'rootedness' so liked by traditional writers on community. Gans writes:

> The community may displease the professional city planner and the intellectual defender of cosmopolitan culture, but perhaps more than any other type of community, Levittown permits most of its residents to be what they want to be — to centre their lives around the home and the family, to be among neighbours whom they can trust, to find friends to share leisure hours, and to participate in organisations that provide sociability and the opportunity to be of service to others. (1967: 412–3)

Clearly for most Levittowners their home was the centre of the community and determined much of its social structure. But as Bell and Newby correctly point out this may well 'be a function of their present stage in the family cycle' (1971: 130). Levittown's young children will eventually grow up and move away to work and marry. At the same time their ageing parents may well change from home-centredness to association or community-centredness. In other words theories of community must be able to account for processes of change over a considerable period of time. Gans has provided us with a model for the emergence of a new community but we also need to know how communities mature and change through time.

Gans has no qualms in referring to Levittown as a community although he points out that by traditional criteria it is not a community. The suburb is not an economic, social or symbolic unit. The residents are not dependent on each other for their livelihood, there is no reason for them to interact on a regular basis and there is little 'sense of community'. But Gans argues:

> If Levittown was a community, and of course it was, it could best be defined as an administrative-political unit plus an aggregate of community-wide associations within a space that had been legally established by William Penn and his associates as a township some three hundred years before. As such, it provides residents with a variety of services and required them to act in a limited number of community roles — for example, as voters, taxpayers and organisational participants — but these roles encouraged division rather than cohesion. (1967: 145–6)

What Gans shows is that Levittown was not made into a community because of 'the pre-occupancy aspirations of the residents' but rather through 'a complex process of external initiative and subsequent internal transformation that produced organisations and institutions which reflected the backgrounds and interests of the majority of the population' (1967: 141). The process of Levittowners sorting themselves out through neighbourhoods, informal associations, formal voluntary associations and government was a central part of the process of *community formation*. Somewhat in line with Weber's view of community (see pp. 35–7) Gans indicates how social solidarity was gradually established by different groups in Levittown on the basis of their common economic, political and social interests. Any 'sense of community' in Levittown was restricted to the house, the adjacent neighbours, the block, friends elsewhere in the suburb, and the particular church or organisation in which they were active (1967: 144).

It is at this level that *community closure* operates in Levittown and the home-centred advantage of the suburb maintained. Nevertheless Gans admits the possibility of a wider process of community sentiment and closure when he writes, 'if the community were threatened by powerful outside forces which would hurt the community as a whole or deprive every Levittowner, an intense identification with the community might be created . . .' (1967: 145). The different groups and classes in Levittown gradually came to consolidating their interests in *associations* both informal and formal. Such associations, whether they be informal gossip networks, churches, sporting bodies or political organisations help to enforce group and class norms.

Clearly both *harmonious* and *conflictual* relationships occur in Levittown — the former with informal friendship groups and the latter in struggles for power in local government. Gans has provided us with an enormous wealth of data and an incipient model for examining the growth of community. What is required is to take this approach further through time to monitor changes in community processes. This can only be achieved through painstaking research which examines what is actually happening. It cannot be achieved by armchair intellectuals who create such exaggerations as the 'myth of suburbia'.

5 The Empirical Tradition of Community Studies: The British Case

As in America, British community studies were strongly influenced by the methods and theories of social anthropology, especially participant observation and functionalist-equilibrium models of society. The initial movements in this direction were Warner's attempts to establish research in Ireland for comparative purposes with his American material and the combination of anthropology and geography in the Welsh school aiming to describe Welsh culture.

In this Chapter I discuss six British community studies which clearly indicate the changing nature of research strategies and theoretical interests in this field over 30 or so years. The studies are Arensberg's and Kimball's *Family and Community in Ireland*; Rees' *Life in the Welsh Countryside*; Williams' *The Sociology of an English Village: Gosforth*; Littlejohn's *Westrigg: The Sociology of a Cheviot Parish*; Stacey's *Tradition and Change*; and Stacey et al's *Power, Persistence and Change*. As in the last Chapter I concentrate on the background of the projects, what the sociologists did, their major findings and their approach to community in terms of the three models outlined in Chapter 2.

Arensberg, Kimball and County Clare

Family and Community in Ireland by Arensberg and Kimball (1940, 2nd edn, 1968) has been heralded as 'a pioneer study' (Frankenberg, 1966: 43) but as Bell and Newby (1971: 132) pointed out it is more correct to see this work as an extension of Lloyd Warner's established approach (see pp. 65–8). Flushed with his success of studying Australian Aborigines and Americans, Warner embarked on a comparative scheme which involved applying similar techniques to the study of diverse communities in varying societies in order to establish some form of classification. Ireland was chosen because the Department of Anthropology at Harvard University was starting a study of Ireland involving archaeology, physical anthropology and social anthropology. Warner was in charge of the work of the social anthropologists and in 1931 during a preliminary survey he chose County Clare as the most suitable Irish county for his needs. The following year Warner and Arensberg, one of his former students who had worked with him on the Yankee City project, settled in Clare and started to collect data. Warner returned to Harvard before the end of 1932 and was replaced by another researcher from Yankee City, Solon Kimball. Arensberg and Kimball continued fieldwork in Southern Ireland for two years.

This background is important for it largely determines the theoretical framework with which they approached the study and analysed their data. Warner's approach was functionist, wholistic and descriptive. Similarly, Arensberg and Kimball followed the functionalist theory of Malinowski and Radcliffe-Brown. As they wrote in their introduction:

> Experience in Yankee City in New England had led the authors to the point of view which is the central hypothesis of functional anthropology. The more they worked, the more it grew certain to them that to a certain approximation it is useful to regard society as an integrated system of mutually interrelated and functionally interdependent parts. A study in Ireland, then, should be a study to test this hypothesis. (1968: xxx)

Clearly, County Clare, a lowly populated rural area, was chosen for study because it was expected to confirm the functionalist thesis. In other words, the authors were adapting tried and trusted anthropological techniques to the study of yet one more relatively small homogeneous population living in a limited and isolated area. Such a situation is extremely receptive to a functionalist approach but it tells us little about social change, the increasing impact of industrialisation and bureaucratisation and the conflictual nature of society.

Arensberg and Kimball went even further to accommodate their data to their theoretical assumptions. They acknowledge that there are two very different types of agricultural activity in Ireland — the large farmers and the small farmers.

> Large farmers differ from the small farmers in their techniques, in their products, in their use of the soil and the land. They differ in the way in which members derive support from their farms. They differ significantly in the organisation of labour upon these farms and presumably in consequence in the relations with other elements of the community. Family labour characterises the small man, hired labour the big fellow. (1968: 3–4)

Despite this important cleavage which has crucial repercussions throughout Irish society, Arensberg and Kimball chose to deal with only the small farmer. Such a decision immediately gets rid of conflict and such macro processes of change as the increasing industrialisation of agriculture with which the functionalist-equilibrium model has problems in explaining and even encompassing. Further, it is to be expected that small-scale subsistence farmers will easily slot into such expectations of the functionalist framework with its emphasis on traditional rather than rational behaviour, the maintenance of stability and order through multiplex ties based on custom and reinforced by strong normative sanctions and an overall static social system untroubled by power, conflict and change. Consequently, such conclusions as 'the forces operative within the structure are of such a nature as to allow the society of which they are a part to continue to function in essentially similar fashion through the welter of economic, political and other events' (1968: 150) are to be fully expected. It is clear that Arensberg and Kimball are dealing with small-scale subsistence farmers in an isolated part of Western Ireland and not with 'society' — Irish society or Western society.

Once these limitations have been recognised, however, *Family and Community in Ireland*, within the functionalist framework, provides us with a rich and detailed analysis of 'the institutional arrangements and the behaviour and values of those participating in them' (1968: ix). The authors successfully come 'to grips with the social and psychological facts in the raw' (1968: 30) and do this through an impressive array of both qualitative and quantitative data.

The study deals with an area which contains several scattered settlements consisting of families of small farmers inhabiting a comparatively isolated farmhouse built on a holding from which they make their livelihood. Their analysis concentrates on the relationships between these dispersed communities and family life. A series of cross-cutting relationships centring on kinship, church activities, schooling, shopping, markets, local government and traditional district allegiances links the families and the scattered communities in the area into a stable, unchanging social system.

According to Arensberg and Kimball the family and the rural community are the two institutions that give Irish rural life and small-farm subsistence their 'characteristic form'. They create 'a master system articulating five major subsidiary systems' (1968: 301) which are the familistic order; the generation order; sex role organisation; the local division of labour; and economic exchange and distribution. Taken together these comprise 'the framework of social life in the countryside' (1968: 303) and no event, issue or relationship can be understood without reference to them. Note that external influences on the social system, such as the growth of capitalist agri-businesses, the role of political power and historical processes of change are ignored. Arensberg's and Kimball's claims are rather grandiose, given the limited nature of their study, nevertheless it has been and remains a widely-read and influential analysis. Many later studies, as we shall see, use the functionalist framework, continue to be ahistorical, and still view the rural community as an unchanging entity.

Life in the Welsh Countryside with Alwyn Rees

Daryll Forde who was the Professor of Geography and Anthropology at what is now the University of Wales encouraged Rees to study the parish of Llanfihangel-yng-Ngwynfa as part of a plan for a series of Welsh studies. Anthropology, geography and a strong commitment to Welsh culture are all combined in Rees' book *Life in the Welsh Countryside* (1950). The anthropological tradition shines through in Rees' desire to find a place where he could study a community as a whole in terms of a more or less self-contained, self-sufficient system. The parish chosen, overwhelmingly Welsh speaking and situated in mid-Wales, was cut off from English culture by class and language and also from the mainstream of Welsh culture by the Berwyn Mountains. The parish was in many respects similar to Arensberg's and Kimball's situation in Ireland. Farms and cottages were scattered around the countryside and three small hamlets provided such services as schools, post office, churches and inns. During the period of the study the population was declining through migration to the cities leaving cottages in decay and fields reverting to rough pasture (1950: 14). It has been suggested that this study was an attempt 'to record the dying Welsh culture before it succumbed to encroaching English influences' (Bell and Newby, 1971: 137). Rees' later work reinforces this view (see Rees, 1973).

As 85 per cent of the inhabitants were born within the area (as were 75 per cent of their parents) kinship relations form the major part of the local social structure. Most households in the parish were joined to each other by kin ties and those not so related were connected to households in neighbouring parishes. For Rees these ties, centred in this locality and reinforced by religion, create a communal solidarity which has played a large part in preventing the farmers of Llanfihangel from migrating. They 'tie him to his locality and make life incomplete elsewhere' (1950: 31). Rees argues that kinship binds the individual to the locality but at the same time places constraints on individual behaviour. The reputation of not only oneself but also of one's relatives are always at stake, consequently kinship is a powerful agent of social control which always reinforces customary norms.

Although there is 'a considerable distinction between the independent farmer of, let us say, a hundred acre farm and a wage earner who supplements his earnings from a small holding' (1950: 145), class divisions and class consciousness are relatively weak and do not interfere with 'the free social contact between families'. Matters of social status, however, are important and centre on non-economic accomplishments. Households seek, gain and maintain reputations for such things as theological argument, card playing, poetry and music. But Rees is aware that changes were affecting these traditional forms of behaviour: 'change has been accelerated by the two Great Wars. During these periods of scarcity money could be made so easily and quickly that it became worth seeking it to the exclusion of all other values . . .' (1950: 145).

Rees implicitly supports the traditionalists' view of the rural-urban continuum. He emphasises 'the completeness of the traditional rural society—involving the cohesion of family, kindred and neighbours—and its capacity to give the individual a sense of belonging' (1950: 170), whereas urban or city life fails 'to give its inhabitants status and significance in a functioning society and [they consequently disintegrate] into formless masses of rootless nonentities' (1950: 170). Clearly for Rees the world of the Welsh village represents the good life and that of the English city the opposite. Given this orientation perhaps we should ask ourselves whether or not Rees has underplayed the envies, jealousies and conflicts that do occur in small face-to-face (or as called by others back-to-back) communities and whether he has totally ignored the communal solidarity found in both 'urban villages' and suburbs (see Gans, 1962, 1967). Rees is pessimistic about the future of such villages as Llanfihangel and he fully expects them to be disrupted by creeping urbanism. He regrets this, for the process 'uproots the ablest members of the community, educates them and scatters them . . . They are birds of passage and their interest in their adopted localities is not, generally speaking, as great as it might have been in their native localities among their own kith and kin' (1950: 165). Such statements exhibit Rees' static, functionalist viewpoint, where the traditional community is seen as an unchanging entity which is under threat from outside forces and should, if possible, be preserved. But traditional communities are not static and change may be endogenous as well as exogenous. The difficulty with Rees is that given his value-laden view of rural and urban situations, he is directed away

from data which does not support his framework. What we end up
with is a partial picture of life in the Welsh countryside and a very
firm view of how Rees would like it to be.

Rees' work had a direct influence on such later Welsh studies as
Frankenberg's *Village on the Border*, Emmett's *A North Wales Village* and Rees' and Davies' *Welsh Rural Communities* but each of
these have taken differing theoretical perspectives where such things
can be discerned, and they are not cumulative in terms of presenting
a fully-rounded picture of Welsh life. Nevertheless, they do provide
us with important insights into, and descriptions of, everyday life in
rural Wales. Rees also trained students in the community studies
field and one of those was W.M. Williams' study of Gosforth in the
north of England.

W.M. Williams' Sociology of an English Village

Williams' study of Gosforth in the uplands of what is now called
Cumbria in north-west England brings together Welsh and American influences but remains within the traditional anthropological
functionalist framework. Williams was a student of Rees and
selected to study a similar type of locality as Llanfihangel, that is a
village of 723 people surrounded by farms dotted throughout the
hills. For his analysis of social stratification in Gosforth, however,
Williams uses Lloyd Warner's hierarchical model of social classes,
or more accurately, status groups.

The social and economic organisation of rural life in Gosforth is
remarkably similar to that described by Arensberg and Kimball for
County Clare and Rees for Wales. This is, of course, understandable when one realises that their functionalist assumptions directed
them towards similar places—communities that were small,
homogeneous, stable, integrated and relatively unchanging. The
family in Gosforth is the basic social and economic unit. Almost all
farm labour was provided by members of the family. Marriage and
inheritance are crucial in this area of upland family farming.
According to Williams 'in the majority of cases, where the eldest
son inherits, he remains at home unmarried until his parents retire.
He then assumes control and is free to marry, and the limited information available suggests that marriage follows inheritance within a very short period. The remaining sons are free to marry more
or less when they choose, subject to the labour requirements of the
holding ... the underlying principle is the maintenance of the family
group as a relatively self-sufficient economic unit and the retention
of the holding within the family' (1956: 50).

The village families do not follow this pattern as they are not productive units but nevertheless, they are part of complex social networks centring on kinship. These ties form 'a framework of reference points which help the individual to identify other people. It explains the stability of the community by linking its present members with those of the past' (1956: 76). The sense of belonging or feeling of community in Gosforth stems from the close-knit kinship networks which have provided population stability in the locality over generations.

The kinship networks provide the basis for the local system of social stratification because it is through such networks that people are known, their actions evaluated and their reputations formed. Williams borrowed Lloyd Warner's method of status placement and divided the Gosforth population into seven 'social classes' on the grounds that, 'The same people were always mentioned in connection with a particular class and never as belonging to another class' (1956: 86). Each class has special characteristics and types of behaviour, consequently Williams sees the system as an interactional or relational one where everyone knows everyone else and all can be socially placed. Each 'class' or 'class' segment has a local label — the nibs, the village aristocracy, the money-makers, the average villager, people who keep themselves to themselves, the immoral element, the worst of the lower orders, and so forth (1956: 107–9). Williams classifies these into Warner's model using the latter's status terminology — upper upper, lower upper, upper middle, middle middle, lower middle and so on. Williams, however, notes that this system is not as stable as it was (the initial stability of the system may be a functionalist assumption as there is little historical information in this study) because of the encroaching influence of new industries in the wider region. This process was beginning to bring to Gosforth people with urban values who did not 'fit in'. Further, as farm labourers left the land to work in the new industries traditional relationships whereby 'goods and services were an important medium of exchange' were altered to those where 'money is the sole medium' (1956: 33).

Williams traces the significance of status differences in formal and informal associations. 'Status within the village organisations tends to reflect the status system within the community generally' (1956: 124). Presidents of organisations are confined to the 'upper upper class' and they occupy more than half of the positions of chairman, vice-chairman and vice-president. The 'lower class' is not represented in any formal positions. As Williams remarks, 'offices are given to people with high status and this enhances and confirms their status. Also, the giving of offices to people of high status enhances the prestige—and therefore the attraction—of offices' (1956: 126). There is, however, the difficulty of some circularity in this argument; if voluntary association membership and activity is a major part of the subjective status placement of individuals and families in the stratification system in the first place (as seems to be the case), then one would expect membership patterns to coincide with the status groups selected. It might have been more fruitful for Williams to compare membership distribution as an aspect of social status with such economic class criteria as relationship to the means of production and/or sources of income.

In a similar way to Rees' view of Welsh country life, Williams expresses dismay at the passing of the traditional way of life—'one could not but regret that the study was apparently made 20 or 30 years too late. Gosforth has changed more in the past two or three decades than it did in the two previous centuries, largely as a result of the increasing influence of urban culture . . . Against this the tra-ditional way of life is static and can offer nothing to replace the loss in community feeling which is a result of these developments' (1956: 202–3). For Williams, then, Gosforth represents a traditional, static and stable way of life but one that is decaying under the influence of encroaching urban values. Clearly Williams does not favour this process of change. The traditional system represents the good life. But it is not at all clear or proven that Gosforth life has been tradi-tional or stable over the previous centuries. What is certain is that the functionalist approach assumes that Gosforth is a static social system being interrupted by a new process of change. In this study, as in many others of its type, values, theory and method are so intertwined that it becomes almost impossible to determine where empirical description and theoretical analysis stops and normative prescription begins.

Littlejohn's Sociology of a Cheviot Parish

Littlejohn's study of Westrigg provides us with a useful advance over Williams' static analysis. Littlejohn, a social anthropologist working from the University of Edinburgh, moves away from many functionalist assumptions and towards a dynamic analysis of class and status in the upland parish of Westrigg. It is worth noting that although this study was not published until 1963 the fieldwork was done during the same period as Williams' work in Gosforth, that is between 1949 and 1951.

A large part of the dynamic nature of the Westrigg study stems from its detailed historical analysis. Littlejohn takes the turn of the century as his starting point and, as well as using oral history, he reconstructs the social organisation of the parish from official records and historical documents. He argues that 'the parish has become less and less a social unit possessing an independent existence of its own, and parishioners have been drawn increasingly into a wider network of contacts and relationships' (1963: 39). Littlejohn avoids the functionalist assumption that the traditional system was harmonious, independent and unaffected by social change. Even around 1900 the parish was 'a unit of local government in a framework established by the State, and the authority of the Parish Council and the School Board derived from it' (1963: 59). Furthermore, farm production was subject to the forces of a worldwide market. Nevertheless, at this time Westrigg 'was a community within which by far the greater part of the individual's social and economic relationships were found. Or rather his relations outside the parish were fewer than they are now' (1963: 121–2).

Littlejohn describes the class system at the turn of the century as a hierarchy of economic power where those at the top exercise power over those below either through owning land and thereby controlling tenants or through owning or leasing farms and having power over manual workers. At the top was 'the county', large landowners with hereditary titles. The Duke of Garvel in Westrigg owned all but three farms. Next came the owners and tenants of the larger farms, the minister, the smaller farmers, the schoolmaster and a few of the more prosperous tradesmen. Below them came the majority of the population — farm workers and tradesmen. Finally, Littlejohn identifies a class which has now all but disappeared and which consisted of tramps and those on Poor Relief (1963: 56).

The fact that Littlejohn emphasises class rather than kinship as the central element of the social structure clearly demarcates his work from that of Arensberg and Kimball, Rees and Williams. There were few family farms in Westrigg. Most were large-scale operations manned by hired labour. As Littlejohn remarks, 'the parish is not the locus within which the kinship ties of parishioners can be effectively studied and ... a study of these ties would not greatly illuminate the nature of the social relationships obtaining among parishioners ... Outside the family the rights and obligations of kinship are neither clearly defined nor of great weight compared with those in other areas of life, particularly occupation, and no-one in the parish at present owes his job to an extra-familial kinship tie' (1963: 7–8). In a discussion of class and kinship norms, Littlejohn concludes, 'there is incompatability between the two sets of norms and [that] where they conflict class norms predominate' (1963: 121–2). Clearly Westrigg is a slightly different type of rural locality from the others described so far but also Littlejohn's theoretical framework diverges from those of the earlier studies. He has moved away from descriptive, wholistic functionalism which emphasises the integrative nature of kinship towards a more analytical and propositional type of approach which draws on the work of Weber and Parsons and centres on the integrative, conflictual and changing nature of class relations. A combination of different empirical data meshed with a theoretical framework centring on class and emphasising history gives Westrigg a special quality which is absent in many other community studies.

Littlejohn examines the major processes of social change and details their impact on the parish. The re-organisation of local government, the extension of the rights of citizenship, a re-alignment of employer-employee relationships towards 'those which obtain in industrial areas' (1963: 69), the development of public transport and a massive increase in the range and amount of consumer goods have all contributed to 'the gradual disappearance of what was once an important social unit, the country parish. Rights, which an individual once possessed by virtue of his membership of this unit, he now possess by virtue of his membership of either the County or the State' (1963: 63). Parishioners' social contacts have widened, consequently they are no longer socially and economically dependent on other members of the parish. According to Littlejohn 'the term "parish" now refers merely to a population living within a geographically defined boundary which has little sociological significance' (1963: 63). Relationships of the local social organisation have gradually been replaced by those of the modern industrial and economic system. Implicit in this view is that 'social class has increasingly become relatively more important than the formation community' (1963: 75). The incorporation of both farmers and farm workers into nationwide unions, the change from personal to impersonal relationships between employers and employees and increased monney wages led to a decline in the number of classes and a redistribution of power between them. The power of the landed aristocracy has declined and that of the working class increased. As Littlejohn concludes, 'relationships among the population of the parish are much more like those among the population of any industrial area than they were 50 years ago' (1963: 75).

Littlejohn used his community study of Westrigg to show the interrelated nature of macro-social processes working on the interrelations of social institutions in a locality. From this point of view his work is a forerunner of the localised social system analysis later advocated by Stacey (1969). By taking propositions relating to class, and examining them in both historical and contemporary situations within the context of a specific locality, Littlejohn's study is more amenable for generalisation and comparative analysis than are many others.

Margaret Stacey and the Banbury Studies

Banbury is the only English town to have been re-studied. The fieldwork for *Tradition and Change* (1960) was undertaken between 1948 and 1951 and for *Power, Persistence and Change: A Second Study of Banbury* (Stacey *et al.* 1975) the fieldwork was done between 1966 and 1968. The first study started from the anthropological tradition. Stacey's aim was to put the 'ingredients of everyday life in something like the perspective in which we view the Trobriands or the Nuer' (1960: v). Stacey was particularly inspired by the Lynds' work on Middletown and decided to adopt their basic approach of seeing how the interrelations between major social institutions worked themselves out in local social relations. At this time some of the difficulties of unfocused, wholistic and functionalist analyses of western urban localities were starting to become plain and although Stacey wanted to test some of the wholistic ideas on a small scale she focused the study on a particular aspect of social change. 'The purpose of the research was to study the social structure and culture of Banbury with special reference to the introduction of large-scale industry' (1960: v).

The main method for both studies was participant observation but this was supplemented by other ways of gathering data for as Stacey comments, 'without the techniques developed by the statistician and the sociologist in their more specialised studies of complex societies, it would not be possible to apply the social anthropologists' methods to a place of this size' (1960: v).

Stacey and her two assistants examined Banbury's published records and used a 20 per cent random sample of 1 000 interviews to obtain data on family and household composition, religious adherence and political activity and attitudes. 'As a main guide to the functioning of the social structure a study was made, by interview of the leading members and analysis of the records of all the formal organisations of Banbury' (1960: vi). The aim here was to show the composition of the leadership and membership of the associations, where leadership overlapped and with what broader social groups the associations were connected.

Banbury was not chosen for its typicality. According to Stacey its choice was fortuitous. She had lived there for several years and was impressed by its suitability for research. It was relatively isolated and was small enough for all its leaders to be known. It was a town with a long history and its own traditions. 'It shows stresses and strains as a result of its sudden growth (in 1931 the population was under 14 000), and the relations of the long-established residents with the large number of "foreigners" who came to man the large-scale modern factory in the 1930s presented an interesting social problem' (1960: iv). But Stacey also was a 'foreigner', a 'non-traditionalist', an outsider who did not share local values. Clearly she must have formed some impressions about the structure and organisation of the town and at the same time been 'placed' by the local people somewhere within that framework. This can lead to certain difficulties, and often barriers, in the fieldwork process but Stacey has little to say on this issue. Working with a team can some-times overcome some of these problems but team research gener-ates its own difficulties as I noted with Vidich and Bensmans' re-search and as I shall explore in more detail below.

Banbury was a market town and for the first three decades of this century it was stagnating and suffered a slight population decline in the 1920s. From 1901 to 1931 the population hovered around 13 000 — small enough for most people to know each other and stable enough to develop a social structure where status was total and pervasive (see Plowman *et al.* 1962; Wild, 1974: 205). Stacey calls this the 'traditional' social structure as it is traditionally legitimised by an appeal to the past — a belief in things as they have always existed. In Banbury there was 'an established group, a group bound together by common history and tradition, with a recognised social structure and having certain common values' (1960: 167). This group was based on a long-standing network of relationships be-tween families and friends, for whom conformity, stability and con-servation of established institutions were keynotes. Although most traditionalists were Banburians not all traditionalists were natives of the town and not all natives were traditionalists. As this society was based on a series of face-to-face relationships it could only accept a limited number of newcomers at a time. Many of these were pre-pared to behave according to the traditional standards and to accept the customary values. But some locally born did not accept their place and were outside the traditional social structure.

The arrival of the aluminium factory in 1933 and the associated influx of immigrants represented an abrupt change. 'Non-traditionalism which had begun to emerge before the days of the aluminium factory, was reinforced and extended' (1960: 170). The opposition between traditional and non-traditional was seen by Stacey as an important key for understanding the social structure and culture of Banbury. This division was not a dichotomy as suggested by some commentators (see Frankenberg, 1966: 155). Non-traditionalists consisted of several groups which did not share any common social or value system—'they include those who have come in with quite other systems of values and customs and those who are developing new ways to meet the changed circumstances of their life and work' (1960: 14).

At the heart of *Tradition and Change* is an extremely thorough analysis of the local interrelation of social institutions. The close-knit networks of pre-1930 Banbury where, 'Family, together with place of origin and associations, such as religion and politics, was the test by which people "recognised" or "placed" each other' (1960: 12) was still apparent in 1950. There were still 'small, private enterprise firms in which the owners take a direct part' (1960: 21), in contrast to the non-traditional factory organised on a large-scale with outside ownership and control. The former places emphasis on particular relationships where, for example, traditional shopkeepers feel they can rely on the personal support of their customers. Such traditional industries were not fully penetrated by trade unions. The aluminium factory epitomised the non-traditional. As Bell and Newby comment, 'Traditional industry . . . was part of a total local social structure in contrast to non-traditional industry which, whilst it was related in particular ways to particular sections of the town, was also related nationally and internationally' (1971: 182).

A major consequence of the expansion of the non-traditional sector was that Banbury 'may less and less be thought of as a whole society, but rather divided with sections, parts of larger wholes in a much wider society' (1960: 3). Economic, social, political and religious values were becoming much less closely linked together as the non-traditional forces increased.

The second important source of social division and tension after the traditional non-traditional distinction was social stratification. Stacey concluded, 'Social class divides traditional and non-traditional alike, although . . . the attitude of each group to these horizontal divisions and their impact on each is different. Each class has ways of life and values and attitudes so dissimilar that interaction between them, except in formal ways, is almost impossible, nor is it sought' (1960: 171). Banbury's social structure then was 'bisected in two ways': vertically by the traditional/non-traditional division and horizontally by the middle class/working class division. Stacey explores the relationship between this pair of oppositions through patterns of voting. She takes Labour voting as a key indicator of non-traditionalism in both classes and the indicator of traditionalism in the working class as not voting Labour. Stacey concludes that the deepest and most significant social cleavage 'is found at the point where the three factors of traditionalism and non-traditionalism, social class and politics come together. This is also the point where the maximum social distance and also social tension between groups is found' (1960: 175). Consequently, the groups at the extremities of Banbury's social organisation are the non-traditional, Labour voting members of the working class and the traditional, Conservative voting members of the middle class.

Although Stacey's approach is wholistic in that 'an attempt was made to relate the parts to the whole' (1960: 5) she is primarily concerned with the configurations of the interrelations of social institutions within this locality and their connections to the wider society. She does not treat Banbury as an isolated unit within a vacuum nor does she claim to deal with every aspect of social life. Banbury is partly seen as an object in the anthropological manner but it is also used as a way of getting at some data to examine some theoretical notions concerning processes of social change. It is this aspect that makes *Tradition and Change* valuable for generalisation and comparative analysis. The dynamic nature of the study is evident in the conclusions where Banbury's social structure is seen to be in a fluid state. Banbury society was viewed as wide open to the challenge of change, but unlikely to experience open conflict because of the many cross-cutting ties. 'What is non-traditional today may well be traditional tomorrow and this new tradition itself open to the challenge of fresh change' (1960: 182). Stacey predicted that the ties of the traditional society were loosening and reducing the intensity of inward-turning social relationships and, at the same time, that demarcation between the locality and the outside world was decreasing and the range of interests and relationships in the town widening.

When a re-study of Banbury was made in the 1960s, this prediction was a major focus of interest as was a concern with what had happened to the traditional society. Further, Stacey was formulating her ideas for the model of the localised social system (see pp. 31–5) where she outlined conditions under which a local social system might develop, be destroyed or changed. The Banbury re-study aimed to examine some of these propositions.

There are however, enormous difficulties to contend with in re-studies. As I have already noted the nature of the data and the research methodology limits comparability in community studies. Time certainly affected the status and perspectives of Margaret Stacey and the new field staff belonged to a different generation and had been socialised into a different sociological world. Much had changed in sociology between 1951 and 1966. The work of such people as Merton, Goffman, Wright Mills, Dahrendorf and others now had to be taken into account. As Stacey comments, 'Any aspect of social relations studied in Banbury in the second half of the sixties had to take account of a specialist sub-discipline' (1975: 5).

Further, there are different types of re-studies. Lewis (1953) distinguishes four. First, those where a second investigator goes to a community with the aim of re-evaluating the work of his predecessor. Second, those in which the original investigator returns to study some aspect of the community not studied earlier. Third, those where a researcher investigates more intensively or from a new theoretical point of view, some aspect of the community studied earlier. Finally, those where the same or an independent investigator goes to a community studied earlier, but this time to study change and uses the first report as a basis on which to measure and evaluate change. These categories are not mutually exclusive. The Middletown re-study, for example, falls largely into the last category but it also includes category three because Middletown in the 1930s was examined through the perspective of a newly developed theoretical approach. The Banbury re-study fits wholly into the last category.

Given these factors the context of the second study was different from the first and the end product is a very different type of work. The first report examined many aspects of the social structure, social processes and culture of Banbury within a wholistic framework. The second report 'concentrates on those aspects where there is something particular to contribute to sociology as a whole or to a sub-discipline' (Stacey *et al.* 1975: 6). The authors have assumed that readers will go to *Tradition and Change* for a full account of life in Banbury in the 1950s which is the base line for the analysis of change. Indeed, without having read the first book, the second would be difficult to follow.

There are several reasons for this. First, the main conclusion of *Power, Persistence and Change* is that it was not possible to discern clear and distinctive patterns in the social life of Banbury in the late 1960s. 'We have now found that the inequalities of power, wealth, income, occupation, education and other resources are surprisingly formless. There is a pattern, but there are no sharp divisions in the pattern of stratification as there were around 1950' (1975: 4–5). Religion has declined in influence and 'does not reinforce other divisions as it once did' (1975: 39). A central feature of Banbury politics in the 1960s is 'the increasing removal of power from the locality' (1975: 56). At the local neighbourhood level three streets were examined by the fieldworkers who lived there for periods of up to two years. They concluded that 'the quality and quantity of neighbour relations is determined more by the institutions of the larger society and by the statuses and roles played by residents associated with these institutions, often outside the locality, than by any physical characteristics of the locality or of propinquity within it' (1975: 84). Finally, with reference to class and status, Banbury society in 1968:

> is complex, linked through many social relations with other parts of Britain and beyond, and pluralist in the sense of being composed of a kaleidoscope of interlocking and overlapping groups and networks ... although it can be seen to be composed of two or three social levels, [it] has no neat social class system but is dynamic, stratified, cross-cut by ties within and without'. (1975: 134–5)

Banbury seems to have lost its uniqueness. It is being swallowed up by the encroaching corporate state and international capitalism. But the theoretical framework for examining this process and for determining the uniqueness of Banbury in response to such forces vis-à-vis responses in other towns is not present in *Power, Persistence and Change*. The propositions they were testing were formulated with the concepts available in the early 1950s and as a re-study the researchers were forced back to the theoretical notions in *Tradition and Change*. Perhaps the Banbury re-study should have followed more closely the Middletown re-study where the Lynds returned to Middletown with a different theoretical focus and produced a more challenging analysis. As Bell comments in his *Reflections on the Banbury Re-study* (1977: 61): 'it is impossible to replicate without some theory of social change. *Tradition and Change* had the rudiments of such a theory; the work that produced *Power, Persistence and Change* destroyed that theory.' The problem is that it did not put anything in its place.

A second reason for the differences between the two studies concerns the nature of the team research. For the first study Stacey lived in Banbury, conducted much of the research and wrote the final report. During the second study she did not live in Banbury, conducted little fieldwork, and although she wrote the final volume, earlier drafts were prepared by the other researchers. Further, two of the fieldworkers were also engaged on higher degree theses using data from the re-study. They 'were "encouraged" to work in areas that would contribute to the project as a whole, but the demands of the project were not always compatible with producing a doctorate' (Bell, 1977: 50). This and the 'sometimes open conflict between the members of the research team' (Bell, 1977: 51) contributed to the disjointed and more abstract nature of the re-study. The latter was further emphasised by the manner in which the report was put together. After fieldwork, team members went to different jobs across Britain and as Bell remarks, 'That *Power, Persistence and Change* was written up at all owes more to the determination and endless energy of Margaret Stacey ... left to ourselves I strongly suspect that we would have individually abandoned the data and the project' (1977: 55). Further, acrimonious meetings concerning such maters as how participant observation data could be married to the survey data and which should be given priority affected the final outcome. The second report clearly depends more on survey material and has less of the 'feel' of Banbury than the first.

A third reason for the flat nature of the re-study concerns the amount of time between the completion of fieldwork and publication. By 1975 neo-Marxists concerns with capitalism and the State, epistemological issues concerning the relationship between knowledge and social structure, and detailed examinations of the social construction of accounts of reality, had all entered the sociological scene and these concerns led to greater theoretical expectations from empirical research. Such expectations are not realised in *Power, Persistence and Change*. Indeed, as one reviewer commented, 'There does seem to be plenty of support in this book for the anti-empiricism of many of the younger [Marxist] sociologists' (Pahl, 1975: 738). The explanatory power of the second report is weaker than the first and its ethnography is considerably less exciting and is more removed from the everyday lives of people. Sociologists considering a re-study of a community can benefit enormously from the problems and difficulties surrounding the planning, execution and publication of the Banbury re-study.

Conclusion

In a footnote Bell and Newby comment somewhat harshly about British community studies: 'Each has something to contribute to sociology yet, as it turns out, they contribute little to each other' (1971: 140). Although this is true to the extent that some studies have not benefited from or developed theoretical themes from earlier attempts, others (such as Littlejohn and Stacey's projects) used both previous studies and the work of Weber to enormous advantage. Further, Stacey's model of the localised social system (see pp. 31–5) and Plowman *et al.'s* framework for local social status (see pp. 182–4) were both built up from the small-scale generalisations established by British community studies. In fact the few discussed here all operate, some more explicitly than others, with some notion of a localised social system. Very generally all are concerned with the interrelationships between certain social institutions that are locality based although, of course, they do not explore these matters with the rigour laid down by Stacey in her model of the localised social system and neither do they attempt to cover all the aspects listed.

An important difference emerges over how the localised social system is conceived. Some, such as *Gosforth*, tend to treat it primarily as an object—as a thing worth examining in its own right and on its own terms—whereas others, such as *Tradition and Change*, tend to conceptualise the localised social system as part and parcel of a much wider entity, such as the State, and use the analysis as a method for understanding broader social processes, in this case, the role of industry in social change.

Newby (1980: 79) is correct when he points to the decline of community as object studies and the rise of community as method approach, but community studies are not one or the other for the best always have a mixture and it is the dialectical tension between the two—between the unique and the general—that provides us with the greatest insights and understanding into social relationships. If *Gosforth* is too much of an object study, and in my view it is, then *Power, Persistence and Change* is too much of a method study. In the latter the team approach and the loosely connected pieces of research theoretically directed towards such sub-disciplinary areas as women, family, neighbouring and religion, largely remove it from the *genre* of 'community studies'. Perhaps such research is better directed at the specific social institution itself (but over a broader canvas) than at a localised social system. The best community studies remain those which combine and elucidate the relationships between object and method, the unique and the general, the local and the national, the objective and the subjective and so forth.

This means that community sociologists must come to terms with a more realistic appraisal of the limits and possibilities of such studies. On the one hand community studies may well be deficient for explaining broad processes of social change or for taking into account the latest theoretical trends, but on the other hand, they are good at providing some understanding of how people go about their everyday lives, of how those lives are affected by wider social structures and processes of change. Community studies also help us to understand the operations of power and status and the relationships of tradition and sentiment, as well as rationality.

6 The Empirical Tradition of Community Studies: The Australian Case

As with the American and British examples, Australian community studies had their roots in social anthropology. The impetus for this research came from A.P. Elkin, Professor of Anthropology at the University of Sydney from 1934 to 1956. He encouraged many of his post-graduate students to undertake research in their own society, perhaps the most well known being the late Jean Martin. Most of this work remains in higher degree theses. One of the few studies published was Allan Walker's *Coaltown: A Social Survey of Cessnock* (1945), a rather sketchy and superficial account of mining life in wartime Cessnock. Elkin was influential in setting up Oeser's and Emery's project on Mallee Town (1954) which Oxley rightly refers to as 'the pioneer publication on a single Australian community' (1974: 13). The community study tradition continued at the University of Sydney, both in research and in teaching, after Elkin's retirement and it was from the Department of Anthropology that, in 1974, both Oxley's *Mateship in Local Organisation* and my own work, *Bradstow*, were published.

In this chapter I examine the four major Australian community studies which are Oeser's and Emery's *Social Structure and Personality in a Rural Community*; Bryson's and Thompson's *An Australian Newtown*; Oxley's *Mateship in Local Organisation*; and Wild's *Bradstow*. I also discuss Pearson's *Johnsonville* — the first, and so far, the only community study completed in New Zealand. As in the previous chapters I include as much material as is available on the background of these studies and on what sociologists did in the field. I also evaluate their findings and consider their approaches in terms of the localised social system, community formation and closure and community, communion and society as described in Chapter 2.

Oeser and Emery in Mallee Town

Background
In 1949 the Social Sciences Research Committee of the Australian National Research Council undertook to sponsor for UNESCO two studies in Australia; one urban and the other rural. They were to be part of an 'international study of communities and social tensions' (Oeser and Hammond, 1954: v). The other countries taking part were India, France and Sweden. The Department of Psychology at Melbourne University was asked to carry out the Australian project. The research was carried out by staff and students associated with a course called Collective Behaviour and resulted in Oeser's and Hammond's *Social Structure and Personality in a City* and Oeser's and Emery's *Social Structure and Personality in a Rural Community*, both published in 1954. Both studies are based on 'the theoretical and methodological foundations of social psychology, and a recognition of the functional interdependence of the parts of any society (Oeser and Hammond, 1954: ix). The studies were carried out under the general direction of Oeser. Emery was in charge of the rural study and Hammond was in charge of the urban one. They were assisted by 4 post-graduate students; 40 students of the Collective Behaviour class and 15 professional psychologists. A.P. Elkin, the Professor of Anthropology at the University of Sydney was an advisor to the project and the anthropological influence, particularly the view of community as a wholistic unit consisting of interacting parts which function to maintain the whole, is especially evident in the rural volume. Here I shall concentrate on the rural study for as the authors comment, it is 'more of a coherent unit' than is the urban study, 'which consists of a number of relatively independent studies' (Oeser and Hammond, 1954: ix).

Oeser and Emery state that they tried to select a locality 'representative of all or a majority of Australian rural communities' (1954: v). Mallee Town, a service centre for a wheat growing area, was chosen first because 'the biggest part of the Australian rural population is engaged in wheat growing', and second, 'because most Australian wheat farms and wheat farming communities are very much alike' (1954: v). These are unsupported assertions and it would take some considerable time and research to establish the latter. I am especially suspicious of the apparent rationality of the choice of Mallee Town when it is mentioned that Emery spent some time working in wheat farming towns in Western Australia (1954: 222). It seems that, as with the Lynds, a town was selected on the basis of prior familiarity.

It is important to emphasise that the Mallee Town study was

based primarily on psychological techniques 'because the research workers were psychologists and because they could not spend enough time in the community to attempt a full-scale anthropological study' (1954: v). Most of the book is concerned with attitudes, ideologies, personality structures and childrens' schooling analysed from a social-psychological perspective and as the authors comment, we 'did not attempt to give a well-rounded picture' (1954: v). However, the first three chapters, and the last, concern the social structure of Mallee Town. These chapters were written initially by G.B. Sharp, one of the post-graduate students and chief research assistant. His sociological and Marxist interests shine through and make these chapters rather different from the rest.

The Report
The population of Mallee Town is 'around 500'. It consists of 12 shops, some 60 houses, 4 churches, a hotel, a school, and scattered workshops which form the boundary between farm and town. The town functions as a service centre for a radius of some 30 kilometres. The first wheat farmers came to Mallee Town in the early 1890s from South Australia because of the shortage of land and a series of droughts in that State. Since that time the area has suffered a cycle of droughts with low prices and good years with high prices. At the time of the research the land tenure had stabilised through inheritance and any new owner-farmers were former tenants who had prospered.

With the arrival of the railway and the land boom of 1910 Mallee Town saw the influx of businessmen, white-collar workers, skilled tradesmen and labourers. Even at this stage there was a marked schism between the Methodists, represented by the farmers who were happy with the status quo as long as they were in control, and the Catholics, represented by the white collar and manual workers who were progressive. The Methodists formed the Progress League in 1910, obtained local control of judicial functions and made several of their members Justices of the Peace. This was followed by fines for drunkeness and disturbances among the workers. As Oeser and Emery comment:

> The members of the Methodist group concerned with establishing a well-ordered and economically well-based community saw progress mainly in terms of the well being of their own class and the acceptance in communal practice of their leadership. Politically they supported those who were prepared to act as representatives of landed interests. (1954: 12)

In the 1920s Mallee Town remained stable and harmonious as

crops were good but the early thirties were disastrous years. The harvests were good but because of the depression the prices realised were below the costs of production and the farmers ran steadily into debt. As the farmers could not pay their bills to the businessmen and tradesmen, relations between townspeople and farmers were tense. This cleavage became wider and more bitter with the Debt Adjustment Act of 1935 which wiped clean the farmers' debts. The storekeepers and tradesmen felt that they should not bear the loss and this situation developed a considerable grudge towards the farmers who made no attempt to pay even when they became more prosperous. Further tension developed between the farmers and the townspeople as farm mechanisation increased putting many rural labourers out of work. This eventually lead to a partial depopulation of the area. According to the authors, 'the extension of this trend (mechanisation and depopulation) on the basis of associated prosperity is of importance in viewing the current phase in Mallee Town's development and the direction of future social change' (1954: 17).

The analysis of the social structure centres on 'the basic relationships established in the course of production ... the organisations representing the interests of those standing in similar productive relations ... [and] religious and leisure behaviour' (1954: 18). Although this sounds vaguely Marxist the units recognised in the social structure are not related solely to the means of production. Their classification of farmers, business people, white-collar workers, and labourers, with the last divided into town and farm labourers, is essentially a status-based occupational division of the workforce.

The farmers form the key unit in the social structure. Whether the locality progresses, remains stable, or declines depends on the economic consequences of the farming activities. To some extent these activities are determined by the farmers but to a far greater extent they are determined from outside the locality by such factors as the prevailing market prices for farm commodities and the costs of equipment, fuel and labour.

The farmers do not locally organise themselves as a group except under extreme pressure which is what occurred during the depression. They occupy positions which, according to the authors, 'produce like interests but they do not have common interdependent interests' (1954: 20) although they go on to point out that present prosperity is tending to bring the farmers closer together, especially the wealthier progressive ones. Under advice and instruction from outside the farm, such as the Department of Agriculture, the progressive farmers plant new crops and introduce new techniques and machinery. Their increasing prosperity has contributed to the rise in the size of properties from about 500 acres (202 hectares) in the early part of this century to around 1500 acres (600 hectares) in the early 1950s. The smaller, marginal farmers are being forced off the land whereas the bigger farmers employ more labour. Oeser and Emery conclude that 'the development of the community is strictly conditioned by the external relationships into which the farmers enter ... [and] what freedom of decision there is within the community is passing increasingly into the hands of a few' [big farmers] (1954: 23).

The business people of Mallee Town arc 'oricntcd towards the needs of the farmers and provide a necessary link between the productive activities of the farmer and those of the outside world' (1954: 23). Although the business people depend on the success of farming activities the farmers also depend on the storekeepers to provide them with necessary goods and with such services as credit. Consequently, the relationship between the two groups is unstable. Prosperity at the time of the study had led to a relatively harmonious relationship, as well as to an increased participation in the life of the town by the farmers, but any recession in the price of farm products would lead to 'a renewal of sharp practices by the business people and consequent hostility on the part of the farmers' (1954: 24).

The core of the business group consists of three long-established families who control the major stores and two agencies and take an active part in town affairs. However, the business group is not as powerful as it could be in local matters because of business competition which has resulted in 'strong interpersonal antipathies', consequently Mallee Town's leaders are able to command a following from only a narrow sector. Unfortunately, the evidence for all of this is slim and rests on the facts that the Progress Association has become inactive, fund raising has broken down from internal dissensions and the construction of the new hall has been held up by interminable disputes. None of these projects or issues are described or analysed, consequently we are left to accept or reject the authors' assertions.

Most of the white-collar workers are temporary residents. They work for such large bureaucracies as government departments and banks and are more concerned with maintaining and improving their position in the bureaucracy than in Mallee Town. Most come from an urban middle class background and exhibit the associated values. They tend to avoid interaction with people of a lower status, sometimes attempt to mix with higher status groups and generally remain within their own clique. In town affairs their relationships are restricted to membership in formal organisations. Their main influence in Mallee Town concerns the introduction of urban leisure patterns, especially in the development of such sports as golf, and the extension of these activities to Sundays. The white-collar workers were largely responsible for changing 'the local conception of Sunday from that of "a day of rest" to a "day of activities"' (1954: 27).

Oeser and Emery divide the labouring category into town and farm workers. The former tend to be recruited from farm families forced off the land and are now employed in such jobs as maintenance of roads, railways and telegraph lines. As with the white-collar workers most are employed by organisations based outside the area but unlike the bureaucrats they are excluded from systems of promotion, graduated salaries, pensions and security of employment and, consequently, do not share the same tie to these organisations. The town workers are linked by kinship and family history to the district and this network of intimate social relations ties them to the area. They command little status in Mallee Town which is reflected in their use of the prefix 'Mr' when addressing people of higher status and their use of first names when referring to the workers. The town labourers' only organisation is union membership but union matters involve extra local issues and rarely impinge on town life.

The small number of farm labourers are unmarried, male, seasonal workers who live on the farms in poor conditions and have little group solidarity.

The authors conclude that these occupational groups follow 'their own interests rather than those of the community as a whole'. The contradictory nature of their interests makes this virtually inevitable and indicates the futility of using the concept of community to refer to a common sense of belonging, as Oeser and Emery often imply, in such a differentiated social system as Mallee Town. Second, the authors conclude that all the major differences in the town 'have been reflected between and within each of the levels discussed' (1954: 30).

Basic group interests in Mallee Town are reflected in the membership of national political parties. The Country Party is based almost entirely on, and led by, the farmers whereas the Labor Party is led by skilled manual workers and supported by the labouring group, lower status white-collar workers and some of the smaller farmers. Support and interest in politics, however, is only expressed at election times. Political activity between elections is restricted to a few formal meetings attended only by a handful of enthusiasts.

Oeser and Emery draw a marked distinction between the open-

ness of the political activities of both parties. Both Country and
Labor Party affairs are limited by the apathy of their members but
the latter is further restricted by marked social hostility. For example, 'during the campaign for the 1949 Federal election the Labor
Party branch was forced to distribute its leaflets secretly by night,
and had difficulty in getting anyone to chair the public meeting for
the Labor Party candidate because its members feared the social
consequences of their actions becoming publicly known' (1954: 32).
The Party secretary was reluctant 'to do anything which would
openly expose him to the threat of social ostracism' (1954: 32).
The authors argue that 'the farmers can enforce a rigorous censorship on the public expression of political view's (1954: 32) but
the only evidence presented to support this is an anecdote from the
hotel where a political comment was quickly quashed by the hotel
keeper with the statement 'no politics here'. Such sweeping generalisations by Oeser and Emery require much more validation with
data collected by different methods.

The authors found 'a widespread belief in and acceptance of the
superiority of the existing political system ... a widespread apathy
rooted in a basic political conservatism common to all sections of
the community and the existence of social pressures against any de-
viation from the politics of the leading farming group' (1954: 32–
3). As I have just mentioned there is not sufficient data presented
to support such conclusions. Oxley criticises Oeser and Emery for
presenting 'factual material which often fails to convince' and because 'we are not told what potential sanctions did the forcing'
(1974: 13). One of the reasons for the lack of this type of data is
that the project was primarily a social-psychological study which
depended essentially on questionnaire surveys. Intensive participant observation over a long period of time is required to provide
substantial evidence for political manipulation. I had been in Bradstow for over a year before I found out some of the subtle and
elusive ways in which manipulation occurred. A few examples indicate the pervasiveness of such matters.

A new pharmacist moved into Bradstow, joined the Liberal Party Branch and became an active member and later an office hol-
der. Yet after I had spoken with him on many occasions he con-
fided in me that in the Federal and State elections just passed he
had voted Labor. I asked him to explain. He said 'Well, its a matter of keeping business. Over three-quarters of my customers are
Liberal supporters and they would go if I was not a member'.
In other words it pays local businessmen to support the Liberal
Party. If they do not then they are very subtly threatened with an
economic boycott and a loss of reputation. If they do then they

become respectable businessmen.

In another case the editor of the *Bradstow Press* supported the dominant conservative ideology. An active Labor Party supporter from a nearby town wrote seven letters to the newspaper opposing Australia's involvement in the Vietnam war and disagreeing with published letters supporting President Johnson's actions. None were published. An eighth letter was published but the order of the sentences and paragraphs had been changed and the letter was virtually meaningless. When the Labor Party supporter complained he was told this action was 'standard procedure'.

In a further issue the same Labor Party member booked the rooms of Bradstow's Country Womens' Association for a meeting. The women withdrew the use of their rooms when they found it was for a Labor Party meeting and the venue was hurriedly moved to the next town.

In my experience political censorship by those in control is a common procedure in country towns and it is this type of situation that Oeser and Emery are attempting to describe. However, the data presented is not sufficient to support their conclusions and perhaps the major reason for the lack of good qualitative case studies was their inability to conduct in-depth participant observation.

The furthering of group interests, the acquirement of social honour and the few controversies that do occur tend to take place within, and between, voluntary associations in Mallee Town. Oeser's and Emery's analysis of voluntary associations which utilises a series of statistics from questionnaires and some case studies shows that 'the farming section has sought to clinch the gain in community status arising from their present prosperity by moving into the leadership of these organisations' (1954: 33–4). For example, the farmers moved into the bowling club until they constituted 68 per cent of the membership. Of these farmers, 80 per cent were staunch Methodists and they formed a solidary bloc. They then passed a motion at a general meeting disallowing play on Sundays and banning alcoholic liquor on the premises. Further, during the period of the study, the Methodist farming families moved into the golf club and the issue of Sunday golf was becoming an important issue as the farmers tried to assert their leadership. The authors conclude that as long as the present prosperity remains or grows and as long as the wage earning groups remain numerically small and politically unorganised the present position of the farmers as a dominant upper status group will not change.

Oeser and Emery attempt to generalise from their study arguing that it has revealed some of the 'essential conditions' influencing the development of Australian rural society. Production for a world market by individual, self-employed farmers who use machinery and non-family labour, and who depend on the commercial, transport and financial services of townships and external organisations have given rise to 'two important features of Australian rural society' (1954: 227). These are that the predominant social relationships and cultural forms in rural society 'are basically similar to those existing in the urban society' (1954: 227). The primary relationships are those arising from the pursuit of economic interests whereas 'kinship, neighbourhood and friendship ... are of secondary importance'. Further, never being self-sufficient Australian farmers 'have always been forced into mutual intercourse with the urban society' (1954: 227), and have consequently accepted its cultural forms and enhanced the spread of cultural conformity.

Because the main focus of research in this study was on the psychological investigation of children it contains nowhere near the sociological detail of other community studies. Nevertheless, the first three chapters and the last do provide us with some useful insights into the social structure and stratification system of Mallee Town. The general picture described, for example, corresponds closely with Vidich's and Bensman's study of Springdale. The prosperous farmers and town's businessmen occupy similar positions and perform similar activities in both towns, and the descriptions of general apathy and political manipulation resemble each other in outline if not in detail. In other words, in comparison with other studies we can see similar social processes operating at the local level which have their genesis in the wider societal structures of class, status and political power.

Bryson and Thompson in an Australian Newtown

An Australian Newtown: Life and Leadership in a Working-class Suburb by Bryson and Thompson reports the results of a study begun in late 1965 when several leaders from a new Housing Commission area on the outskirts of Melbourne approached Professor Max Marwick, an anthropologist and chairman of the Department of Anthropology and Sociology at Monash University, to ask for some help with research. These leaders were members of Newtown's (a pseudonym) Civic Group which consisted largely of such middle class service professionals as ministers of religion, social workers and school teachers. They were interested in community development and felt that some research would assist their plans.

In their book (Bryson and Thompson, 1972: 319) the authors

provide three reasons for agreeing to help the Civic Group. First, they wanted to 'provide a picture of life of "average citizens"; second, the leaders' eagerness meant a ready access to data; and third, the research promised 'practical value as well as theoretical value'. In a later paper Bryson and Thompson (1978: 95) discuss some of the difficulties involved in deciding to do this research. They were unsure about doing a study in a 'problem' area and were worried about possible publicity sensationalising the research. Further, they thought that if they were going to undertake a community type of study then it would be better done in an area 'with a greater cross-section of socio-economic status'. Nevertheless, they 'were anxious to cooperate with people in the "real world"' and went ahead. I think perhaps a further factor was at play in this situation: The Department of Anthropology and Sociology was only in its second year of existence and Marwick as the new professor was keen to establish a reasonably large-scale research project, especially one where his Department could be seen to be concerned with community needs and development. Marwick set up the research and 'saw it as providing the basis for a series of studies that might be undertaken by staff and post-graduate students in the future' (Bryson and Thompson, 1978: 95). Marwick applied for, and received, a grant from the Australian Research Grants Committee, which was used for research assistants and travelling expenses. Gradually Bryson and Thompson, who started work on the project as research for higher degrees, took over the study from Marwick and were aided by several research assistants at different stages. The authors provided 'mutual support' and completed the study 'with a firm belief in the advantages of joint projects' (1978: 96). As Vidich's and Bensman's experiences and the saga of the Banbury re-study show, not all team research is as successful. Clearly team research is much more successful when there are two people, and preferably no more, who are able to work and write together.

The main methods used were participant observation and a household survey. 'The decision to do participant observation must be seen as one influenced by our anthropological leanings ...' (1978: 98). Theoretically the authors 'adopted a conflict model of society' (1978: 99). Given these two factors immediate difficulties arose with the researchers' relationships with the Civic Group. The Group and its activities were part of the study yet they were also friends-colleagues and because they initiated the study they possibly felt as though they were in a privileged situation to provide information. Although the Group explained their interest in the research, Bryson and Thompson began to wonder whether these views represented those of the working-class residents. Their conflict model directed them to examining the different interests and views of the middle and working classes.

The household survey was used to obtain representative data on the characteristics and attitudes of the residents, and secondly, because 'the Civic Group had requested one' (1978: 99). Ninety under-graduate students were used for interviewing consequently 'the quality of the completed interviews was very varied' (1978: 100). I consider it unwise to use students untrained in interviewing for a relatively large-scale and publicly-financed sociological study. At best it leads to distortions in the data and at worst to total fabrication, as has occurred in some instances. Further, it removes the main researcher(s) even further from the material, and therefore, from a thorough subjective understanding of the social situation.

In framing the questionnaire Bryson and Thompson experienced some of the limitations and constraints, also described by Vidich and Bensman, that are involved when prior commitments are made to a specific section of the population (see pp. 75–6). In this case the Civic Group wanted the survey to ask questions about community development and services which, as Bryson and Thompson comment, 'left us very little room to indulge our own "purely sociological" interests, a limitation that certainly proved a restriction on the final analysis' (1978: 101).

Whereas Vidich and Bensman reacted to such constraints by withdrawing from the official project Bryson and Thompson took their commitment even further. They suggested that the Civic Group survey all the formal groups in Newtown using a 'community self-survey technique'. This involved the Group members in locating and interviewing the formal groups. The aims were to provide a detailed picture of formal activities and to bring Group members into contact with local groups thus enabling them to find out other opinions concerning community development. This was not a success. The Civic Group members tended to collect information from only those groups with which they had some prior contact. Only 42 of the 128 groups isolated provided information about their organisation and opinions concerning Newtown. Further, there was enormous variability in the quality of the material collected and because there were about 50 people involved Bryson and Thompson found it impossible to exercise control over their activities. Perhaps worst of all was that the Civic Group just collected the data in a routine fashion and made no attempt to develop any liaison with the other groups. This in turn meant that no foundation was laid for any future community-wide social action and it indicates that the Civic Group was pursuing its own interests, sometimes at the expense of other organisations.

In a further attempt to help the Civic Group, Bryson and Thompson suggested to the Group's welfare sub-committee that as they already had a considerable amount of data on welfare at their fingertips through their experience in community work what was required was a pooling of this knowledge so it could be analysed. After solving problems of confidentiality of data, case history questionnaires were designed and the welfare personnel completed them for their own cases. Bryson and Thompson were surprised when the raw data was handed to them for analysis. As they comment 'we were left holding the baby' (1978: 106). They were perceived by the Civic Group as 'expert University researchers' consequently, as far as the Group was concerned, they were the ones who should do the work. Bryson and Thompson's expectations, however, were different and they wanted the Group to take primary responsibility because they assumed that the Group had the interests of the whole of Newtown at heart, wanted to find out about the workings of the area and desired some social action to alleviate 'social problems' and develop the locality. Such assumptions were misplaced as the Civic Group was primarily interested in imposing its values and interests on Newtown.

An Australian Newtown clearly shows the problems and difficulties of including inexperienced and untrained people in sociological research, whether they be students or members of the population under study. It also indicates that the sociologists themselves were inexperienced and ill prepared to tackle a project of this scale. It seems clear that the authors were not familiar with the fieldwork difficulties described by such researchers as Vidich, Bensman and Stein (1964), Whyte (1955), Stein (1960) and Gans (1962) *before* they embarked on the research.

The demands of the Civic Group continued to affect the project even after the fieldwork was completed and the data was being collated. At this stage the research assistants had gone and Bryson and Thompson were the only people working with the material. The Civic Group members were intensely concerned with practical matters and they wanted immediate analysis and some solutions to their perceived difficulties. They had little understanding of the slow and arduous process of organising data, coding it, putting it on computers; of re-coding and re-running it through new programmes; and finally of writing it up within some coherent framework. Nor, of course, should such people be expected to know such things. The Civic Group had these expectations because the sociologists initially took on the project on their terms rather than in terms of a sociological problem. Once again a compromise was reached and Bryson and Thompson, 'to take the heat off the situation', produced an interim report. This was an unsatisfactory measure for as the authors comment, 'it is not clear that it was used and certainly we could not feel satisfied with it' (1978: 109).

The Civic Group had also, unwittingly, contributed to an imbalance in the data. Because Bryson and Thompson spent so much time with these leaders, they obtained a large amount of material concerning their attitudes and values. They did not obtain the same amount of information about the attitudes and values of the ordinary residents of Newtown. This is further evidence for the lack of thorough planning for a fieldwork-participant observation type of study. The survey covered a sample of Newtown residents but the participant observation was skewed towards the Civic Group. For a successful blending of survey and participant observation data the latter must cover the same range of social situations as the former.

In this study, the sociologists' relationships with their 'sponsor', the Civic Group, was crucial. It largely determined the initial scale and topic of research, created difficulties in the research process and affected the writing up. One of the most problematic themes in the whole project was the difficulty in reconciling sociological and practical aims, and as Bryson and Thompson remark, 'the situation was compounded by the fact that the leaders' practical aims turned out to be based on different premises from our own' (1978: 11). The Group's ideology predisposed them to favour solutions that attempted to adjust individuals to their circumstances whereas Bryson and Thompson's aims were more to alter a person's life chances through significant social and economic changes.

According to Bryson and Thompson the Civic Group had already worked out a community development programme before asking the University to conduct research. What they really wanted was some validation for their activities both for then and for in the future. Social research can provide legitimation for many activities, and further, it removes responsibility onto more distant, and so-called impartial, experts. In such situations only those findings that conform with initial preconceptions are accepted and this partially explains why the Civic Group was unprepared to make use of most of the research findings. Perhaps as informed service professionals they did not doubt that this research would confirm their opinions. Here is a good example of professional community workers not understanding the role played by value judgements in both social action and research. As Bryson and Thompson somewhat pleadingly comment, 'We tried to make clear our own view that the most that can be expected from research is information, which can then be used to inform the value judgements that ultimately must be made with regard to action' (1978: 111).

Bryson and Thompson identify several tensions between social action and sociological research that are not easily reconciled. People of social action are often people of strong convictions who are not easily moved by research findings unless they support their initial position. Researchers and practitioners evaluate knowledge differently, have a different time perspective on projects and are divided over such matters as a skeptical approach to knowledge versus a confident and accepting one. It was for these sorts of reasons that they suggest that their findings were not heeded by the Civic Group and, with an air of frustration, they conclude, 'Perhaps they should be persuaded that research is not what they need' (1978: 113).

This I think misses the point for research is what is needed but not in this context. The authors started this study with the assumption that their sociological research could help a community group, and more generally, 'improve' society. This is a naive view that can distort judgement and make sociology the handmaiden of political and economic interests. After all the Civic Group used the project to further their own interests. If the project has arisen from a sociological problem, from an issue in sociological theory, then it would have been easier to see the differences between the theoretical and the practical from the outset. Instead they remained muddled which in turn adversely affected the study. There is an important difference between the pure and the applied and this difference may be ignored only to the detriment of both. According to Durkheim, 'If we separate carefully the theoretical from the practical problems, it is not to the neglect of the latter; but, on the contrary, to be in a better position to solve them' (1960: 33). To repeat the old analogy, theoretical contributions to mathematics and astronomy, by increasing the precision of navigation, have saved more lives at sea than any possible tinkering with the carpentry of lifeboats. It seems that Bryson and Thompson were constrained by the Civic Group, and the obligations made to the members, into being primarily carpenters. Sociology can contribute to social reform and facilitate the tasks of reformers, but it is not itself reform nor should it be deluded by the criterion of immediate utility. Bryson and Thompson became aware of these issues *after* the research and hopefully other sociologists can learn from their sometimes painful experiences.

The publication of *An Australian Newtown* raised some ethical issues for the authors and once again these centred on the Civic

Group. The leaders were clearly recognisable through their positions and 'some of them were bound to be upset by our interpretation of their activities and their relation to the working-class residents' (1978: 114). What to publish and what to leave out became complicated because of initial commitments to the Group and because friendly and colleague type of relationships had developed between the sociologists and Group members during the course of the research. According to Bryson and Thompson, 'We agonised about our interpretation of the situation, about the breach of trust that might seem to be involved, and long and hard over whether or not we were justified in publishing' (1978: 114). On the completion of their respective Ph.D. theses Bryson and Thompson circulated them to some key members of the Group and discussed some of their reactions. Some agreed with the interpretation, others rejected it and still others felt personally affronted. The authors were clearly worried about adverse effects on the members of the Civic Group for in a version of the report that they made available to the local library they omitted the activities of the Group. The constraints felt by the sociologists were strong enough to impose censorship on the research findings: in my view such censorship is rarely ever justified especially when it concerns such a central part of the analysis. Sociologists should attempt to strive for the freest possible conditions of reporting within the strictures of what they consider their responsibility to the people (see Wild, 1978b: 198–200; Becker, 1964: 267–84; Vidich and Bensman, 1964: 327–43). Because of the initial commitment to the Civic Group, Bryson and Thompson were not able to establish for themselves the freest possible conditions for publishing their findings.

When the book was published, however, most of the Civic Group had left the area and Bryson and Thompson decided to go ahead and publish the section on the Group's activities. Some of the Group's members read the book and were irritated by its interpretation of their activities; two members wrote articles in Melbourne magazines attempting to refute the analysis but others responded favourably.

Bryson and Thompson experienced some difficulties with the participant observation method. They found the approach taxing, full of ethical complexities and containing 'the contradictory demands of participation and observation' (1978: 117). The most exhausting and demanding aspect involved being flexible with respect to other people's timetables. Yet it is arguable whether or not participant observation should be a major method in a project where the researchers do not live with the people being studied. Living elsewhere and travelling long distances to hold interviews or carry out an afternoon's participant observation is not the best way to conduct a community study. Participant observation is a full-time and demanding methodology that really requires the researcher(s) to live with the people. Only then does it become a rewarding and satisfactory method which can provide data which is unobtainable in any other way and at the same time give the researcher(s) a thorough qualitative understanding of the social situation.

In the end Bryson and Thompson were unsure as to whether the project was really worthwhile. They found out two things which characterise almost every community study ever published: first, that, 'The local residents, whom we naively wished to assist, seem to have been supremely unaffected by the work'; and second, 'That some real estate agents and land developers have found the information useful (1978: 117; see also Wild, 1978b: 213). But their pessimism is unfounded because *An Australian Newtown* has been an extremely valuable book at least at two different levels. First, it has helped many people working in the welfare field to question some assumptions which they had previously taken for granted, especially the point that there is often a disparity between the values of professionals and most of their clients. Second, on the academic level, it tells us a lot about the everyday life of people — about their characteristics and values, their hopes and despairs — in an outer Housing Commission suburb. Further, it contributes an instructive lesson for young sociologists in what they should not do. Most of the problems surrounding this project stemmed from the initial acceptance of, and commitment to, the Civic Group's wants and demands, and from Bryson's and Thompson's lack of preparation and ambivalence which 'had its origins in the fact that we were largely "conscripted" to the task and somewhat reluctantly drawn further and further into a web of responsibilities and loyalties' (1978: 116). Any sociologists who are considering embarking on social problems contract research should ask, 'Who wants the problem solved?', 'Who wants them left alone?', 'And why?' (Stein, 1960: 333; Bryson and Thompson, 1978: 119). Such questions must be asked for sociological research is in itself a social and political activity as well as a technique to be applied to the world 'out there'.

The Report on Newtown

In 1954 the Victorian Housing Commission decided to develop the Newtown site. As two large industrial complexes existed in the neighbourhood and a car manufacturing plant was planned, there was ample work for the people who would live in Newtown. The first houses were occupied in 1955 and by 1966 the Commission had completed its building programme of some 2500 dwellings. Within the area there are status distinctions based on such things as the age of the houses, their building material, the lie of the land and whether the houses are rented or being purchases. Newtown's natural setting is attractive with hilly land and some open countryside close by and it is well supplied with basic facilities. There are seven churches, three pre-school centres, four primary schools, two secondary schools, a hotel, a totaliser agency, two infant welfare centres, a private medical clinic, a public hall, a police station, several sports reserves, two halls for youth activities, and a swimming pool.

Newtown is a predominantly working-class suburb. Seventy-five per cent of the male householders are manual workers. There is a small middle class of managers and semi-professionals, and a few deprived families and pensioners form a lower class. This class framework forms the basis of Newtown's social structure and is the main organising principle for the interpretation of the findings.

In the bulk of the report detailed statistics outline the occupations, financial positions, club memberships, ethnic and religious composition, kin relations, opinions about the place and social problems of the population. Newtown, for example, has a high proportion of immigrants and approximately half of its adults were born overseas. Fifty per cent of the immigrants are from the United Kingdom. The next highest proportions come from the Netherlands and Germany. This predominance of north European immigrants is partly a result of the Housing Commission policy which advises Britishers 'to register with the Commission in the first weeks of arrival' whereas 'a European has to [first] take out papers of intention to naturalise' (Jupp, 1966: 31). This situation has now changed somewhat since the Labor government of 1972 equalised immigration and naturalisation legislation. The Newtown picture is also partly the result of cultural preferences. Zubrzycki (1960: 81) refers to a tendency for southern Europeans to congregate in inner-city areas and for Dutch immigrants to be attracted to outer city and more rural zones. Newtown's population includes hardly any southern European families. In more recent years this general pattern has changed with many second generation southern European immigrants moving to suburban and outer-suburban centres.

Newtown's population is youthful with almost half under 15 years of age and only seven per cent over 50 years at the time of the study. The typical Newtown household (85 per cent of all households) consists of a married couple and their dependent children. The number of children per family is high with the Newtown mean at 3.47 compared to the equivalent State figure of 2.48. In 1966 more than half of the residents had lived in Newtown for four or more years and only seven per cent had been there for less than one year.

Neighbouring and social participation have been major themes in housing estate and working-class studies (see for example, Willmott and Young, 1957, 1960; Berger, 1960; Brennan, 1973). Bryson's and Thompson's data show high rates of neighbourliness, friendliness and interaction with kin, especially among those who have been there for more than two years. Only two per cent said they had no contact with neighbours, whereas 41 per cent had very close contact with considerable help (1972: 119). 'Our data on neighbouring suggest a range of interaction with a majority having considerable contact ... it is likely that the degree of interaction among neighbours in Newtown will increase with time, since length of residence is an important variable' (1972: 124–6). Almost 90 per cent of families were in regular contact with kin apart from their own offspring, over a third had kin living in close proximity, and in 5 per cent of these cases the household unit was an extended family (1972: 113). Such findings support Gans' conclusions (see pp. 76–7) that the view of suburbia as a collection of socially isolated nuclear families is indeed a myth.

Bryson and Thompson suggest that these high levels of neighbouring and kin contact may be moving Newtown 'closer to that illusive settlement type, "a community"' (1972: 126). But this view of community as neighbourhood interaction — in a sense a traditional working-class view of community — is remarkably different from the middle class leaders' and Civic Group's view which sees community centring on levels of participation in formal associations within Newtown. It is to the latter I shall now turn.

Membership in voluntary associations is often used as an index of social participation and Bryson and Thompson employ this measure in analysing their data. They found that 28.7 per cent of all adults belong to a formal organisation (1972: 170). Around 28 per cent is a common figure for working-class membership (see Brennan, 1973: 121; Wild, 1974: 75; 1978a: 83, Oxley, 1973: 124; Oeser and Emery, 1954: 34) and can be regarded as high for a new housing estate where family life-cycle stage inhibits external activities, and where many working-class people prefer neighbourhood participation rather than the middle-class preference for formal associations. Bryson and Thompson found that women join less often than men and predominate in religious, civic and service organisations whereas the heaviest male memberships are in sporting, recreational, social and political bodies. Bryson and Thompson conclude that it is 'domestic variables', such as stage in the family life-cycle, that largely determine membership patterns rather than such variables as class and religion. I shall return to this point later when I discuss the authors' conception of class. The authors also point out that the local middle-class leaders bemoan the poor response to formal groups as they consider that formal participation is the way to generate 'community'. But the working class does not want to join (does not see the relevance of) the service-and activity-oriented groups of the middle-class. As Bryson and Thompson comment, the one way to increase participation is to develop associations which are popular and in line with the working classes' existing interests but which are unavailable within the area, such as clubs with social and sporting facilities. The policies of the Civic Group are opposed to such developments, consequently 'the long-term prospects for social participation within Newtown to be substantially increased as the present population ages must be considered extremely slender' (1972: 186, 303).

The findings on neighbouring, kin contact and association memberships encapsulate two views of community. For the working class, community centres on family and neighbours whereas for the middle class, formal participation is the main criterion. This clash of values brings us to the main theme of *An Australian Newtown* which concerns the 'caretaking' role played by the middle class over the working class majority. Caretaking is a concept used by Gans in his analysis of inner-city Italian-Americans (1962) and refers to the 'agencies and individuals who offer aid which they believe will benefit members of the society' (Bryson and Thompson, 1972: 11). Caretakers may be internal or external. The former come from a similar social situation and share the values of those to whom assistance is offered. The latter come from a different social situation and hold different values.

In Newtown the middle class hold the positions of leadership and authority. The most active are the local government councillors, the members of the Civic Group, and the Protestant clergy. These are the main caretakers in the social organisation of Newtown. Bryson and Thompson specifically mention that these leaders are also those who actually make most of the key decisions affecting the district. Familiar patterns of invisible government and indirect influences from business and politics behind the scenes were not apparent in Newtown. The low socio-economic status of most of the population virtually guaranteed that they would be unable to affect public decisions. Because of the absence of informal power and influence most power and authority was concentrated in two organisations: the Shire Council and the Civic Group.

Newtown elects three representatives to the Shire Council. At the time of the study these were a secondary school teacher, an accountant and a foreman in a car factory. Although they are of a higher socio-economic status than most of the population they generally support policies which are approved of by most residents, consequently Bryson and Thompson refer to them as internal caretakers. Councillors are the most widely recognised leaders even though most of the residents were uninformed about the activities of local government.

Individually, the councillors are different and reflect some of Newtown's variations in values and interests. The school teacher is also an endorsed Labor Party candidate and although he espouses a dichotomous view of society based on power and conflict, his experiences as a professional make him well aware of the different views of society middle class people hold. According to Bryson and Thompson he has 'a fairly broad basis for appeal as a leader' (1972: 264) in Newtown. The accountant, along with many residents, believes that politics and local government should not mix. He looks to economic measures to solve problems and positively identifies with the people and the district, especially with his fellow members of the Catholic church in which he holds a key position. The foreman is oriented to the middle class and upward mobility. He is active on many committees, especially the Youth Club. His activities reflect a development towards a middle-class view of issues and remedies. As a result of the contradiction between his job and his values, he is often a leader for people with different values. The practical outcome of their combined effects is in basic accord with the wishes of most residents and concerns the building of a swimming pool, improvements to existing facilities and the development of recreational reserves. In other words, they have effected policies which represent internal caretaking for most of the population.

Unlike the councillors the members of the Civic Group are not elected. As the Group does not have a constitution, there is no formal way to join it. These professionals who are concerned with community welfare and development have recruited people like themselves. Most Newtown residents are not aware of their activities — in only 2 per cent of responses to the household survey was the Group mentioned (1972: 31). The members have a significantly higher socio-economic status than most residents but in contrast to the councillors 'their middle-class values tend to affect their interpretations of local problems and their selection of remedies. They do not always seem receptive to working-class points of view and so in civic affairs they often act as external caretakers' (1972: 31).

The Civic Group's role as external caretakers comes out clearly in two spheres: their ideology of community and their desire to establish a fee-paying counselling service. The most active members of the Civic Group were preoccupied with how to create a 'community' out of Newtown in terms of their values. They want to institute their version of the good life. Essentially this means getting the working class to join and take part in formal associations. The professionals attach little or no importance to working-class ideas of neighbourhood based on kinship, marriage and friendship. Unfortunately Bryson and Thompson have little material on the values of the working class because of their lack of participant observation in this area, consequently they have to admit to not knowing the extent to which the working class embrace an ideal of community (1972: 207). What is clear, however, is that the working class want improved economic conditions and practical physical facilities and are not especially interested in the middle-class ideal of formal participation.

In 1967 the Civic Group established a counselling service for marital problems because they regarded the existing services to be insufficient. An immediate obstacle was the consultation fee. Further, Bryson's and Thompson's data show that Newtown's residents are not concerned about counselling services — 60 per cent did not know about them at all and 27 per cent believed them to be adequate (1972: 253). The desire for the counselling service by the Group members 'represents a trend which is quite general among personal service professionals. As such it must be linked with class attitudes which the Newtown residents do not share' (1972: 253). There is, then, a broad discrepancy between the concern shown by the professionals towards marital problems and the unconcern of the large majority of the population. Counselling techniques may well be appropriate for middle-class clients whose ways of thinking and coping with personal problems are similar to the counsellors' but they are not necessarily the best way to deal with those of the working class whose problems and perceptions differ. Bryson and Thompson show that the most successful welfare workers in Newtown were residents and non-professionals who shared the values of the majority of the population. One such worker employed by the council had enormous success in giving effective, practical assistance and clearly part of the secret of this success was because she behaved as an internal caretaker (1972: 251).

Five of the six resident clergy and the deaconess were members of the Civic Group and four of these were extremely active. Bryson and Thompson refer to these ministers of the Presbyterian,

Anglican and Methodist churches collectively as the PAM clergy. They are ecumenically oriented and consider that their responsibilities reach into every aspect of the world, both sacred and secular, in which they live. This philosophy makes community affairs a central part of their work, consequently the programmes and policies of the Civic Group have been created and developed by these church people. Their central goal is the development of a 'community' in Newtown. They want to use the middle-class ideal of community as a vehicle for Christian values. The Newtown clergy are not acting in response to pressure from the working-class majority in their attempts to create a 'community'. 'Rather, their goal of trying to convert a working-class population into "a community" summarises the pervasive elements in their approach which makes them external caretakers in the district' (1972: 272). Whereas the working class recognise the need for, and desire, better physical facilities and practical help, the clergy emphasise the ways and means to establish and develop the quality of social life which they believe ought to exist in a 'community'. They further assume that such an aspiration can be promoted by participation in formal groups, especially those groups aimed at developing local services. It follows from this orientation that in their plans to encourage community development the PAM clergy paid little attention to working-class sources of community ties, such as kinship, marriage and friendship among neighbours.

The PAM ministers and the Civic Group as a whole were not aware that they were involved in a degree of cultural conflict with those they were trying to help. Most professionals are aware of cultural differences between their own and other societies and, for that matter, between the divergent values associated with ethnic groups in their own society. It was, however, extremely difficult for the Civic Group to see and acknowledge that legitimate cultural differences based on class and status exist in Australia.

This cultural blindness is evident in the PAM clergy's project to establish a youth centre. Both the residents and the clergy see facilities for youth as having high priority consequently the ministers had a good opportunity to act as internal caretakers. They did not act this way, however, because of their tendency to function as an elite. They relied on each other to evaluate their propositions rather than to find out what the residents wanted. They showed little interest, for example, in exploring any youth activities that could take place outside the framework of a formal club. The PAM clergy's notions centred 'on unstructured mixed clubs with mixed programmes which would develop the personality of their members' (1972: 275). The PAM clergy, who were members of the Newtown Community Youth Club executive, prepared their youth project carefully in consultation with experts and presented it at the annual general meeting of the Club hoping for an endorsement of their policies. Many of the residents attended and they were not sympathetic to the clergy's project. Although the project was not actually defeated it received a distinct rebuff. The PAM clergy were hurt and withdrew to establish their own teenage club. Clearly Newtown's working class is less interested in the joys of a fully integrated personality in a democratic society through participation than is the middle class.

The PAM clergy's and the Civic Group's idea of community development reflects their values rather than the aspirations of the residents. Consequently they have allocated their priorities to civic measures which they believe will improve the quality of life in Newtown, and perhaps lead to the normatively prescriptive good life. As a result of this they have paid little attention to projects concerned with improving the physical facilities and economic conditions with which the majority of Newtown residents are concerned. The choices of the professionals reflect a largely middle-class view that the major causes of social problems lie within the individual and that it is possible to solve or prevent them by taking individual action. Consequently, they support programmes such as counselling and club participation which are directed towards improving the competence of individuals. They have little insight into the structural constraints felt by the working class. The feeling of the lack of control over the direction of their lives, especially in the work situation, and the problems of economic survival from one week to the next mean that many of Newtown's working class are not interested in Civic Group or similar projects. They are more concerned with helping their families through better physical facilities and economic conditions, and in free or leisure time relaxing away from such external constraints as formal clubs.

Bryson and Thompson draw both broad and narrow conclusions from their findings. Among the former they include suggestions for programmes tailored to the interests of the working class. They argue that the middle-class view of community is unrealistic in Newtown because of the high rate of mobility in and out of the area. Ironically the middle class itself has the highest rate of mobility. The authors emphasise the need for more participation by the workers at the leadership level and suggest that the best way of doing this is through the neighbourhood. They call for the establishment of local social clubs (like the New South Wales Rugby

League clubs), and underline the need for greater flexibility in community organisations such as using schools outside normal hours for child minding, adult education and sports. They conclude that if the caretakers want to convert the working class to a middle class style of life then they need to provide the necessary economic conditions and social circumstances.

The broad conclusion is a more sociological one that strikes at the heart of the matter. The higher class is the leaders and they rule in terms of their own values and interests. They offer help but dictate the type and conditions, and therefore, reinforce their own positions of power. In other words, the caretakers act as agents of social control over the working class.

An Australian Newtown is similar in many respects to Young's and Willmott's (1957, 1960) studies of East London done in the middle fifties. Such studies provide a useful collection of data on which to base welfare policies but as I noted in the discussion of the background to *An Australian Newtown* the report had no effect on either the residents or the welfare professionals. It takes more than sociology to change vested interests.

Unfortunately, from the sociological point of view, Bryson and Thompson have not improved on the Young and Willmott studies. The questionnaire schedules are similar. They have little to say about the impact of the wider society and general social processes, such as bureaucratisation, on the suburb. They argue that the key decisions affecting the area are made by the caretakers but that this ignores the role of such State bureaucracies as the Housing Commission and Social Security as well as the policies of the various church hierarchies, and how these affect such suburbs as Newtown. Although they started the study from the methodological position of participant observation their report depends heavily on the household survey (with all its methodological weakness see pp. 54–5) and especially on the measurement of numerous objective variables at the expense of the observation and interpretation of social relationships. This statistical dependence results in most chapters being made up of paragraphs joining and describing tables of figures. The longer chapter on caretaking departs from this model and examines caretaking relationships in an interpretive manner obviously based on thorough participant observation of the Civic Group. It is unfortunate that there is not a similar type of chapter on the working class. Perhaps Bryson and Thompson could be seen as sociological external caretakers in that they concentrated their research on the middle class at the expense of the working class! As they point out in the conclusion, 'our efforts can also be construed as part of the system of social control' (1972: 311).

Perhaps the most important criticism is that they reduce such complex relational concepts as class and status to the distribution of occupations, and reduce power to leadership in formal organisations. We are told, for example, what the occupations of male householders are, their opinions of them, the length of time they have held the job and their educational attainments but we are not told anything about their work relationships with their employers or with those in authority. Are they proletarian, deferential, affluent or privatised workers in their actual relationships at work and in the community? (See Goldthorpe *et al.* 1969.) Such relations play a central part in determining a worker's orientation to such things as voluntary associations and neighbouring and welfare agencies, as well as to their views of the stratification system. Further, in discussing membership distribution in associations, Bryson and Thompson conclude, 'it is apparent that the extent of parental membership is affected by both the number of children and their age distribution. It seems that it is domestic variables which hold the key to understanding memberships in Newtown rather than the major traditional ones of class, religion and culture' (1972: 184). But if class is viewed as a relational concept (see Wild, 1978a: 22, 68–75), rather than conceptualised as the distribution of occupations, it can be strongly argued that many domestic variables themselves are largely determined by aspects of class, status and culture.

There is a brief appendix on class which attempts to outline some of the relational complexities of the concept but there is no attempt to explain any of their data in these terms. As I wrote in a review of *An Australian Newtown*, 'it seems that the theoretical problems came after the study instead of before it' (Wild, 1972: 23). Now that we have the paper 'reflecting' on the Newtown study and outlining the genesis of the project, it seems that my remark was fully justified. As a consequence there is little fruitful interplay between theory and data and the bulk of the report consists of describing and interpreting the household survey. In Baldamus' terms (see pp. 46–50) there is not sufficient 'double-fitting theorising' and too many facts are left to speak for themselves at the descriptive level. Nevertheless, *An Australian Newtown* remains an extremely valuable study which tells us a lot about suburban life in Australia. It is essential reading for students in the field of community studies and it has yet to be surpassed as an account of life in a new suburban area.

Oxley in the Two Towns

The background
Oxley, an Englishman, arrived in Australia from South Africa in 1961 to take a position in the Department of Anthropology at the University of Sydney. It was his South African experience that led him into the research which eventually formed the basis for *Mateship in Local Organisation*. The following information is from personal communication.

After arriving in Capetown without much money Oxley secured a job as a clerk and started an evening course for the Chartered Institute of Secretaries. His lecturer in Commercial Law required some help with his 'pet do-good project' of a coloured slum boys' club. This situation provided Oxley with a little money, bed and board at a coloured theological seminary-teacher training college near the boys' club and free courses in social welfare work at Capetown University. Difficulties of obtaining transport with his coloured friends meant that Oxley arrived at the University too early for his course consequently he looked around for a subject to fill in his time. 'I picked anthropology because I didn't know what the word meant, and wanted to find out because it tickled me'. In rapid succession Oxley became tired of social work, got the sack because he could not 'stomach the do-gooders or their pet delin-quents' and became intensely interested in anthropology.

The Professor of Anthropology at Capetown University, Monica Wilson, a specialist in African tribal societies, sought to dissuade Oxley from doing honours in the subject. 'She said, quite correct-ly, that I "would never make a first-rate anthropologist".' In the meantime Oxley came top of his finals in economics and could have taken the economics prize to carry on with fourth year. Being the sort of man he is, Oxley decided to go ahead with anthropo-logy.

In fourth year he had to pick two culture areas on which to base a whole series of essays and he selected blacks and poor whites in South Africa. He was informed that there were no sociological community studies on South African whites and that it would be valuable if he would do one for his M.A. According to Oxley, he was put in such a position that he had to do one, so he did. It was the experience of doing this study — 'Wyksdorp: A Study of a South African Village' — that made Oxley into what Colin Bell once referred to him as a 'primitive sociologist'; a sort of Grandma Moses of sociology. This, incidentally, is a label that Oxley accepts, and I suspect, enjoys.

During the writing up of his M.A. Oxley worked as a local

organiser for the South African Institute of Race Relations and as racial issues were hotting up he found himself 'getting on too many of the wrong files'. He decided to get out of South Africa and applied for jobs in England, Nigeria and Australia. He took a job at the University of Sydney and looked around for a community project for his Ph.D.

Oxley went to the two towns of Rylstone and Kandos for the following reasons:

(a) I wanted somewhere near enough to Sydney to commute weekly while keeping family in the field; (b) I wanted somewhere sufficiently isolated and sufficiently small to manage; (c) my car's exhaust-muffler system fell off on a dirt road during the preliminary over-survey, and I came up the mainstreet of Kandos like a whole Bikie procession, and the Kandos roofs looked so bright and Mediterranean in the sun (cement dust) and I was so pleased to find a garage, that I liked the place on sight; and (d) Kandos had just what I wanted, to wit a bloody great factory with a nice neat job hierarchy.

The anthropologically-based desire for isolated wholes comes out clearly in this process of selection and is a point to which I shall return later.

Oxley's initial aim was to study how positions in work-group hierarchies influenced leisure time relationships in such things as voluntary organisations. But what he found was that one of the most firmly held beliefs in Kandos was that work-group relationships should not be allowed to influence relationships outside work. There are, of course, slips between beliefs and practices but as we shall see Oxley has considerable evidence to support this generalisation. Given this situation Oxley decided, 'If you cannot study what you wanted to study, study the reasons why you cannot'. Consequently, Oxley ended up studying egalitarian beliefs. This required 'a heavy crash course of reading' on such areas as egalitarianism, community power studies and so forth. Australian egalitarianism made a substantial impression on Oxley, especially after studying social stratification in South Africa. 'It was these impressions which led me to a theoretical interest in egalitarianism and, hence, to a town which is probably atypical in exhibiting it so well' (1974: 26).

Oxley installed his family in a Kandos house from late 1962 to mid-1965. He lived with them during University vacations and for three days a week in termtime. From 1965 to 1968 he made several visits, staying with friends. He also re-visited the town in 1971, after the Ph.D. thesis was completed but before the manuscript for the book was prepared.

According to Oxley another crash course of reading led to the final writing up which lends further support to his being labelled a 'primitive sociologist' and provides an insight into the processes of 'double-fitting' (see pp. 46–50).

> Having worked out ideas and distinctions which made sense in the field I would hunt through the literature and pick brains in order to find somebody who had brought out something like the relevant idea in a sufficiently stodgy work; then I'd say 'I develop the idea of so and so, which was very relevant to . . .' and all like that. I suspect we all do it this way, but sociologists' 'true confessions' seldom say so.

The report

Oxley attempted two main tasks in his study of Rylstone and Kandos: 'the first job is to describe as completely as possible a particular segment of social life at a particular time and place; the second is to make a theoretical statement valid for various times and various places' (1974: 1). He aims to describe voluntary organisations and community improvement projects in this industrialised rural area of the Central Tablelands region of New South Wales. Kandos, with 2100 residents, was established around 1910 and expanded around a cement factory. Rylstone, some eight kilometres distant and a century older, is a shopping and Shire Council centre of some 800 people.

Oxley draws distinctions between the towns and also between the 'Two Towns' and the rural hinterland. The variations between Kandos and Rylstone indicate the importance of different stratification arrangements and their contrasting historical developments for determining social relationships and attitudes. Rylstone people are conscious of the fact that their town is the Shire centre and has a long history, whereas Kandos is a new industrial centre. But Kandos has developed more successfully, leaving Rylstone as 'a mere middle-status suburb' (1974: 86). Such differences are stereotyped by the townspeople, some of whom see Kandos as 'a brawling urban world alien to the respectable calm of the countryside; an uncouth place with uncouth people in it' (1974: 87) yet these people still depend on the workers for custom and help in town projects. Others see Rylstone as 'backward and narrowly parochial, full of people overly status conscious and stand-offish' (1974: 87). At another level, however, the 'Two Towns' are united in opposition to the countryside. Graziers tend to be cut off from the towns 'spatially, socially and politically' (1974: 88). Many are of higher class than the townspeople and the latter believe that they avoid town affairs through feelings of superiority. Not all those farming the countryside, however, are wealthy. Some of them own land and capital worth 'half a million dollars or more' whereas some of the small farmers 'own no more than many urban labourers' (1974: 64).

Both rural and urban areas come under the one Shire Council of six members, two representing each of three ridings. Councillors are chosen 'according to their personal repute rather than their political party' (1974: 72) and, unlike Bradstow, they are regularly replaced. Throughout the time of the research three graziers and three townsmen were councillors. Also unlike Bradstow (see Wild, 1974: 130–145) the operation of local government in the Rylstone Shire 'approximates very closely to formal prescription' (1974: 73). The Council is not covertly controlled and councillors act in accordance with popular consensus. They are in Oxley's term 'honest men' because 'dishonest men have no incentive to seek office' (1974: 74). I return to this point later, (see pp. 136–7). At Federal and State levels the Shire is represented by Country Party members but in Kandos votes favour the Australian Labor Party three to one, whereas in Rylstone votes are more evenly divided. Little party political activity takes place between elections.

This is the setting in which Oxley examines voluntary organisation participation and leadership. He does this from a fairly traditional anthropological perspective. Oxley's approach centres on the 'interstitial structures' of the wider and more formal framework of economic, political and social institutions. 'These are the small-scale and highly personal groups which serve, and may specifically exist, to circumvent, manipulate, make workable, or merely render palatable the impersonal order of large-scale institutions' (1974: 5). They include cliques, old-boy networks, kinship and neighbourhood groups, voluntary associations and committees of various kinds. This is a concern with what Oxley calls the 'social minutiae' of complex societies and he argues that the anthropological technique of participant observation is especially suitable for this purpose. Oxley is well aware that such small groups may be studied for their own sake — in relation to each other, in relation to higher level structures or in terms of the attitudes and beliefs of the members — but he makes it clear that his concern is with the last. As I show later the restriction of analysis to this level inhibits the generalisability of the conclusions.

Oxley's main theoretical concern centres on the relationship between social stratification and egalitarianism: 'stratification is a set of structural facts associated with an ideology, and egalitarianism is an ideology associated with certain structural facts' (1974: 2). As his model of social stratification Oxley takes Warner's 'model of status seeking and status symbolisation' and remarks that 'it corresponds surprisingly closely to a lot of popular thought on the subject' (1974: 32). There need be no surprise for Warner's ahistorical stratification framework was built solely from popular perceptions collected in his American towns (for a critical discussion of this approach see Bell and Newby, 1971: 101–11, 189–204). In other words, the core of this model consists of what people think and say about social status. As C. Wright Mills (1963: 41) once wrote about Warner, this view of social stratification as one vertical dimension of status ignores the structural realities of two other dimensions, namely economic class and political power. Oxley's use of the Warnerian approach limits his analysis of social stratification largely to the *ideology* of status and consequently ignores the 'structural facts' of economic class and political power.

Oxley sees egalitarianism as 'an ethical doctrine ... a set of ideas which guide action in terms of some basic concept of the human condition and destiny' (1974: 44). He distinguishes between a doctrine of equal opportunity and one of intrinsic equality. The former is only meaningful in the context of unequal rewards and could be used to legitimise any non-hereditary system of social stratification. The latter, however, denies people equal rights to compete. As all people share an essential sameness it opposes unequal rewards. Oxley is solely concerned with intrinsic equality and uses the term egalitarianism for this type of doctrine. The ideology of intrinsic equality, then, is counterposed to the ideology of status, and *Mateship in Local Organisation* is primarily concerned with charting the different contexts of these ideologies in the Two Towns.

Oxley divides the population into a series of occupational categories and collapses these into three occupational strata on the basis of informants' data and because 'they would make sense to most of the people' (1974: 66). We are not told how many informants there are or of their position in the social structure, nor are we told how many 'most of the people' are. This is one of the shortcomings of the more traditional anthropological community studies which do not use random sample interviewing to support their generalisations. At the top is a small elite of wealthy graziers who live very comfortably in imposing homesteads. They belong to exclusive clubs in Mudgee (a regional centre) and in Sydney. Their children attend the best private schools. They take little part in town life but when they do they mix with the town's professionals, senior factory management and wealthy businessmen, which helps to give this group 'an aura of exclusiveness' (1974: 85). This group, along with some smaller graziers, forms an upper stratum below the grazing elite. The middle stratum is composed of small businessmen, junior factory staff, and such white-collar workers as bank clerks and school teachers. The working stratum is formed by skilled and semi-skilled workers.

'The great majority of townspeople see their community as divided into strata' (1974: 78). The workers, for example, see the factory executives as 'the boss class'. Townspeople think the graziers avoid town activities because of their feelings of superiority; the senior executives and graziers do not drink at the R.S.L. or fraternise with the middle and lower strata in the public bars. Kandos has its 'Nob Hill' of company houses for senior staff, 'some high-stratum families (in the towns) send some or all of their children to private schools' (1974: 78–9) and, as in many other places, Rotary 'has nearly all the best-known voluntary organisation leaders' (1974: 135) and acts as an organisational base for these influentials. There is 'no notable mixing' of strata through intermarriage. Nevertheless, according to Oxley, it is commonly thought and stated that the strata mix well. Further, 'the facts of stratum differentiation are not very obtrusive in the everyday life of the towns' (1974: 78). The author argues that stratum differences and social separation are restricted to the private realm of social life such as in several small exclusive voluntary organisations, friendship cliques and private parties. This is the world of women who are the most 'notable status-game players' (1974: 79). Most of the exclusive organisations are for women and status seeking and symbolisation play a central role in their lives.

The bars in the Two Towns represent the centre of the male world and symbolise equality. It should be made clear at this point that Oxley's discussion of egalitarianism is restricted to what he observed in the Two Towns and does not refer to the graziers. Egalitarianism in Kandos and Rylstone is closely connected to male solidarity and superiority. Men of whatever town strata tended to be treated as equals whether they liked it or not. Most of the wealthier men compromise in such situations 'and play the unpretentious equal' (1974: 94). Voluntary associations, community projects and licensed clubs function as stratum mixers and emphasise conviviality, male independence and egalitarianism. But within this broad egalitarianism of townspeople there is a narrower and stronger egalitarianism of workers. This asserts claims to collective honour, opposes individual pretentiousness and disapproves of social climbing. The workers are immediately suspected of social climbing if they join any voluntary association with a substantially high-stratum membership. As one of the workers' wives commented about another, 'She joins so that she can try to make friends with the graziers' wives'. According to Oxley, 'The broader egalitarianism obliges the high-stratum person not to reject advances from below; the narrow egalitarianism requires that the low-stratum person should not seem too eager to make them' (1974: 97). But even the narrow egalitarianism is shallow. Male friends are seldom intimate and are often limited to particular contexts. This is not the traditional mateship of two or three men developing close ties through the experience of hardships together, rather it is 'a wider but shallower brotherhood of all' which 'has a pronounced aura of impersonality' (1974: 101).

Oxley's examination of voluntary association membership shows that a minority of organisations are limited to particular strata and help to perpetuate social stratification whereas a majority aid stratum mixing and emphasise egalitarianism. The wealthy graziers' wives control the Red Cross and the association is seen as their property. The same is true for the Country Women's Association. Rotary is exclusive because it limits membership to the top positions in particular occupations. The Kandos Cooperative Committee and the Town Band have long been identified with the workers. Stratum mixing is most universal in the committees and work groups of such special community projects as The Kandos Festival and the building of the aerodrome.

The Munn family appeal is a good example of a community welfare project which generated stratum mixing. Munn, a council labourer, died of a heart attack leaving 11 children and a widow in a rented house with few savings. Before the funeral two influentials, Smith the dentist and Charles the barber, called on Howard, the police sergeant and President of Rotary, to persuade him to call a public meeting. Howard was also approached by Munn's Methodist minister and the Shire President. The meeting which was held in the Kandos community hall attracted about 40 people and they decided that the project should provide Mrs Munn with a house. Howard became the project's president and all present formed the committee.

The first stage was the fund-raising. Union leaders organised pay deductions totalling $500. The dentist ran a dance and a chocolate wheel at the golf club for $400. The R.S.L., Apex, and Rugby League raised about $80 each. The Guides' Committee, Infants' Mothers' Club, and Kandos Country Women's Association raised $150 from street stalls. Most organisations in the Two Towns gave something.

With the $2300 raised the committee, under Howard, decided to purchase a rundown Council house for the book-value of $1175. The next phase involved voluntary renovations. Most of this was done by Apex under the direction of Britt, a councillor and a master builder, but many others did odd jobs and organised working bees. The last of the money was spent on furnishings and sending Mrs Munn and her children on a holiday. The whole project took no more than four months.

Clearly considerable stratum mixing took place during the course of this project although the leadership came from the Two Towns' higher strata. Such projects as this 'reinforce ideas of interstratum equality' (1974: 209) but leadership is anti-egalitarian, consequently some techniques are used to render leadership as innocuous as possible. Stress is put on decision-making by public meetings and committees. Further, anyone who chooses to turn up is accepted onto a committee. Leaders must work as much as, and preferably more than, ordinary members. Only certain sorts of higher-stratum members are chosen as leaders. They are those who avoid the exclusive high-stratum organisations and are often associated with lower-stratum groups. Consequently, the factory management and graziers provide few leaders and most come from the professionals and businessmen. Further, those emphasising egalitarian attitudes have two explanations for accepting leaders. First, such people as school teachers and bank managers are expected as part of their job to take leadership roles, and of course, they are often used as scapegoats for things that go wrong. Second, many minor and temporary leaders are regarded as having special expertise perhaps in negotiation or raising money and there is no shame in following orders from an expert. Overall in the Two Towns, leaders (especially those active in more than one field) are suspected of wanting to run or control things and are treated with ambivalence.

Nevertheless, the Two Towns' influentials do have their own exclusive club which marks them off from the workers. Rotary has more than half of the Two Towns' most infuential people among its membership. It has 16 from the top 30 of a reputational survey conducted by Oxley. Further, its members include some of the more prominent graziers, most of the major bureaucrats, and virtually all of the senior executives of the cement companies. It has all of the best-known voluntary organisation leaders.The club meets weekly for dinner, club affairs and fellowship. As Oxley remarks, 'there is plenty of opportunity for informal discussion and the seeking of support, and this does occur' (1974: 135). A Rotary influential has many advantages such as channels of communication and support among many organisations, easy access to experts for voluntary work, direct connections with company executives, contractors, bank managers and Shire Council bureaucrats for financial and other supports, and immediate help from Rotary's own funds. Rotary membership goes no lower than the upper end of the middle stratum and consequently supports and directs community leadership by the higher strata.

The ideologies of stratification and egalitarianism in the Two Towns coexist and are 'inextricably intertwined'. Oxley explains this situation in eight points (1974: 205–7): (1) 'Both ideologies are used by the same people in bolstering claims to social honour'. The workers stress egalitarianism but take pride in their children's upward mobility. Wealthier people enjoy their superior position but are capable of using egalitarian attitudes and ways of behaving. (2) Both lower and higher groups 'make special claims to honour on the grounds of supposedly peculiar virtues, and each set of claims is partially accepted'. Many of the higher-stratum men take pride in physical prowess and manual skills whereas the lower stratum acknowledge the worth of professional skills. (3) As I have already mentioned, 'there is a narrower egalitarianism of lower-stratum people within a broader but weaker egalitarianism of all'. (4) 'Stratum distinctions and absence of stratum distinctions are each associated with specific types of group activity'. The stratification ideology is emphasised in work situations and in such affairs of the home as marriage and private parties, whereas egalitarianism reigns in bars, sporting matters and community projects. The social distance separating these activities prevents the two ideologies from conflicting. (5) 'Shortfallings from the egalitarian ideals can be blamed on the womenfolk'. Egalitarianism is an expression of male solidarity, especially those males at the lower end of the status hierarchy. According to Oxley the males in the Two Towns leave the defining of their families' status positions to the wife whereas they act as complete egalitarians. (6) 'Interstratum egalitarianism is assisted by prevailing impersonality'. Impersonality enables people to emphasise their common attributes and ignore their differences, thereby creating an all-embracing but superficial mateship. (7) 'Honour can be sought in terms either of stratification or of the egalitarian frame of reference'. People have the choice to 'set oneself above the common herd' or 'symbolise identification with the common man'. Such a situation advantages high-status people because they can have the best of both worlds. (8) 'For the principles of egalitarianism and stratification to be fairly balanced, it is necessary that the former receive special support'. This is because Oxley sees egalitarianism as on the decline largely because of increasing affluence and egalitarianism's anti-intellectualism which cannot cope with educational improvements (1974: 27–8).

Egalitarianism is especially reinforced in the Two Towns because of their economic base in mining and industry, the graziers as an outside group which thereby emphasises unity within the townspeople, the small number of high-stratum townspeople, self-confident workers resulting from strong and effective unionisation, the role of the licensed clubs, and the Australian legend itself.

In the second edition of *Mateship in Local Organisation* published in 1978 Oxley and Nancy Rew, a colleague, report on changes in the Two Towns based on one week or fieldwork in June 1977. Oxley considers changes in local organisation and Rew examines the position of women. Both looked for changes created by the publication of the first edition but were unsuccessful for as Oxley comments, 'search as I might, I could detect absolutely no effects whatsoever' (1978: xiii).

The general recession of the mid-1970s hit the Two Towns hard. Shops were closing, the population had declined by 20 per cent and there was increased unemployment as one of the cement works had halved its workforce and in the following month it closed altogether. Some things had not declined: the three licensed clubs had all increased membership and returned higher profits; four new community projects were underway and although they were following a similar path to the enterprises described in the first edition, Oxley noted 'the enthusiastic amateurs of past leadership have increasingly yielded place to bureaucrats and professionals' (1978: xix).

Oxley carried out a small reputational survey and found that many of the old influentials had been replaced. Seven of the old names reappeared and more women were named probably because of their prominence in the new projects and the effects of international concern with women's affairs. The graziers maintained their superior position and were no more active in town affairs than they had ever been. The author concludes that 'leadership [is] almost completely fragmented among special interest groups' (1978: xxii).

No change is noted from the male viewpoint concerning the balance between the ideologies of status and egalitarianism in everyday life. Oxley's predictions for the future are pessimistic. Not even a national economic recovery could bring the mid-sixties' prosperity back to the Two Towns for there is now new machinery and techniques for the production of cement. Consequently, 'the Two Towns of the foreseeable future promise to be a continuing charge on the social security bill' (1978: xxviii).

In her piece on women Rew criticises Oxley's book because of its 'male-oriented bias' and proceeds to examine 'what the women of the Twin Towns are doing and who are their leaders' (1978: xxx). She points out, as does Oxley, that egalitarianism excludes women (it also excludes blacks, migrants, the young and the old). Most of the data presented in this section, in fact, supports Oxley's earlier statements. Rew found that the women of Rylstone and Kandos were not 'overly concerned with their position as women' (1978: xxxvi), that female solidarity was 'expressed in the home and neighbourhood' (1978: xxxvii), that women are largely involved in maintenance type of activities, such as hospital and school improvements, rather than new projects (1978: xli), and that women 'play the status game much better than men' as can be seen in home life and in the predominance of exclusive associations with solely female membership (1978: xlix–li). Rew notes, however, that women in this area, as elsewhere, have 'emerged in a new perspective' largely because of 'better education and more controlled contraception' (1978: lv–lvi). This can be seen in the increasing number of female leaders, both at the community-wide level and within women's affairs. The Shire Council in 1977 had a woman councillor and the engineer was also female. Rew provides two examples of 'minor charismatic' leaders within women's matters, one is a leather craftswoman who is giving classes at the new evening college and the other is a quiet worker in some six organisations, who, interestingly, was a vocal critic of Oxley's use of real names in the first study because of possible hurt to the people concerned. Rew comments, again in support of Oxley, that male solidary egalitarianism is on the decline as younger couples 'no longer subscribe to sex segregation ... Perhaps the new generation of Australian males are reflecting the influence of a more pluralistic society and are breaking away from the mateship cult' (1978: xxxviii). Before accepting such sweeping generalisations more information is required. What are the class and status situations of these particular couples? Are they involved in a middle-class process of privatisation or is this development common to all strata? Overall Rew concludes that although some changes have occurred much tradition holds sway: the women are busy with their maintenance, the men are seen as the 'decision-makers and innovators' (1978: lvi).

Most of the problems in Oxley's study stem from the limitations of the traditional anthropological approach when it is applied to an analysis of advanced capitalist societies. The desire for an 'isolated' and 'self-contained' (1974: 4; and see p. 125) social system, the treatment of the townspeople in relative isolation from the wider social structures of the region (especially the graziers) and the State, and the emphasis on studying 'social minutiae' in terms of 'the attitudes and beliefs of members' (1974: 10, 38), all stem from the initial traditional anthropological frame of reference. In this same tradition is the lack of any historical analysis examining the production, development and reproduction of the social structure, the dependence on such assertive statements as 'most people ...' rather than random sample data-based generalisations on attitudes to class, egalitarianism and politics, and Warner's status model.

Oxley begins by seeing social stratification as largely structure and egalitarianism as primarily ideology. However, by adopting Warner's stratification model — what people think and say about social status — structure is down-played and the *ideology* of status symbolisation takes over. In other words, Oxley ends up counterposing two ideologies and ignoring the underlying social structures of class and power. We are provided with such structural facts as occupations but these are used only in terms of status and prestige and not in respect to class as market capacity or relationship to the means of production or in terms of power and authority such as the capacity to hire or fire labour. In the first edition of *Mateship in Local Organisation* for example, Oxley briefly refers to a five-week strike at the cement factory. He comments that the strike primarily concerned factories '*outside* the shire' ... and ... 'caused less annoyance between the strata than between fellow workers of striking and non-striking unions' (1974: 198, emphasis added). In the preface to the second edition Oxley refers to the tension between the cement executives and the workers when retrenchments started but later 'a consciousness of common helplessness against *outside* forces ... smoothed these relations' (1978: xxiii; emphasis added). Further, in a discussion of influentials Oxley argues that if company directors close a factory on economic grounds 'they are acting as participants in a national economic system. Their decision belongs to the realm of community decision-making no more and no less than would a government decision inundating the town with the water of a new dam' (1974: 39–40). In each of these cases Oxley is isolating the local social system from the wider class and political systems of the State and the nation. To fully understand what goes on in such places as Kandos we must know more about the external structures and processes that largely determine the overall social organisation of our society. More attention needs to be paid to the processes that link such national and inter-national structures as class, bureaucracy and party politics to matters at the local level. The anthropology of advanced capitalist societies cannot be as narrowly focused as the anthropology of primitive and tribal societies because many wider issues impinge at the local level. The anthropology of complex societies must be concerned with the localised social system, the broader social structure of the society and with relating them together. Unfortunately, Oxley's primary concern with the isolated local level and his emphasis on examining the 'social minutiae' of life in the Two Towns prevents him from coming to grips with this problem.

There are also one or two problems with the 'social minutiae' in *Mateship in Local Organisation*. From participant observation Oxley makes many assertive statements which are not supported by data. Now participant observation is an excellent method for gaining a thorough understanding of social situations, for describing patterns of social relationships and so forth, but it is especially weak for obtaining a wide spread of quantitative data on such matters as attitudes, income levels, education, voting and so forth. Consider the following statements: 'Most farmers and graziers regard Rylstone ... as the local town peculiarly their own' (1974: 62); 'Nearly all the shops are managed by their owners' (1974: 64); the division of farmers into three groups 'is based on a cutting of the income-property continuum according to estimates of rural informants' (1974: 69); 'Informants usually describe the strata firstly in terms of "ordinary worker", " businessmen", "bank people", and so on' (1978: 79); and finally, 'The great majority of townspeople see their community as divided into strata' (1978: 78). These statements and others like them are quantifiable by some form of sample survey and the 'informants' could be identified by the number spoken to and their place in the social structure. This again is a weakness of the traditional anthropological method whereby selected informants are used as special sources of knowledge and no surveys are carried out to collect factual data such as family size, income or land ownership, or to collect material on attitudes and beliefs. Modern community studies should use a skilful blend of both participant observation and sample survey data. Participant observation provides social understanding, valuable insights, case studies and the bases for a relational analysis. Sample survey data supplies useful quantitative data which can be used as a basis for generalising the more qualitative propositions established by participant observation.

According to Oxley local government in the Two Towns operates according to formal prescription. The Council is not controlled by bureaucrats or by a self-appointed clique, and the councillors 'are honest men; and dishonest men have no incentive to seek office' (1974: 74). We are also told that the graziers 'have a clear

interest in keeping down council expenditure on town amenities'
(1974: 88) in order to keep the rates on their large properties low.
There is a fine line indeed between pursuing economic interests
and dishonesty and if a grazier can follow his economic interests by
being a councillor then there is some incentive for dishonest men
to seek office. Considerable corruption has been revealed in many
local government councils (see Wild, 1979a: 25–26) with most of it
centring on councillors and bureaucrats pursuing their economic interests. The problem with *Mateship in Local Organisation* is that
there is no analysis of council meetings or of major council issues
such as the raising or lowering of the rates. It is mentioned
(1974: 198) that on a re-visit to the towns in 1971 there had been a
reduction of general rates but we are not told how or why. There
is just not enough information to come to any significant conclusion concerning the activities of the Rylstone Shire Council.

There is enough information in Oxley's report, however, to
attempt a slightly different interpretation and this is always the sign
of a good community study. The structural facts of inequality in
the Two Towns — Nob Hill, bosses versus workers, graziers versus
townspeople, exclusive clubs, male versus female, income and educational differentials, the lack of intermarriage between status
groups, and so forth — are hidden or diminished by an egalitarian
ideology, which is especially strong within the working stratum. As
Oxley concludes 'the two towns offer a good advertisement' for the
ability of *Gesellschaft* type of relations to contribute to social participation (1974: 206). An impersonal egalitarian ideology allows
people to associate on grounds of common interest, while their
structural inequalities are hidden behind the ideological facade.
The mateship belief, however, is not sufficiently extensive to include the wealthy graziers, factory executives, women, the old and
the young, which emphasises the complex and diverse nature of relationships and ideologies in this area.

Wild in Bradstow

For a detailed discussion of the background to the Bradstow study
the reader should see 'The Background to Bradstow: Reflections
and Reactions' published in the revised edition of *Bradstow* (1978)
and also in *Inside the Whale* (Bell and Encel, 1978: 182–215). Here
I shall briefly sketch some of the more important matters. Community sociologists have tried 'to capture some segment of an elusive reality which would be true to the world of the observed as seen
by the particular perspective of the observer' (Vidich, Bensman and

Stein, 1964: ix). Consequently, there is an intimate connection between the research worker, the methods of investigation, the results
and the researcher's own intellectual development. The theoretical
frame of reference and the data gathered partly depend on the experiences, the abilities and the personality of the fieldworker.

Bradstow was not designed as a project in three weeks or even
three months. It was, rather, the result of a slow ten to twelve years
growth of interest in different cultures, especially at a local level,
and in social inequality.

My interest in other cultures developed first. I was born and
raised in a cotton and linoleum manufacturing town in north Lan-
cashire and my grandfather and father worked in the local factory. I
remember one day talking to one of my school teachers about a
geography essay and he said he had a book at home that would
interest me. The following day he presented to me as a gift Daryll
Forde's *Habitat, Economy and Society*. This was my first contact
with anthropology and it generated in me a powerful interest in
other cultures. During my years at the local grammar school three
events further consolidated my interest in localised populations.

First, I spent three months with a Brathay Exploration Group
studying glacial movements in the Jostedalsbre mountains of Nor-
way. I spent as much time getting to know the Norwegian hill farmers as I did measuring the rate of ice flow. Second, I was awarded
a scholarship provided by a shipping company which sponsored exchange tours between English and West African school boys. Third,
on a geography excursion we visited a field centre in the Welsh
borderlands. I was intrigued by the nature of Welsh village life.

In 1962 I won a Drapers' Company scholarship to study in any
University in the Commonwealth. I arrived at the University of Sydney in February 1963 ready to study geography and anthropology. I
had, by this stage, a well developed curiosity about different peo-
ples, but was not fully aware of the nature and importance of social
inequality.

In my undergraduate course in anthropology I was profoundly
influenced by honours seminars on sociological theory which discussed the writings of Marx, Weber, Simmel, Durkheim and Pareto,
and the contemporary interpretations of them by Parsons, Dahrendorf and Aron. As Dahrendorf pointed out it was question about
'The Origin of Inequality among Men' (1968) that were the first to
be asked by sociology and were the primary concern of these early
writers. This theme of social inequality, of social stratification and
differentiation, was important to me because for the first time it
made me fully aware of my own social situation during my upbring-
ing.

I was brought up to accept the social structure with its inherent inequalities as being right and given, and to believe that one must do one's best to rise within this system. In other words it is possible to be almost totally unaware of gross social inequalities because they are accepted as the natural order of things. The sociological theory, particularly of Marx and Weber, came to life for me in the ethnography of my own background.

Two further factors helped to formulate my interest in localised populations. First, anthropologists have always been concerned with small groups or categories of people whether it be a family, a tribe or a village, and those who turned their attention to modern societies studied such things as a small Welsh village or a slum area of a metropolis. Second, I was influenced by seminars on community studies and I was attracted by the ethnography of Middletown, Gosforth and Springdale as well as their implications for wider theoretical issues. I felt there was a need for closer relationship between some central theoretical issues in social stratification and the ethnography of localised social systems, and Stein's book *The Eclipse of Community* assured me that this was a possible and useful way to proceed.

With the idea of centring a community study around some theoretical propositions concerning social stratification I started to look at a number of small towns. For practical purposes I wanted a town that was a political unit at a local level rather than part of a wider entity such as a shire. As the smallest municipality in New South Wales has an approximate population of 2500 I was limited to places with a greater number of people. I also wanted a place where I could get to know and talk to a large proportion of the inhabitants. As a single fieldworker with few resources this limited me to towns with a population less than 10 000.

A member of the Department of Anthropology was mid-way through a study of a predominantly working class, single industry town and we thought it would be useful, for comparative purposes, to select a different type of locality. I listed several towns in New South Wales that fitted these criteria and went to visit them. Many people have asked me why I did not select a typical country town. In a country with no tradition in community studies the only measure of typicality is in terms of average statistics. Some towns in America have been selected for study on the basis that their occupation, income and education statistics correspond closely with the average figures for the state. At the intensive level of anthropological research and at the level necessary to understand the core features of stratification phenomena, this type of typicality is hardly relevant. I selected Bradstow because I felt an empathy with the place I had not experienced elsewhere. Perhaps it was because the area reminded me of parts of England or because I met a friendly historian who told me about former times. It was probably a combination of many of these sorts of things but whatever it was I felt that I could do some valuable research in this town.

After catching up on some reading and organising accommodation in March 1967 I moved to Bradstow with my wife of several months. One of the first things I did was to write an article for the local paper saying that I was a postgraduate student conducting an anthropological-sociological research project on various aspects of town life. I spelt out the areas in which I was interested and mentioned that at a later stage I would be doing a random sample household survey. Being chronically short of copy, the *Bradstow Press* ran this article on the front page with a photograph. Consequently, most people in the area knew what I was doing although there were different levels of understanding. For some people I was 'just writing a book on the town' but others had a much more accurate perception. When I first met one of the solicitors he said to me, 'I know what you are doing. I did anthropology at Sydney University and I can tell you they would have made your job a lot easier if they had sent you to the Trobriand Islands. You will have a difficult job finding out how this town works'.

Initial contacts were important because they introduced me to different sections of the social structure. I shall restrict my remarks to the status system because this dimension of stratification emphasises the many different types of social situations which can occur. My first informant was the real estate and stock and station agent who arranged my accommodation. Where the research worker lives can be important for determining people's initial reactions. There were two houses available for rent. One was a small cottage near the railway line and the other, which we took, was a two-storey gatekeeper's lodge about one and a half kilometres out of town on the south-eastern outskirts: it was a National Trust classified building on a half hectare of land which had been subdivided and sold when the main house and property were taken over by a convent. The house was close to Grange, but sufficiently marginal so as to be able to avoid close identification with that exclusive residential area.

Our agent was regarded as a professional man (because he charged fees) as against the local businessmen who were seen to be in trade. This was an important distinction in Bradstow because it determined who was eligible for membership of the exclusive Bradstow Golf Club. As a professional, this agent mixed socially with the people from Grange who were primarily retired professionals or businessmen from Sydney, retired colonial service personnel, and wealthy Sydney folk with weekend villas and grazing properties. In the first two or three weeks the agent invited us to various cocktail parties and I met a wide range of people from this status group.

During this period I had several long conversations with the deputy town clerk, a local historian, whom I had met on one of my earlier visits. As well as being able to clarify aspects of local history he knew all the municipal council aldermen and almost all the businessmen and tradesmen. He introduced me to many of these people and invited me along to the council meetings and others, such as the historical society, the gardening club, and the senior citizens' homes committee. The contacts I made through him, particularly the mayor and a number of aldermen, invited me to Rotary, Lions, and Apex meetings, and I arranged through these people to sit in on the town's biggest committees, the Flower Festival and the Swimming Pool.

I have played the game of soccer for the greater part of my life and I now had an opportunity to use this game to help my research. I joined the Bradstow Soccer Club and made many friends among unskilled, skilled, and clerical workers. The status of my educational background, which had been accepted by the Grange-ites, could have gone against me in this situation but this did not happen and I was accepted into their social circle on the basis of my playing ability and, perhaps, partly because of my obvious pleasure in drinking at the pub after the match. I became secretary of the club and the coach of a junior team.

During the first few weeks we met a small number of people who became and remain close personal friends. These folk were primarily artists and potters who were living in the district because it was a pleasant place. Most lived outside the town, took little or no part in town affairs, and formed a fringe group. Some were referred to as 'weirdos' by the townspeople because they 'had beards', 'did not work', and 'refused to have their children christened'.

The Bradstow District Hospital is large for a small town but serves a wide area. My wife, a nursing sister, had arranged a job there helping to deliver the town's babies. Coming from a big Sydney hospital she was highly valued by the general practitioners, who run the hospital, as she was conversant with all the latest techniques and drugs. Consequently, she established good relationships with the doctors. Through these contacts I had an easy entry into their social circle and was able to see the important position that the doctors and solicitors held within the social structure. These professionals are among the small number of people who can cross the central status cleavage between the Grange-ites and the townspeople (1974: 47–8).

During the first few weeks I made contact with, and was collecting data from, a wide range of status levels. But there were two further status groups that had eluded my first impressions and these were at the very top and bottom of the status hierarchy.

At the beginning I viewed as synonyms such terms as the aristocracy, the blue-bloods, the Golf Club crowd, the Grange-ites, the old family group, the landed gentry, the wealthy elite, the silvertails, the better class of people, the poo-bahs, the snobs, and others. By some people these terms were used as synonyms. But there was an important distinction here which first struck me when I was standing in the main street on a busy Saturday morning talking to the owner of a junk shop. An old lady walked past and climbed into a vintage Daimler which was parked at an odd angle with its bonnet pushed into a small parking space and the back section protruding onto the road. He turned and said to me, 'That's Mrs Legge-Smith'. I asked who she was. He replied in hushed tones, 'She's one of the old families, she's real aristocracy. This crowd out here (nodding his head towards Grange) are just nouveau riche who have come to live here to pretend to be landed gentry. And what's more that car never gets booked.' This casual conversation outlined the distinction between the Grange-ite nouveau riche and the gentry. This enabled me to ask further probing questions about this cleavage and I was able to isolate a small core group of long-established gentry families, most of whom had three to five generation connections with the district.

In the first weeks no-one mentioned the existence of what one informant later called 'the low ones who are really low' and who are generally referred to as the no-hopers. I was aware by looking at the housing conditions near the railway and in Stone Valley (a shanty area reclaimed from swamp land on the extreme eastern edge) that there were some poor people, but on first impressions I thought they were probably the poorer fringe of the manual workers. Several families living in these areas turned out to be in this position but there was a small category of families who were generally despised by the rest. One particular incident made me fully aware of this distinction.

A businessman challenged a man leaving his shop. The man produced a packet of biscuits from his pocket, apologised, put some money on the table and ran from the shop. The owner called the police and charged him with stealing. As it was a repeated offence he was gaoled for six months. The man and his wife were both invalid pensioners and had several children. This incident received wide publicity including a photograph in the *Bradstow Press*. The businessman cut out several of these press reports and pasted them over the front of his shop window. When I discussed this incident with two other businessmen one said to me, 'Oh, there are a few no-hopers like him in Bradstow. They are just lazy bastards. They'll never do a day's hard work. There are about a dozen families like that. Most of them have been in prison and some are prostitutes. I can tell you I'd like to kick them all out of town.'

One of the main problems after the initial two months was to gain entry and acceptance by such disparate status groups. Some were easier than others. I was collecting data almost straight away from the blue and white-collar workers with whom I played soccer. An interest in art, music, drama, history and gardening was essential for any rapport with the Grange-ites, especially the women. My keen interest in local politics and service clubs activities provided me with an entry into the businessmen's circle and the political cliques. My boyhood and adolescent experience as a boy scout enabled me to fill in as a scoutmaster for a period and provided immediate entry into a number of tradesmen's, businessmen's, and schoolteachers' homes. However, it was difficult to obtain information from the gentry and the no-hopers.

I solved the first problem quite by chance. One afternoon I met a distinguished looking old gentleman taking a stroll close to my house on the outskirts of town and we started talking. I eventually found out that he was the owner of a very big shipping and retail business and that his family had moved onto the land in Grange when they had become wealthy after the turn of the century. After this chance encounter I used to join him for afternoon tea on the sun verandah on his 20-odd room house which overlooked some one and a half hectares of immaculately kept gardens. At other times I was invited for drinks — always the best scotch whisky served promptly at five-forty every evening in the library. This contact became perhaps my closest link with the gentry (1974: 41–2).

I did not have the same success with the no-hopers and at one stage it was only a wife's restraining arm that stopped her husband from hitting me for 'asking damn fool questions about my private life'. It soon became obvious that I was not going to get much information just by trying to talk with them at home or even in the pub. In the public bars they were sometimes ostracised by the other workers. I struck on the idea of trying to get some information from their children. I knew one boy in the soccer club who mixed with some of the no-hopers' children, some of whom played rugby league. I got him to take me along to a particular hotel where they monopolise the lounge with a pop band and dancing on Friday and Saturday nights (1974: 93–5). I attended for several weeks at the end of which I had gained sufficient acceptance to obtain general information on such things as style of life, leisure activities, how a typical week was organised, attitudes to local politics, and so forth.

One further major difficulty I had with gaining acceptance was with a small crowd of people about my own age (24 at the time) who had established their own businesses as painters and decorators, plumbers, welders, and builders. This group drank regularly at the Bradstow Hotel and one evening I introduced myself to them in the saloon bar. A painter and decorator, who was their main spokesman said, 'You are the bloke who is writing the book are you? What's it all about?'. I replied, 'Well, I am writing a book partly about local history and partly about how the town is run and organised today, local politics and things like that.' He answered, 'And you get paid to do that by the University? What a bloody waste of time. And anyway who sees that you get up at eight o'clock and start work on time? I think all this bloody education is overrated. Look at me, I left school before my Intermediate and I employ seven blokes now and make a fair crust.' I replied cautiously and pointed out that people are interested in different things and he had obviously done well in the area he had chosen. But it was clear I was not making any headway. I could not get them to answer any probing questions.

I went to the same bar of the hotel for almost two weeks. I drank with them and eventually got to play in their games of darts but I was still not getting the information I required. Finally, on one Friday night I was invited to join them at the Country Club after the hotel closed. At the Club we played snooker and table tennis as we drank on until after one in the morning. Before we were about to leave the painter and decorator came up to me and said, 'We all thought you were a prick when we saw you. We didn't like your hair, and the way you talked, but you've had a few beers with us, (over eighty middies in the past two weeks in fact) and you're not bad at darts, so we think you're not a bad sort of bloke.' He then extended his arm and we shook hands. On leaving the Club the youngest member of this crowd whom I knew through the Soccer Club turned round and remarked to me, 'They've accepted you now. It's a sort of initiation that goes on for a while but you're in now and you won't have any more trouble.' He was right: a few weeks later I interviewed in depth two members of this group.

It should be clear by now that to gain acceptance and obtain information from disparate status groups entails playing many different roles. Trying to prevent clashes which occur between one's normal behaviour and one's role expectations in a particular social situation can be difficult, and the investigator may have to become almost devious in avoiding such incidents. The observer may also, in some situations of conflict for example, have to avoid being seen by the members of one group when he is mixing with those of another.

In such situations as these, personal relationships have to be developed, established, and kept up for instrumental purposes. This is one of the more difficult, and least attractive, aspects of this type of research. Such situations develop even more tension when the status gap between the investigator and the respondent is particularly great. Two social dramas, one centred on the Golf Club and the other on the teenagers' pop lounge, indicate the types of social situations at vastly different status levels with which a participant observer has to cope (1974: 84; 93–5). In the Golf Club drama I was dressed in a dark three-piece suit, white shirt, and University tie. I drank double scotches and the conversation centred on politics and business. In the pop lounge I wore corduroy jeans, desert boots, and a purple floral shirt. I drank schooners of old beer and talked about sport, cars, and women. The more the researcher can equalise the status differences between himself and his respondent the more, and better quality, data he will obtain.

Gans has suggested that the researcher plays at least three roles: total researcher, researcher-participant, and total participant (1967: 440). I played the first role on very few occasions. My attendance at the municipal council meetings, for example, took this form but after the meeting over drinks in the Mayoral Room I took on the second role. I played the role of researcher-participant in most situations. I became a total participant with several close personal friends, and also when I was playing soccer, running the scout troop, and helping with various projects. What may begin as a researcher-participant situation can become a total participant one. As a total participant investigators must exercise particular care because they become less observant and their own biases intrude in a more forthright manner. Further, as a total participant, that is when researchers have forgotten their research role and are acting as a 'normal' person, it is easy to offend people. Once this has been done it rebounds on the research role and makes future interviewing and participant observation more difficult. I found that in most participant observation and interviewing situations it paid me to take a neutral stance and to act as though I knew nothing about the topic. In these circumstances most respondents keep on talking to avoid the silences. Essentially, participant observers have to sell themselves to the respondent or group in order to obtain the type of information they require and they are likely to be more succcessful if they take a neutral or sympathetic position.

So far I have discussed some of the difficulties I encountered in the early part of the fieldwork when I was collecting data on a wide range of topics. During this first year I was also collecting data on the political system. I attended municipal and county council meetings, interviewed politicians, followed through several case studies of controversial issues and town projects, and conducted a reputational survey of political power holders.

Two general methodological points, of which I was unaware, emerged from this work on politics. First, I found that it was impossible to remain passive and uncommitted in a controversial political issue. People were constantly asking my opinion: did I think for example, that a T.A.B. office should be allowed to open in Bradstow. In such situations it is as bad to be passive as it is to be provocative. I found that if I argued carefully people would listen and either agree or proceed to argue against my points. Further, in such discussions other useful data that were previously ignored, and would not have been explored with even the best prepared questionnaire schedule, were often introduced.

Second, I found that I had to be constantly aware of what I was saying even in the most casual conversations. An anthropologist obtains some data from general gossip. Different groups have different norms or rules about gossip and these have to be learned and followed. This was fortunately brought home to me early in the fieldwork period. Three weeks after arriving, my wife was having a casual conversation with a patient in the hospital. Referring to an item in the paper the patient said, 'The council are still on about garbage collection. God, they are a hopeless lot.' My wife replied, 'Yes, I agree with you. I've been to two of their meetings and they never get anything done. I think a benevolent dictator would go well in this town.' It was an incidental conversation that was soon forgotten, at least for the moment. Two days later the president of Marston Shire Council, which adjoins the Bradstow Municipality, said to me, 'I believe your wife has been making acid comments about our civic fathers.' I asked him to explain and he recounted the story informing me that the patient was his daughter-in-law. I replied that my wife had been to a council meeting and was entitled to her own opinion. I could not have said much else as it was obvious from his attitude that he thought my wife's comments originated from me. In this case the matter was soon forgotten and I had several discussions with him on later occasions but it indicates why investigators must try to be aware of the possible consequences of all their actions as well as those of their spouse.

During the second year of fieldwork I directed my attention to more specific areas on which I required more data. I selected a number of clubs and societies from different status levels, became a member, played an active part on their committees and analysed their membership and organisational structure as well as the part they played within the stratification system. I collected comparative data on local politics from a nearby town and continued taking notes from general participant observation.

By this time I knew many people in Bradstow and I had a lot of qualitative data as well as some quantitative data from the census and from the reputational, issue, and positional analyses of the political power system. I required, however, more quantitative material on such basic facts as amounts and sources of income, levels and type of education, family backgrounds, and so forth. I also wanted further data on people's attitudes to class, politics, and religion. I planned and carried out a random sample of 20 per cent of the households which consisted of 326 interviews. I used a formal questionnaire and each interview lasted between one and three hours depending on the interest of the respondent. A response of over 94 per cent shows that I was certainly accepted by the people at this time and the other 6 per cent included those who were sick and whose houses were empty as well as the few who refused to be interviewed. Surveys such as this carried out on the basis of a thorough knowledge of the historical and socio-cultural context of the area can provide valuable, if somewhat limited, data. Mass surveys carried out without any knowledge of, or reference to, the socio-cultural context, often provide misleading and meaningless statistics within a social vacuum, especially when they are concerned with such qualitative phenomena as class, status, and political power. The survey was the last part of my fieldwork and I then started to collate the data and present it within an historical, social and cultural context.

After fieldwork most anthropologists find themselves with data that may harm people if it is published: the harm may be real, as for example, in counter-insurgency anthropology, or it may be in the people's minds. Both are significant. In the writing of Bradstow I considered what might rather pretentiously be referred to as two broad ethical tenets in order to help me determine what I could publish and in what form. First, I was concerned with scientific inquiry and interpretation, that is, the pursuit of knowledge, of free inquiry, and free publication. Second, I took into account my own responsibility to the people and the confidences they shared. If this responsibility is not taken personal confidences will be divulged, privacy will be infringed, and reputations may be damaged.

In *Bradstow* I left out several social drama situations because they could have been a source of severe embarrassment to some people. One of them, for example, later involved legal proceedings. I changed all local place names and all personal names in an attempt to retain the privacy of as many people as possible and to avoid any undue publicity on publication. I did not suppress details such as occupations, club memberships, case study material, or similar data, for to have done so would have been to distort the social context. Some people in Bradstow will, of course, recognise those who are described in the book. This is unavoidable in a study of this nature. Most of these people, however, are in public office or concerned with public affairs and should be accountable for their actions.

A further issue relating to this discussion concerns the restrictive laws of libel found particularly in New South Wales, and in Australia generally. Under these laws it is impossible, for example, to publish such examples of political corruption as Vidich and Bensman used so well in *Small Town in Mass Society*. I had to spend several sessions with the publisher's lawyers re-writing sections, omitting one case study, and pruning some quotations. I fought successfully against some alterations and agreed with others to enable most of the data to appear.

One effect of this has been to weaken one of my arguments and, therefore, partly affect the quality of scholarship. Another effect was the delay in publication. The manuscript was completed in 1971. It took several months for Sydney University Press to reject it 'because of the legal problems which relate to possible defamation'. Several more months passed before Cheshire Publishing decided to reject it because 'our sales research indicates that we could not sell any more than a few hundred copies'. It took further time for Melbourne University Press and McGraw Hill to reach the same conclusion. When Angus and Robertson finally accepted it, the legal difficulties caused some delay, the re-organisation of the publisher's educational section created a further deferment, and finally the first print run disappeared under the Brisbane flood. The book eventually appeared in July 1974.

The Report
Bradstow is primarily concerned with examining some propositions from sociological theory concerning social stratification within the context of a localised social system. I had no intention of studying or describing the 'whole community'. Bradstow is not a wholistic

study examining the 'community as object' (see pp. 00; Bell and Newby, 1971: 41) in the tradition of some of the earlier anthropological community studies rather it represents 'community as method', that is, it uses community as a localised social system to get at some data concerning social stratification. In the process, of course, it also tells us a lot about Bradstow in particular, as well as about social stratification in general.

At the theoretical level I started the Bradstow research with the notion of examining the relationship between class, status and party (called political power in the report) and finished with the comprehensive model briefly outlined in the Introduction. In the concluding paragraph to *Bradstow* I contend that this amplification of class, status and party provides 'the most inclusive and comparative model of stratification available' and suggest that it may be applied, and further developed, in other places and at other levels. I have utilised and developed this model in *Social Stratification in Australia* (Wild, 1978a) where I applied it to studying Australia's national system of social stratification. In the following discussion I shall restrict my comments to some of the central aspects of status, class and party and their interrelationships in Bradstow.

The Status System
Following Weber, I mean by status groups those who share a common style of life and generally accepted forms of conduct in so far as these provide bases for interaction. The recognition of signs and symbols, such as dress and accent, the evaluation of common behaviour, and the application of such sanctions as membership restrictions in voluntary associations, afford such foundations for interaction. The symbols, qualities and virtues that constitute a social status are accorded honour or prestige by differential evaluation. The resulting hierarchy forms the status system.

In a localised status system, claims to prestige are generally organised as rules and expectations that control who successfully obtains it, with reference to whom, in what ways, and on what criteria. Such demands are expressed in conventions and patterns of consumption that compose the styles of life of various people at different places in the hierarchy. The things done and the things not done are conventions that relate to dress, speech, place of residence, type of house, make of car, club membership, standard and type of education, religion, occupation, ideology and so forth. Status equals tend to maintain free association among themselves and simultaneously limit it with others.

By definition social prestige rests on subjective attitudes such as esteem, deference, admiration, exclusiveness, honour, respect, condescension and dignity. Such qualitative relationships cannot be briefly described or accurately measured. Consequently the investigator must observe and interpret social interaction and attitudes as well as examine the distribution of occupations, incomes and other status attributes.

During ·my first few weeks in Bradstow it became apparent that many people recognised, and discussed in evaluative terms, a number of reasonably well-defined status groups. They evaluated them in relation to behaviour, general style of living and attitudes, and based their judgement on personal knowledge or hearsay about family background, occupations and other criteria. There was a general consensus that some groups were high and others low, that some were superior and others inferior, and that some should be accorded deference, some condescension and some aversion. There were the 'snobs who are well off', the 'ordinary respectable people like ourselves', the 'down and outs who just don't help themselves', and others in between.

Using data from participant observation and in-depth interviews, I isolated six basic status groups with a recognisable membership and arranged them in a hierarchy. Although the persons belonging to each one consider the rest to have specific attributes and behaviour patterns it must be kept in mind that there is a certain amount of overlapping. Some divisions are more rigid than others, and some people are not members of any. The six are rather core status groups that have specific attitudes to others, exhibit certain forms of behaviour, are referred to by labels that are recognised and understood throughout the town, have an identifiable style of life, and share certain common attributes. These core groups, by determining many social relationships, form the basis of the social structure.

Each of the social clusters is referred to by various expressions, and I shall use some of these labels to name them. They are, in the order of the status hierarchy, the gentry, the Grange-ites, the bosses, the tradesmen, the workers, and the no-hopers. It is clear that these are value-loaded names and I do not necessarily subscribe to all their implications, but they provide a picture of a status system that helps us to understand reality in a way that the first six letters of the alphabet would not.

The gentry are of two types. The first are descended from the explorers and pioneers who were granted tracts of land by various governors; the second are descendants of the wealthy retailers, shipping merchants and industrial magnates who made their fortunes in the middle of the nineteenth century and then moved on to the land as the respectable thing to do, while still retaining an interest in commerce. The original graziers have for one reason or another gradually lost their wealth. The others have remained obviously rich.

The gentry are much concerned with kinship and lay great stress on background, traditions, continuity and ancestry (albeit that goes back no more than four or five generations). They like to live in the ancestral house, surround themselves with heirlooms, and have reunions on festive occasions. It is usual for the children to attend the same schools as their parents and follow the same calling. Some have written books and historical articles on the lives of their forefathers. This concern with the family gives the gentry their solidarity. The lack of such ancestry makes others, especially the nouveau riche, realise that they cannot in their lifetime rise to this status level.

The gentry's aping of English upper-class affectations helps to create social distance between themselves and other groups, except perhaps for some of the Grange-ites with whom they share some of these attributes. Unlike the earlier gentry who were active in community affairs, today's gentry are rarely seen in the town; they do not attend gatherings or meetings, they never seek any form of publicity, they belong to few voluntary associations, and they rarely seek any office. This is an indication of their declining numbers and wealth. The men belong to the exclusive Bradstow Golf Club (which does not permit local businessmen to join) and the Liberal Party branch, and shun most other organisations. They are members in Sydney of the Australian and Royal Sydney Golf Clubs. The women belong to the Liberal Party, the Golf Club, and the local branch of the Red Cross. These are the most esteemed organisations, but running them is left to the Grange-ites.

Other status-conferring qualities such as wealth, occupation, type and level of education, house type, gardens, clothes, residential area, and accent cannot alone confer sufficient prestige for inclusion among the gentry despite the fact that a certain type and amount of all these characteristics seem almost necessary criteria. To the gentry it is kin that is the major link. All the other things may be necessary criteria for membership, but without family they are nothing.

The Grange-ites form approximately 18 per cent of the population. Some are retired, some have independent means, some live in Bradstow but work in Sydney, and still others have grazing properties. Most of them live in Grange, which is, as the name implies, a prestigious outer residential area.

Two subgroups may be recognised. One consists of people who have often been described as self-made men. These have accumulated a lot of money and moved to Bradstow to seek respectability and legitimate their newly-acquired riches. They define success as wealth and evaluate everyone else on this basis. The educational level is generally low, and rarely beyond the Intermediate certificate, but their speech, if it has not already done so, soon acquires what the townspeople call 'that snobbish sort of voice'. One thing most essential for the self-made Grang-ites when they first arrive is to join a small number of clubs of which the most important is the Golf Club. Membership provides an immediate reputation both within and outside the community. Within the town it separates the townspeople, except for the professions, from 'those who just come to the town to live'. As membership is considered most acceptable among many Sydney folk, social honour is conferred on the member over a wider area than Bradstow. The wealthy Grange-ites rarely link up with any associations that involve interaction with the townspeople.

The self-made Grange-ites are ostentatious. They live in big houses that are surrounded by acres of carefully tended gardens. They may graze a few beef cattle or keep one or two race horses in the paddocks nearby. Their cars are almost without exception Rolls Royce, Bentley, or Mercedes Benz. In dress they emulate the gentry: heavy tweeds, cavalry twill, and good corduroy are fashionable. One may see the floppy tweed hat with the occasional trout fly, the plus fours, a shooting stick or a silver-topped walking stick, and a monocle or two. Some of these self-made men who have lived in the town for 15 to 20 years or more often mix with the gentry at social gatherings and bridge parties, but there is never total acceptance. A woman member of the gentry once remarked, 'Our close friends are all family friends. The older families that we have known for years. We have other friends that we meet at the theatre or the Red Cross but they are not close friends; they are acquaintances, I suppose.'

The second subgroup might be termed the professionals. They have been successful and have retired to live comfortably on investments and superannuation. They were company secretaries, high-ranking public servants, politicians, chartered accountants, medical practitioners and the like. Some still work in Sydney a few days a week. They tend to evaluate people according to occupation, education, and common interests rather than wealth. Generally they are better educated than the wealthy Grange-ites; obviously many would have had to take a university degree. A majority speak in 'educated Australian', although many imitate what they believe to be an Oxford accent. To the townspeople both seem obnoxious and assumed.

As well as being members of esteemed organisations like the Golf Club and the Liberal Party they also belong to such cultural organisations as the Arts Council and the Art Society, charity committees, for example the Red Cross and Legacy, hobby societies similar to the Gardening Club, and other reputable bodies such as the Pony, the Picnic Race, the Horse Show, and the Polocrosse Clubs. In these societies they see themselves as mixing with people with common interests. Some of them mix with the townspeople who share similar values. However, this interaction tends to be restricted to the town professionals, some of whom are Grange-ites, and others who are more sociable with the local bosses.

The professional Grange-ites are less ostentatious. Their houses are generally smaller, with no more than six bedrooms. The gardens are smaller but well cared for by the owner or a part-time gardener. Their cars are the smaller luxury ones such as Jaguars and Rovers.

I have stressed the difference between the types of Grange-ites but it must be kept in mind that this is not a categorical distinction. There are many visible similarities, and townspeople often subsume both under the one term. The most discernible resemblances are the comfortable style of life that evinces financial security, dress that emphasises conspicuous leisure, speech that indicates type of education and acts as a badge of solidarity and respectability, and club memberships that stress exclusiveness.

The local bosses consist primarily of those who have been successful in commerce locally and so have made a lot of money, particularly since the Second World War, but the circle also includes those in administrative and managerial posts such as the town and county clerks, the headmasters, the editor of the newspaper, and the senior welfare officer. There are two major differences between the successful retailers and the administrator-managers. The latter have a better formal education, sometimes with university degrees. The successful businessmen, however, are wealthier.

The bosses are active in everyday affairs. They dominate local government, the Chamber of Commerce, such social service organisations as Rotary, Lions and Apex, the Country Club which is the townspeople's 'Golf Club', and the Flower Festival and Swimming Pool Committees. Proprietors and managers work together in these societies, play squash together in the evenings, eat at one another's houses, and spend holidays together.

Generally the wealthy retailers have bigger houses, more elaborate gardens, and more expensive cars than the administrator-managers, but they live in the same residential areas either in the town or on Harris Hill, which is said to be 'the businessmen's answer to Grange'. Their clothes are similar and their speech is little different, although the retailers tend to have a broader Australian accent than the more educated administrators.

The bosses form a solidary core status group. They claim and receive a reputation for their interest in social and political affairs. They have a particular circle of club memberships and share a common lifestyle. There are differences, particularly with respect to education and income, but it is the system of social relations built around community projects that provides unity. The bosses are known as the ones who can get things done, and they control most of the projects.

The concept of the man in trade is a central element of the status system. By the tradesmen group I primarily refer to skilled manual workers, both self-employed and employed, small shopkeepers, and some white-collar workers. It is almost twice the size of the bosses group and forms approximately 23 per cent of the population. The younger self-employed tradesmen and white-collar men are keen to work hard to earn money and a higher occupational standing. This enables them later to move into the bosses' circle. The older tradesmen and small shopkeepers have realised that they will achieve little more or are happy with their station and form the basis of this status group. A perceptive observer referred to their latching 'on to the Bowling Club: they have given up the status race altogether and put all their energies into building up the Bowling Club.'

Most of the tradesmen attended State schools but left either before or immediately after the Intermediate examination. Usually they follow the same occupation as their fathers—plumbing, building or whatever it was—or they were apprenticed at the cement works, the brickworks, or the county council. Others became clerks. Many of the younger men are members of Apex and without doubt some will eventually more into Rotary and Lions as they build up a reputation. The older tradesmen focus their social life on the Bowling Club. Some also belong to the Country Club and some to the R.S.L. in a neighbouring town. It is within this group that such sporting clubs as cricket, rugby league and soccer are popular, and many tradesmen hold offices in these clubs.

Most members of this group live either in the town or on its outskirts. The younger men bought land just outside to the east and have built new brick veneer or weatherboard houses. They have small gardens which usually consist of an area of lawn surrounded by a border of flowers. There are rarely any fully grown trees which are so typical of the gardens in the older-established areas.

Other tradesmen live in older houses closer to the centre of the town.

The Grange-ites view this status group as part of the townspeople or those in trade. 'The Grange people talk about going in to the village and about employing a tradesman for a job just as if they were back in England where most of them never were anyway; it's the influence of the English tradition in this town that does it', remarked one of them. The bosses refer to this group as those who have not made it, but the workers see them as the Bowling Club crowd or the ones who are comfortably off.

The workers are the biggest group: they make up almost 40 per cent of the population. Their occupations include tradesmen, semi-skilled drivers and operatives, white-collar service workers, and unskilled labourers. Most of the employed work at the brickworks, the cement factory, the municipal and county councils, and the local shops and stores. There are some former wage-earners who live on old-age or widow's pensions. All the workers attended the State schools, which the vast majority left before the Intermediate examination. After leaving, a small number were apprenticed, though the majority moved immediately into semi-skilled and unskilled jobs, which they often change. Those who became shop assistants and storemen tended to keep the same job, possibly because there are so few jobs.

The most popular clubs with the workers are the rugby league and the R.S.L. a few kilometres away, though many do not belong to any club. Others have joined the Bowling Club and such sporting bodies as the Basketball Association, the Pigeon Racing Club and the Car Club. A small number are members of the Country Club. Few workers hold any offices.

The workers live in the town, in the eastern outskirts and in the railway-industrial area, where they are most numerous. In the town they tend to the northern end, which merges into the railway-industrial area. On the outskirts they are a long way off, near the housing commission land and Stone Valley. The houses vary from one to four bedrooms, and most are built from fibro and iron roofs. Many of the houses in the town have no gardens, but a few have a tiny strip of lawn or concrete bounded by a wall or a fence. On the outskirts they usually have a lawn or a patch of grass. The houses and furnishings of many of the older workers, especially the pensioners and widows, are dilapidated but the younger workers are in different circumstances. Many live in new or near-new fibro houses and most have a television set, a washing machine and a car — all obtained on hire purchase. In these cases the husband works as much overtime as possible and the wife also works to help pay for them.

Some of the workers, many of whom are middle-aged, keep one room for special occasions which is a continuation of the English lower class front-room or parlour custom. It contains the best furniture, carpets, curtains and mirror, and is used only for important guests.

The workers who are not members of clubs, and some of those who are, form public bar cliques. They drink, usually at the same hotel, every night and discuss such topics as rugby league, beer, women, cars and work. They may also play games of darts. The bosses and tradesmen often refer to them as the pub crowd or just the workers.

The centres of social interaction for the workers are the work place, the clubs, particularly the R.S.L. and the rugby league, and the public bars of the hotels. They rarely invite people to their houses. It is possible to see some aspects of the process of embourgeoisement among some of the younger worker families, especially the ones in which the wife is employed. But there are still many poor workers who find it difficult to house, clothe and feed their families.

The no-hopers are generally well known among the townspeople and spoken of disparagingly by the bosses and the tradesmen. The members comprise less than four per cent of the population, and most are unskilled labourers, though a few are semi-skilled drivers and operatives. Many have a reputation for always being in trouble with the police. During the period of fieldwork one was jailed for repeated shoplifting and another for breaking and entering.

Few no-hopers belong to any voluntary associations, and those who do join the R.S.L. in a neighbouring town. Most are well known around the public bars of two particular hotels. The other hotels have a slightly higher standing and cater for the tradesmen and bosses.

The no-hopers live near the railway, in the northern part of the town, and in Stone Valley. Their houses are usually small, dirty and dilapidated. The gardens are small and untidy with all types of rubbish lying amongst overgrown grass. Most left school after one or two years of secondary schooling, though a minority had only a primary education and a few are illiterate. Many earn above the basic wage on labouring jobs, but they often work for a time and then take a few weeks off. Most own a car, usually an old American sedan or a Holden.

The no-hopers are aware of what others think about them. Their response is either an attempt to opt out of the system or to be hostile and live up to their bad reputations. Sometimes the children act out these responses. A doctor's son had to be removed from the high school 'because he was constantly teased and beaten up by the sons of these drunken labourers on account of his father having two cars and living in Grange. I mean that is nothing but inverted snobbery.'

Many no-hopers' comments about other groups are bitter. 'This town is full of bloody snobs. They stick their noses in the air because they think they are richer than everyone else and the ones that are flash are always going off to some club or other.'

Each status group, then, exhibits a number of distinguishable social characteristics, including forms of behaviour, attitudes to the status system, networks of association, typical paths of social careers, and style of living. The deepest and widest cleavage occurs between the gentry and the Grange-ites on the one hand, and on the other the bosses, tradesmen, workers and no-hopers. The upper-status groups, following the supposed pattern of the English rural squirearchy, represent in their own minds everything that is formal, respectable, conservative and in good taste, and the middle and lower groups, preferring to appear as natural dinkum Aussies, represent everything that is rough, coarse and unrefined. At the same time, some townspeople have attempted to imitate the upper groups in order to gain respectability.

As I mentioned, there are individuals and fringe groups who blur the edges but I have abstracted what I consider to be the prime constituents of status. Each status group occupies a distinctive social milieu, where its members share experiences within an area of social reality, within the common occurrences of everyday life, and where they interpret their circumstances and those of others in relation to these experiences.

The particular historical development of Bradstow has enshrined a number of values, such as conservatism, the upholding of certain alleged English customs, an emphasis on conspicuous leisure, the desire for private education, and a concern with respectability and reputation. Such values, accompanied by a slow population growth, the lack of industry and associated trade union affairs, and the absence of any labour or radical political organisation, have contributed to the maintenance and continuity of this traditional status system.

A number of changes are slowly taking place within the status system. The decline of the gentry has been going on since the 1930s and certainly will continue. The Grange-ites of today are unacceptable as replacements because they do not have the necessary length of pedigree, but their grandchildren could perhaps become the gentry of the future. The Victorian saying that it takes three generations to make a gentleman may well apply. It took one well-known family three generations to entrench itself as gentry and forget that the founder of the dynasty was a shopkeeper in Sydney. It is rumoured that one of the earlier members of this family was refused membership of the Golf Club because of his trading associations.

The circumstances of the bosses has also changed slightly, especially since the Second World War. A fast-developing economy has produced several who are as wealthy as many Grange-ites. They have been able to imitate some aspects of the Grange-ites' sub-culture, but the fact remains that they have not been accepted socially, and not one local boss is a member of the Golf Club.

The status hierarchy is a traditional system with a much greater emphasis on persistence and maintenance than change, and it has remained a predominantly closed traditional order dominated by the upper groups. The question I shall now turn to is, how do these groups relate to the class system, and therefore, the distribution of economic power.

The Class System

I use class in the Weberian sense to refer to people who share 'similar life chances and common economic interests under the conditions of the commodity or labour market' (1948: 181). Both Marx and Weber recognised that ownership of the means of production was central to the analysis of class, and both laid stress on the fundamental distinction of the propertied and the propertyless.

In the analysis of class in *Bradstow* I combine simultaneously three separate dichotomies concerning relations of the means of production and the market. These are the propertied and the propertyless; the employers and the employees; and the leisured and the workers (see Ossowski, 1963: 69–88). The overlapping categories form the intermediate classes. So at one extreme is the class that owns the means of production — employers who do not work — and at the other the propertyless class — employers who work. In between are such classes as the property owners who are not employers and work and the property owners who are also employees. Using this framework and other indices, such as the source of income, I examine the class system as one of social relations with varying connections with the means of production.

Four major classes can be isolated in Bradstow. These are the leisured owners of property who are employers; the working owners who are employers; the working owners who are not employers; and the non-owners who are employees. There are a number of other intermediate positions such as the part-owners who work and are employees and the owners who work and are employees, but in this discussion I am concerned with the four major classes, their relationships to criteria of social honour, and their significance for interaction.

Probably the most important class cleavage is that between the leisured and the working. This partly coincides with the status division between the gentry-Grange-ites and the townspeople. The idle-working class dichotomy has clear affinities with the distribution of prestige and forms a major link between the class and status systems. Many of the leisured are living on independent means or are retired. This class cleavage partly determines patterns of social interaction because it coincides with a major status division rather than because it is a class line. Other class dichotomies such as the propertied and the propertyless and the employers and the employees cut across the division between the leisured and the working. But, at the same time, this class division is crucial in its own right because it relates people to different class systems. The leisured are mostly related to modes of production outside the town, whereas the workers are related to production within the town and district and, therefore, within the local class system.

Clearly the class categories overlap to some extent with the status criteria. The leisured owners who are employers make up the whole of the gentry, many of the Grange-ites, and a small number of some partly-retired bosses. The working owners who employ labour are some of the Grange-ites, most of the bosses, and a few tradesmen. The working owners who do not employ labour are most of the tradesmen and a few workers. Those who are non-owners and employees are most of the workers and all of the no-hopers. Class position can provide a vertical tie between the two or three status groups. An example is a new arcade building on the main street. It has shops on the ground floor and offices above. A retired army officer who is a grazier and a Grange-ite joined with two wealthy bosses to provide finance. All three are working owners who employ labour. The shops and offices are rented to tenants. Thus the Grange-ite and the bosses had the same source of income. A further example is that of two owners who work only part-time and employ labour. One is a local building contractor and a boss, and the other a Sydney solicitor, grazier, and Grange-ite. Both own a number of flats and houses and rent them to tenants. In both these examples a common class position has created a vertical tie between two status groups. Although socially the Grange-ites and bosses do not associate, in the economic system they share a similar place. In some cases economic agreements can and do operate outside the status sphere.

During and after World War II three developments that had important consequences for the class system took place. First, on account of the war, a number of wealthy Sydney people built houses in Grange and other, less wealthy, established small businesses in Bradstow itself. This development represented the first movement towards urbanisation. Today a number of professionals, semi-professionals, and manufacturers live in Bradstow and work in Sydney. For them, the place has become a dormitory or weekend suburb. This further emphasises the effect of the metropolis on rural settlements and country towns. Bradstow's class system, then, is becoming even more closely tied to that of Australia's largest city.

Second, after the War, B.H.P. established a cement factory at Hornby, and national industry extended roots into the local economic organisation. Simultaneously there was a decline in many of the old family estates as a result of death duties and other economic difficulties. Some were taken over by international companies and others formed the nucleus of private schools or were subdivided and tenanted. Woolworths and other national chain stores moved into the town and were quickly followed by self-service grocery chains. The biggest locally-owned general store was bought out by a national company, and the same thing happened to the cinema. Industrialisation and commercialisation had taken over, and many people were working for absentee owners in branches of national organisations.

Third, local government increased, as did branches of the State government concerned with education, health, decentralisation, and agriculture. The county council was established in 1954 to cater for the distribution of electricity and now has more employees than the municipal. Schools and the hospital have expanded and taken more workers into their bureaucracies. More and more employees have been brought into relations with people in authority in the work situation and have been taken away from relations with the owners of property. But the significant class relationship concerning the control of labour by employers in authority remains and it has been developed by bureaucratisation.

If, following Weber, we see bureaucratisation as administration in the hands of officials who possess the necessary technical knowledge (and this is a procedure of organisation that is general in applicability) then the bureaucratic aspect in the economic sphere can be seen as a development of Ossowski's employer-employee dimension of the class relationship. Thus for white-collar workers the important relationship is between those holding and not holding authority rather than between the owners and non-owners of property. The significant class relation in the authority-non-authority relationship is the control of labour. The person with authority in the bureaucratic hierarchy has control over labour and is the employer. In local government, for example, the town clerk and mayor, as holders of authority, control labour and act as employers in the employer-employee relationship. In this way the bureaucratisation of economic organisations is not an inhibiting factor to the class system but rather a development of one aspect of it.

Further, the growth of bureaucratic structures can lead to an emphasis on status. The hierarchy of positions in a bureaucracy provides levels of increasing importance and prestige. People attempt to move up into more prestigious positions and associate with people on similar levels.

These three features have helped to integrate the local with the class systems of the wider society and simultaneously have partly led to an emphasis on status as a major determinant of social relations. But such factors must not be over-emphasised. In many spheres class position is still an important criterion in determining social relationships.

An example showing that a class perspective is often central is a conflict over air pollution concerning a property owner and employer and a number of manual workers who live in the railway-industrial area. Since 1962 several petitions have been sent to the municipal council complaining about the soot that covered their houses and washing. Air pollution samples were taken but the petitioners received no reports. As one of the organisers of the petitions remarked, 'The ordinary person doesn't get a chance of getting anything done here. You have to be well in with the business clique before you can get anything done in this town.'

The organisers also asserted that they had written letters to the council about air pollution but that none had ever been read out at a meeting. When I left in 1969 a new petition was being organised, and the conflict continued.

Every issue in this conflict has been resolved in favour of the employers and property owners. This class cleavage between propertied employers and propertyless employees also runs along a status cleavage between the bosses and the workers. When it coincides the division is of greater significance and, as in this issue, it often comes to the surface.

The class system has developed from a simple dichotomy to a complex system of class categories each having varying relations with the fields of production. During the first period of settlement there was the landowner and convicts or emancipists he employed;

but today, through the processes of industrialisation, bureaucratisation, and urbanisation, the local class system has become complex and closely interrelated with the class system of the wider society.

If, as it seems, adjacent groups share similar economic characteristics, and therefore occupy similar class positions, then there is a potential for class ties between them. There is a possibility that an awareness of these relations may produce a class consciousness, that is, an awareness of their general social position and the problems and opportunities that surround it. Here there is a close link between the class and status systems because some cultural elements (that is some bases of prestige evaluation), such as labels of identification, become part of the class consciousness. In other words, class consciousness and styles of social honour can share some elements. Thus the fact that the gentry and many of the Grange-ites are owners, leisured and employers enables them to play golf every afternoon. This cultural element becomes part of their consciousness of their common class position as against the people who work and do not have as much free time. So Ossowski's leisured-working dimension of the class relationship has clear affinities with the distribution of prestige and forms a further link between the class and status systems.

Five major conclusions can be established from the analysis of class in Bradstow. First, there are many different types of production; some link the locality to an international economy, others are localised. Therefore, class in Bradstow as a system of social relations of production is both extensive and complex. While the connections with wider class systems has become increasingly crucial, there are still many local aspects, particularly within the overlap between the class and status systems, that remain of the utmost significance.

Second, the class system has been undergoing change under the impact of such forces as industrialisation, bureaucratisation, commercialisation, urbanisation and the effect of governments and other national organisations. Many enterprises once locally owned have been taken over by outside organisations and absentee owners. This process has accelerated the bureaucratisation of production and administration. The owner non-owner dimension of the class relationship has been partly modified by the managerial revolution, and simultaneously by the employer-employee dimension which contains the essence of bureaucracy, (emphasising control over labour) has been developed. The same process has also been partly responsible for the increasing stress on prestige and status. If any future developments can be forecast, then it seems that these processes will continue to strengthen the vertical class relations between Bradstow and the wider society and further weaken the horizontal class relations within the community.

Third, common class positions form vertical ties with adjacent status groups. Class position helps to form a unity through common economic interests between adjacent status groups but further alienates disparate status groups through clashes of economic interest. Further to the extent that adjacent groups share a class position, then there is potential for the development of a class consciousness. In addition to perceiving a common economic state, consciousness also perceives prestige entitling properties that act as labels of identification for a class. It is here that the class and status systems are closely related.

Fourth, when class conflicts emerge from the complexities of everyday life, the divisions tend to run along major status cleavages that closely follow the class dichotomies. The working leisured dimension of the class relationship has close connections with the distribution of prestige as may be seen between the upper status groups and the townspeople. Further, if adjacent status groups share a class position and, in some circumstances, develop a degree of class consciousness, as do the gentry and Grange-ites, then it is here where the most significant link occurs between the class and status systems.

Finally, the growing influence of such processes as modern technological developments, bureaucratisation, and urbanisation have led to an accentuation of status as the primary source of social relations and a decreasing emphasis on class. This is paralleled in the workplace by the increasing stress on the sphere of consumption and the decreasing emphasis on production. Mallet (1963: 9) has highlighted this crucial distinction. Regarding consumption 'the level of living [of the working class] and its aspirations for material comfort have led it out of the ghetto in which it was confined at the beginning of industrialisation. The worker ceases to regard himself as a worker when he leaves the factory'. But in the modes of production, 'the fundamental characteristics which distinguish the working class from other social strata seem to have remained unchanged'. Class relations have not disappeared, there has been no end to ideology; rather, at the present time class relations are taking second place to relations based on status. In the cases where class relations emerge, they often appear in the guise of status.

The Political Power System

Weber (1948: 180) defined power as, 'the chance of a man or a number of men to realise their own will in a communal action even against the resistance of others who are participating in the action'.

This is a wide concept, and in *Bradstow* I am chiefly concerned with political phenomena. Politics refers to interest in the distribution, maintenance, or transfer of power in the sphere of public relations. Further, I analyse both its actual and potential effects.

In an attempt to isolate the major influentials in local Bradstow politics I used three separate approaches. The 'reputational' approach consisted of asking several community knowledgeables to list those they considered to be most influential in community affairs. From their replies a master list was constructed. This was regarded as representing people who have a potential for power whether or not they use it. The 'issue' method entailed the detailed examination of a number of political events and community projects in order to determine which persons realised their aims. In 'positional' analysis the officials of formal voluntary associations and other bodies were identified, and the part they played in political affairs was examined. The methods (1974: 146–80) isolated three types of influentials — the boss influentials, the concealed influentials and the Grange-ites influentials — and I shall outline their main characteristics.

The boss and concealed influentials share similar class positions. Most are owners or part-owners of property; the majority are employers of labour, all have some control over labour, and all work. The Grange-ite influentials differ in the respect that two are leisured and a further two are partly leisured and work only part-time. All the Grange-ites have or had control over labour, and all are owners or part-owners of property. No influential is a wage-earner and none is an employee without any control over labour.

The boss influentials were born and raised in the district. They are successful and financially better off than the concealed influentials but not generally as wealthy as some of the Grange-ites influentials. They have close relationships with several concealed influentials and together form the bosses influential clique. The concealed influentials are itinerants, businessmen or managers. Generally they have a higher educational level than the boss influentials but not as high as the Grange-ites. They are younger than both the bosses and the Grange-ites. The Grange-ite influentials are older, professional men or wealthy businessmen, some of whom have retired. They take little part in the everyday affairs of the town but can and do organise themselves on particular issues, especially when their interests are challenged. They have few relationships with the boss and concealed influentials. All the influentials are Protestants. All the Grange-ites and most of the boss influentials are Anglican, an indication of this church's high standing. Most concealed influentials are Presbyterian or Methodist. Seventy-five per cent of all influentials are members of the Liberal Party. All influentials except one concealed influential unaffiliated with a political party, voted Liberal in the 1963 and 1966 Commonwealth elections. The differences between the categories of influentials becomes even more evident with the positional analysis.

Many people hold official positions in voluntary associations and other councils and committees, although there is an extensive overlapping of offices. Here I am concerned with only those bodies that make decisions of consequence for the whole community. The service clubs such as Rotary, Lions, Apex and the R.S.L.; the Liberal Party Branch; the Flower Festival Committee; the Chamber of Commerce; and the local government councils and committees make the important formal decisions. It follows that the office-holders in these organisations have more potential influence and authority than those in lesser and more specialised associations.

The members of the bosses clique hold many of the major formal positions in the town and so control the formal mechanisms for initiating, deciding, and implementing policy in community-wide affairs.

The concealed influentials in the bosses clique work closely with the visible boss influentials in community affairs and hold official positions. Almost all the bosses clique belong to the Rotary Club, where they meet each week. As one informant put it, the clique have 'their hands on the pulse of the community. They always know what is happening and if they don't like it, they can do something about it before anyone is any the wiser'. The other boss and concealed influentials join the bosses clique on different occasions as their interests and committee memberships are concerned.

The Grange-ite influentials hold few major formal offices. They tend not to participate in everyday political life and consequently have little direct say in the management of community affairs. If the Grange-ites decide to take a stand on a topic they can dominate, but this derives more from their high status position and extra-community contacts than from authority in local organisations. Generally, then, those reputed to have the most influence in local politics are the same as those holding the major positions of authority.

I examined several major political events and community projects to identify which persons were overtly active. This analysis indicates the nature of political participation and the actual wielders of power. Unfortunately I do not have space here to detail all these issues, so I will outline the main points with the help of one example.

The great majority of people concerned with the controversies and community undertakings were listed on the first reputational survey. The reputed influence or potential power assigned to them is actually wielded. Further, the most active participants were those classified as boss, concealed, and Grange-ite influentials, giving further validity to the reputational technique. Also the same people hold the major positions of authority. Altogether some 25 people, 0.5 per cent of the total population, play the central roles in initiating, deciding and implementing political matters.

Although the bosses influential clique runs local politics the Grange-ites and gentry still have a dominating influence. They take little interest in run of the mill local affairs unless something specific directly impinges upon them. They then employ intra- and extra-community contacts to have their way. More important than this, however, is the pervasive influence of their potential power and of their ideology about the sort of place Bradstow should be. The town clerk, amongst others, supports the Grange-ites' view that it ought to remain a rural village with supposedly English traditions free, from industry and manufacturing. They have invariably been successful in achieving their ends, as the following example indicates.

On a request from the Army, the municipal council invited it to establish a training depot in Grange. The Grange-ites organised a big petition, obtained the support of the town clerk, and by employing extra-community contacts, got the Army to move the depot to another town. All this was against the motion passed by the municipal council.

Another example that did not proceed as far but which indicates the potential power of the Grange-ites concerned the establishment of an irrigation-sprinkler factory in an old house near the river on the western extremity of Grange. The river frontage was necessary for testing and no other site was suitable. The factory expected to employ about 30 people. When the town clerk read the application at the council meeting the following discussion took place:

Mayor This is right in the heart of a top-class residential area.
Ald. Gare We could have a lot of trouble with this.
Town Clerk We haven't got sufficient information here to make a decision.
Ald. Sim Do you want industry here or not—that's the basic question?
Ald. Farrell What more information do you want? Here's a chance for a good light industry.

Ald. Gare You can't put it in a good residential area like Grange.

Ald. Lewis We have to decide quickly because the house is up for auction on 6 December.

Ald. Wilson Let's have a deputation and try to get them to go to another area more suitable for industry.

Ald. Gare This land would have to be re-zoned, and the big problem is the people of Grange. We'd have another petition on our hands.

Ald. Sim I think the greatest industry here is tourism. [Ald. Sim owns a motel.] Machinery is a red herring. It would spoil our tourism. Also at Grange. This makes a precedent. It is a better area for residential than for light industry. Perhaps we could accommodate him somewhere else.

Ald. Cooper We need tourism and also light industry for our rising generation. We need both.

Ald. Sim I propose that no action be taken.

Ald. Gare I'll second that.

Mayor Other areas in the municipality might suit. This area is near nice houses and will cause annoyance to residents.

Ald. Wilson I'll move an amendment that a deputation be sent to Thorne [the entrepreneur] to put this industry on another site because this is the sort of industry we want.

Alderman Sim and Alderman Gare agreed with the amendment, which then became the motion. It was carried unanimously. The deputation was never formed, although the mayor spoke privately with Thorne who was not interested in other sites without water. Nothing further was mentioned and the matter was shelved.

It is evident that the bosses in this issue were searching for a way to have this industry without offending the Grange-ites. The bosses want this type of development; the Grange-ites do not. The potential power of the Grange-ites was sufficient for the bosses to search for alternatives and eventually shelve the proposal. In other words, the Grange-ites got their way through potential power without even entering the actual situation. For many years the Grange-ites have successfully determined the question of decentralisation against the wishes of the local bosses.

It is clear that core status groups act as *loci* for the concentration of political power. The boss influentials form part of the bosses core status group, holds a high degree of influence and authority through their control of such bodies as local government, Rotary and the Chamber of Commerce, and manage everyday political affairs.

The Grange-ite influentials, part of the Grange-ite core status group, have widespread political connections through exclusive clubs and school-tie networks. The Grange-ites, and especially the gentry, remain distant from everyday affairs, but their opinions are known, respected, and often acted upon. They enter the local political arena only in such specific circumstances as the decentralisation controversy, when their values appear in danger of being undermined. The upper status groups use their dominance which is based on class and status to acquire the compliance of the middle and lower groups. As with the status system, political organisation is traditional and marked by continuity and conservatism.

In Bradstow, status, class and political power reinforce each other to a high degree. The status hierarchy is the most central and unchanging dimension. It is a reflection of the past, but it is also a major determinant of social relations in the present. Yet changes are occurring in the status order. As I mentioned, the gentry are slowly disappearing, and although the Grange-ites remain, they are not moving into the place that is becoming vacant. The class system has not softened or diminished; rather, it is taking a secondary place to status, while underpinning much of it in a time of unprecedented affluence and stability. The political system reflects more accurately a movement away from the traditional order. Most believe that the present political system is ideal and should not be criticised. But local politics are partly removed from this sphere. Local politics are removed from party allegiances and take place within the traditional status system. Local political conflicts run along status cleavages not along party political or ideological divisions. In national politics, then, the townspeople follow the conservative ideology of the upper status groups, but local politics become enmeshed with status divisions. The upper groups dominate the rest of the population with their immense social and economic power and through this power they are able to influence political affairs and keep the town in its accustomed mould.

Pearson in Johnsonville

The Background
As in the case of Oxley's work Pearson has not published anything on the background to his research in Johnsonville and the following material comes from personal communication. According to Pearson:

The Johnsonville study, akin to many other community studies, grew out of an intangible mixture of theoretical interests, auto-biographical details and sheer fortuity. The study was never planned insofar as I did not rationally sit down and select a re-search topic, cast around for funds then execute the research with smooth precision.

Pearson studied sociology at the University of Leicester in Eng-land as a mature-age student and emerged with the following tenets '(a) that one has to understand the past in order to explain the present, and (b) that social life is always shaped, at least in part, by its own unique cultural setting'. His first research for his Ph.D. was a study of West Indian community politics in Britain. He lived amongst West Indians in Leicester and married a Trinida-dian. Pearson conducted anthropological style fieldwork, for as he comments, 'I have always believed in getting my hands dirty in the research process because ultimately I believe sociologists have to relate their work to real people'. It was this fieldwork experience that moved Pearson towards community studies, 'because despite my strong awareness of the classical problems attached to the method, it is one of the few social science approaches which allows one to take out a slab of life, experience it and then seek to de-scribe and explain it from a variety of methodological perspec-tives'.

After the West Indian study Pearson and his wife decided to go abroad. He took a lectureship in sociology in New Zealand just be-cause the job was available. Pearson intended to study race rela-tions but 'discovered that social scientists seemed to know far more about the Maori population than themselves. There appeared to be little sociological or social historical investigation of New Zealand's past and very little rigorous research on the present'. He became increasingly intrigued by this society where everyone talked about being equal but signs of stratification were all around.

Pearson lived in the suburb of Johnsonville in Wellington and although it may sound like a pseudonym (compare Warner's Jones-ville) the name is real. In 1975 some local service clubs approached the Sociology Department to 'do a survey on community needs'. Pearson was presented with the request just because he lived in the area. His initial reaction was skeptical, 'I wasn't the least bit in-terested in surveys and could someone tell me what "community needs" were?'. He did, however, go to a meeting to discuss the project and 'discovered that the plan to get a community centre for the area dated back to 1916 and the politicking side covered a clas-sic scenario of local power games'. He became interested in the stories told by the club leaders and the social situation of working-class Johnsonville adjacent to a high-status suburb and an old, established farming area. Pearson ended up doing the survey and saw it as a small exercise in community politics. But as he read more history and followed up local records, he 'became immersed in the data to the point where it became a major research project'.

During the research Pearson was often reminded of his own background but the images presented were quite different from those in studies of the British class structure. He comments,

> My background was semi-rural and on the margins of the working class. Most of my relatives stemmed from 'respectable' working class families on the lower reaches of the middle class — and my own father's family in particular hailed from working class rural backgrounds. In short, I had always been intrigued by his feelings of class ambiguity and here was a society, New Zealand, where many people came out of similar backgrounds.

Gradually the research took on a systematic approach with funding, a research assistant and student help with interviewing. The project was becoming 'a well-rounded community study with its multi-methods of participant observation, interviewing and immersion in the historical record'. No-one else was doing this type of research in New Zealand and there was little contact between sociologists and historians. Consequently, Pearson suffered from a problem familiar to many lone community sociologists.

> My greatest problem was isolation and the sheer graft of working away in a research vacuum ... For me the Johnsonville study became an exercise in comparative academic solitude — an exercise which is intrinsically satisfying but frequently nerve-wracking... I remain convinced that many sociologists never venture out of their offices and *do* fieldwork simply because this method puts your ability to handle social relationships on the line.

Pearson shares my own strong conviction that community studies are an enormously vital part of sociological work. This does not mean that they do not have limitations or that there are no bad community studies. It is one of the aims of this book to provide a realistic assessment of what community studies can do and to establish theoretical and methodological guidelines within those limitations. But community studies do have that little extra which is absent from so much of sociology and Pearson puts it well when he comments, 'Above all I believe community studies can be productive simply because so many of them do grow out of the autobiography of the social scientist'.

The Report
In 1848 Johnsonville was 'a collection of rough houses' (1980: 16) on the outskirts of Wellington. By the 1870s its population was still less than two hundred. As with many other places the opening of the railway in 1885 transformed Johnsonville physically, economically and socially. The place grew as a service centre for the surrounding farming and growing suburban areas on the city's boundaries. The advent of the motor car, the electrification of the railway and the building of public housing by the government contributed to further development until the early 1950s. Then came a period of rapid growth that transformed the landscape from countryside scenery to suburban housing. In the 20 years between 1956 –76 the population jumped from 2272 to 9230 and Johnsonville emerged as truly 'metropolitan in character and appearance' (1980: 32). Associated with this growth was a change in the class character of the locality from a predominantly working-class neighbourhood in the early period up until the 1950s to what is now a more 'lower-middle/middle-class residential/industrial blend' (1980: 53). The influx of white-collar workers with young families, the abundance of voluntary associations and patterns of friendship and neighbouring that reflect 'individual contingencies rather than a consistent pattern' (1980: 51) make Johnsonville 'a useful microcosm of the Wellington urban area' (1980: 53).

In a manner uncharacteristic of many community studies Pearson details the changing nature of property ownership and social inequality since first settlement:

> As the nineteenth century unfolded, the contrast between the fine wood-frame dwellings or homesteads of the more affluent, and the far more humble accommodation of the majority, soon became evident. The pattern of inequality in Johnsonville manifested itself in home-ownership or tenancy, landed wealth or bare subsistence'. (1980: 56)

The farmers and the store-keepers were the wealthy in Johnsonville but their affluence was modest in comparison with that of the pastoralists and entrepreneurs elsewhere in New Zealand. By comparing property values from 1905 to 1928 Pearson shows the narrowing of inequalities. 'Professionals and businessmen were four times better off than labourers in 1905, whereas the average in 1928 was half this figure' (1980: 61). Further, there was a narrowing of differentials between clerical, craft and unskilled workers. An analysis of income levels in 1926 supports these conclusions. Nevertheless, a small elite of local notables managed to maintain their superior position with respect to property ownership. 'By

1928 fully 10 per cent (compared with 13 per cent in 1905) of property owners held land worth twice the average or more for the township, with certain families owning land valued at four to ten times the norm' (1980: 65).

An influx of tenants swelled Johnsonville's population after state housing construction started in the 1930s in an attempt to alleviate some of the difficulties of the depression. These people 'enjoyed similar or even superior amenities to the less affluent private owner' (1980: 67). Many tenants purchased their houses from the State and 'by the early 1950s when national prosperity had returned, the subtleties of property inequalities—at least for the majority in Johnsonville—retained only the broadest structural features of pre-depression days' (1980: 67). The data on incomes, in common with property ownership, clearly separates the most and least affluent but emphasises the homogeneity of the middle ranges. This process of homogenisation has not been carried into the present where Johnsonville's clearly observable housing hierarchy— State housing, old and newer standardised private dwellings, and new architecturally designed houses—is considerably reinforced by residential segregation. Pearson found 'a high coincidence' between property values, occupation and the residents' personal impressions concerning the prestige allocated to housing areas. 'The general pattern of property ownership in contemporary Johnsonville marks a return to past eras when local inequalities were firmly illustrated by residential separation' (1980: 74). Further, international and national corporations have taken over the commercial centre of Johnsonville emphasising 'a new entrenchment of outside interests which can be considered as at least one sign of the demise of "localness"' (1980: 74).

Local politics in Johnsonville, initially rudimentary and ad hoc, were formalised around the turn of the century. 'A local "elite", largely consistent with patterns of wealth and prestige dominated political decision-making, church affairs and, to a lesser extent, the organisation of recreation' (1980: 95). National party politics and local political affairs were seen as separate spheres. Johnsonville was an island of Labour Party support in a conservative electoral district. 'Political impotence at the national level tended to diminish the importance of party politics in the locality and foster an even stronger commitment to Town Board affairs' (1980: 95–6). In the 1930s and 1940s when the Labour Party gained national power there was 'a much closer correspondence between the local character of office holding and broader national political trends than any time previously' (1980: 96) but this disappeared after the Second World War with the profusion of voluntary associations which broadened the base of political participation even if it did not eradicate the elitist tradition of local leadership. Perhaps the most important change in recent years has been fragmentation in areas of local leadership.

It is no longer common to find social figures prominent because of their local economic standing, almost automatically influential in local politics, church affairs and the patrons of sports clubs ... The new major influentials ... know one another; but many local residents are largely ignorant of the network of activists. (1980: 97)

In other words politics in Johnsonville follows the general shape of social inequality described above. As Pearson concludes, 'Those at the top have most say, those at the bottom very little, whilst the majority in the middle hold a tenuous balance between elitism and pluralism' (1980: 98).

Many community studies in the past have just assumed their populations to be geographically and socially stable. Such assumptions are often built into the very concept of community. Johnsonville is one of the few community studies to carefully examine geographical and social mobility over a considerable time span. Pearson uses such documentary sources as street directories and marriage records and his own survey to establish patterns of residential movement and persistence, occupational inheritance and mobility and marriage and mobility. Nineteenth century New Zealand was a transient society as new immigrants moved from job to job and place to place. The people of Johnsonville reflected this process as many stayed for short periods on their way elsewhere. Less than a third of those living there in 1875, for example, were still there in 1885. Today many of the young suburbanites in white-collar jobs are as transient as their forebears but Pearson found 'a small core of old-timers within Johnsonville and a sizeable local population with Wellington attachments' (1980: 103).

The data on occupational inheritance from father to son indicates that most tended to move up or down the occupational hierarchy within a comparatively narrow occupational spectrum. Very few (less than 10 per cent) managed to bridge the gap between manual and professional-managerial status. The marriage statistics support this general pattern and illustrate 'the subtle conventions of social and geographical distance, which continue to separate the highest and lowest rungs of the local status ladder' (1980: 117). An examination of marriages over 70 years indicates that approximately 60 per cent of the men tend to marry into the same family background as their own occupational status. Marriages between professional-managerial and lower manual households do occur but the chance of it happening in Johnsonville is about 1 in 12.

Although the general picture in Johnsonville is one of a mixture of transience and continuity, 'a minority of households *do* remain in the vicinity long enough to construct and maintain local institutions, and cement identities for themselves within discrete geographical and social environs' (1980: 120). As Pearson points out, this raises the intriguing question of how much persistence and continuity is required to foster the illusion or create a reality of local identification and communal settlement?

Pearson pays considerable attention to perceptions of Johnsonville society, for people's images 'not only reflect(s) objective conditions, but also shape(s) them in the continual process of relating culture to social structure' (1980: 122). He draws on literary sources, reminiscences from in-depth interviews and personal observations. Unfortunately, the interviews do not form a statistical sample, and although I agree with the author that participant observation and intensive interviewing are the best methods of investigating social imagery, the ability to link this material to a sample of questions on local perceptions across classes or status groups would produce greater reliability, and possibly, further insights.

In the nineteenth century Johnsonville was portrayed as being modelled on an English form of structured inequality but leavened by inter-personal egalitarianism developed through the colonial experience. In the mid-twentieth century Johnsonville had developed into a solidary localised status system 'with its own modes and manners of parochial distinctions' (1980: 146). A shop assistant described the depression as 'a terrible time but we all pulled together' (1980: 130). As Weber remarked, (see pp. 35–6) external threats contribute to community formation and solidarity. The new State housing tenants were aware of the distinction between old-timers and newcomers and they were expected to fit in to the traditional way of doing things. Present day Johnsonville suburbanites are seen as more affluent, more fragmented, and more privatised, and therefore, anonymous. For the old-timers Johnsonville is the transformed village, for the newcomers it is just another suburb. Accompanying these changes are alterations in the nature of status awareness. In the localised status system of the 1930s most people knew each other and status centred on a system of localised social *relationships* but as the 'village' became a suburb with a greater population and a bigger scale of local activities more formal *distributive attributes* of status, such as residential area, house type and motor car, grew in importance. Increasingly more reliance was

placed on visible indicators of status and display became more crucial than intimate knowledge.

At this point Pearson attempts to link these patterns of *status*
awareness concerned with lifestyles to images of *class* awareness
based on life chances. He isolates three 'models of class'
(1980: 142) used by the residents interviewed. First is the 'power
model' which perceives a direct clash of interests between us and
them, workers and bosses, and so forth. Such images promote a
view of class conflict but only a small minority, invariably manual
workers, adopted such a model. Second is the 'prestige model'
which emphasises a graded hierarchy of groups usually based on
such criteria as money, job and education. An overwhelming
majority of Pearson's respondents verbalised this type of hierarchical model. But can such an image be referred to legitimately as
a 'class model'. Surely this is a status model emphasising distributive attributes of social status. The value of the analytical distinction between class and status is diminished by referring to such
perceptions of status as a class model. Third is the 'classless model'
where the very notion of a class society is severely modified or dis-
owned. A small number of respondents claimed that class did not
exist or that 'we are all middle class now'. Once again such images
are often a denial of status differences rather than class interests
(for a useful comparison of status and class images see Wild,
1974: 11–29). It seems to me that most people in Johnsonville are
aware of status groups and have some idea of status differences
and status identity but that only very few are aware of classes and
class differences and even fewer of the possibility of class conflict.
This is a slightly different conclusion to Pearson's (1980: 144) and
is based on a sharper analytical separation of status and class.

Pearson approached Johnsonville with a concept of community
that visualises this local urban milieux as a response of territorially-
based populations to their environment, rather than viewing it as a
remnant of what was a localised society, (see Suttles, 1972: 233).
Such a view of community emphasises *processes* of social change
and sees community studies as a sociological *method* useful for
identifying the significant processes of change and their direction.
Pearson identifies three dimensions of community: territorial
boundaries, social interdependencies and ideology. He attempts to
show how the changing nature of each helps to explain what Johnsonville was and has become.

Traditional boundaries related to familiar landmarks have now
given way to suburban sprawl but 'such changes have *not* destroyed
a sense of common territory *per se*, they have merely transformed
them' (1980: 156, original emphasis). Changes in the landscape

continue to affect images of community. Older residents still refer to changes in the village whereas newcomers treat their subdivision as 'a newly emerging territorial entity'.

Such boundaries may be reinforced or weakened by social inter-dependencies. Changes in Johnsonville's economic and political affairs described above indicates a growing dependence on external factors at the expense of local autonomy and as such may be seen to represent a dissolution of communal boundaries. Further the fragmentation of communal activity into specialised spheres contributes to the same process. Nevertheless, there remains some continuities at the local level. In the past as well as the present 'a minority of local residents have performed the role of a community custodians' (1980: 163). In the pioneering period these custodians were the prominent farming and business families whereas today they are professionals and businessmen in service clubs and local government. In other words 'there has always been a representational community process which implicitly or explicitly separates the local from the extra-local and reinforces communal sentiment' (1980: 163). Community as ideology, therefore, can create a crucial basis for continuity. Such terms as 'our village', 'our past' and 'our place' provide communal continuity and at the same time emphasises the ideological dimension of the concept of community. Perhaps the major difficulty with this notion of community as ideology is that it does not distinguish between tradition and sentiment. As outlined in Chapter 2 (see pp. 39–40) it is analytically useful to separate tradition from sentiment; that is, community from communion, in order to better understand the relationship between the two and to examine the contributions of each to processes of change and continuity. I shall take the issue of whether or not a tavern should be established in Johnsonville as an example (1980: 92–96; 165).

Two groups of residents, one opposed to the tavern and the other in favour of it, argued their positions over several years. Those supporting the tavern claimed that new amenities, such as a swimming pool, would eventuate from tavern profits which would, by legislation, be channelled back into the township. Those in opposition emphasised the peace, quiet and safety of the past and the present, and demanded this be maintained. A poll won the day for the supporters of this tavern. At the same time a new shopping complex was planned for the centre of Johnsonville and as the tavern was adjacent the developers envisaged problems with parking and social disorder. The complexities of this matter took five years to sort out with negotiations between residents, big business and the State bureaucracy. In the meantime those residents formerly divided 'became united in their anger, triggered by incessant delay and the degree of perceived outside controls' (1980: 93). The residents 'eventually perceived an "us" and "them" situation, as the locality ... defended itself against the external interests of big business and the lethargy of State bureaucracy' (1980: 165). Pearson explains this issue in terms of 'the ever-expanding inter-relationship between local, regional and national spheres of influence' (1980: 93), and community as ideology as 'a clarion call for local residents' (1980: 165). Although this may well be so I think we get a deeper understanding of this issue if we examine it in terms of the community, communion, society model described in Chapter 2.

Initially the residents' group supporting the tavern represented *rational societal* interests by emphasising progress and development through profits. The opposing group attempted to maintain *community* by emphasising tradition — the way things always had been. Larger-scale societal interests in the guise of big business and State bureaucratic red tape took over the dispute and provoked a reaction among the residents — *communion*. This wave of *emotion*, developed as a reaction to impersonal, large-scale rational-legal interests; it united previously opposed residents and emphasised the qualities of 'togetherness' and 'localness'. But communion is precarious; it cannot be maintained and is rapidly routinised into community and/or societal orientations as the residents have little power to make decisions, and the issue is formally and rationally resolved by State bureaucratic procedures and judicial decision-making. The separation of community as tradition and communion as sentiment, and the recognition of society as representing rational-legal relationships, enables us to identify the complex processes in this issue and, at the same time, link them to the broader processes of change at the societal level.

In the final chapter of *Johnsonville* Pearson illustrates through his material how this community study as a method of analysis can help to understand New Zealand's broader social processes. The gap between the local and the national is not as great in New Zealand as in most other capitalist societies because of the smallness in scale of urban life and work situations which tend to produce a predominant 'small-town capitalism'. Such a situation 'promotes a parochial identification which is more concerned with *inter-personal* relationships than broader, structural concerns of a more universalistic nature' (1980: 173, original emphasis). Only with very major crises do people in Johnsonville confront universal issues, and even then, as in the depression, 'a collective system of mutual assistance coalesced around a community identification which severely diminished the importance of more transparent class divisions' (1980: 173).

The majority of Johnsonville residents, along with many New Zealanders (Franklin, 1978: 80), exhibit the outward signs of bourgeoise middle-class affluence in their styles of life but class differences relating to the market capacity of major occupational groups and to authority patterns in the workplace have not fundamentally changed. Although occupational mobility, for example, has always been a consistent feature in Johnsonville's history it 'has always been within strict short-range upward *and* downward limits' (1980: 179, original emphasis). Further, class backgrounds remain important in both local and national politics. To the extent there is inter-meshing between the working and middle classes, it is in the area of lifestyle and consumption patterns, and therefore, relates to status rather than to class relations which centre on life chances and production. As Pearson argues, this brings us back to a central concern, 'the interrelationship between lifestyle and life chances', that is, between class and status. (For a discussion of this in the context of another community study see Wild, 1974: 112–7; 201–3).

This recent community study is especially strong on linking historical material of many different kinds of contemporary survey data and in its skilful treatment of the relationship between theory (especially class, status, egalitarianism and community) and data. It is, unfortunately, less strong on the participant observation side which accounts for some of the lack of a close 'feel' for the place and the people. Nevertheless, it is through its strengths that Johnsonville clearly shows the advantages of using community studies as a method of analysis and it illustrates how and why such studies are not atheoretical or idiosyncratic.

7 Extending Community Studies

Perhaps the commonest criticisms of community studies are that they are non-cumulative and idiosyncratic (Glass, 1966: 148) and that 'they contribute little to each other' (Bell and Newby, 1971: 140). But such comments can be applied to many areas of sociology. Community studies are, perhaps, better than other branches sociology at showing the heterogeneous nature of social life rather than emphasising processes of homogeneity. These criticisms remain exaggerations in that some significant attempts have been made to demonstrate the cumulative possibilities of community studies, both for sociology generally (especially macro-social processes) and for the development of future community studies. In this chapter I attempt to show how Stein's *The Eclipse of Community*, Plowman's Minchinton's and Stacey's paper *Local Social Status in England and Wales* and my own discussion in *Localities, Social Relationships and the Rural-Urban Continuum* have tried to demonstrate the value of community studies for understanding macro-social processes and such specific concepts as status, bureaucratisation and power, as well as, hopefully, to delineate theoretical directions for future studies.

Stein and *The Eclipse of Community*

Maurice Stein was primarily concerned with establishing 'a perspective for treating community studies as case studies showing the workings of fundamental social processes in specific American contexts' (1964: 304). In the preface to the 1964 Torchbook Edition he comments, 'I discovered that I could identify generalisable institutional configurations and generalised patterns of change in the separate studies ... [and] that these separate patterns of change could be linked with each other through viewing them as examples of the major social processes studied by classical social theory' (1969: 5). In other words Stein was confronting the difficulty of generalising from individual community studies and was attempting to establish a theoretical framework within which to locate the studies in a process of social change. 'I wanted a theory that combined the search for systematic generalisations with a search for significant historical patterns and a search for critical commentary on American community trends' (1964: 6). The first part is a thorough attempt at theoretical generalisation from empirical description but as we shall see in his 'critical commentary' he slides into normative prescription.

Stein is aware of the difficulties in theorising from vast amounts of empirical data and refers to it as 'a challenging and even frightening task'. The writer:

has to be prepared to omit much that seems important in them to him but which does not yet fit into his evolving theoretical framework. Finding an adequate level of generality is an ever present problem, as is remaining satisfied with any given level once it has proved useful. This theory attempts to stay as close to the empirical materials as it can while still establishing the relationship of the trends they reveal to the major social processes of our time. (1964: 98)

Stein's theory is that localised communities are losing their local autonomy and becoming increasingly interdependent through the effects of the social processes of urbanisation, industrialisation and bureaucratisation. He uses Park's work on Chicago to demonstrate urbanisation, the two studies of Middletown by the Lynds to elaborate the effects of industrialisation and Warner's analysis of Yankee City to illustrate the process of bureaucratisation. Stein did not regard these case studies as 'representative communities in any statistical sense but rather [that] they were undergoing processes of structural transformation that affected all American cities and towns to one or another degree, and therefore could be used as laboratories in which to study these representative social processes' (1964: 94). He continues this approach in the middle of the book and examines slum life through Whyte's *Street Corner Society*, bohemia through Ware's *Greenwich Village*, the Deep South through Davis' and Gardner's *Deep South* and so forth. These discussions contain many useful insights, parallels and small-scale generalisations.

In the conclusion however, Stein goes much further than the empirically-based generalisations warrant. He writes:

American communities can be seen continuing the vital processes uncovered in Muncie by the Lynds. Substantive values and traditional patterns are continually being discarded or elevated to fictional status whenever they threaten the pursuit of commodities or careers. Community ties become increasingly dispensable, finally extending even into the nuclear family, and we are forced to watch children dispensing with their parents at an ever earlier age in suburbia ... individuals become increasingly dependent upon centralised authorities and agencies in all areas of life ... personal loyalties decrease their range with the successive weakening of national ties ... Suburbia is so fascinating just because it reveals the 'eclipse' of community at one of its darkest moments (1964: 329).

There are four problems here. First, the last statement is empirically false as demonstrated by Gans (see pp. 76–80) and it gives an insight into Stein's value-orientation towards community.

Second, he has moved from empirical description and generalisation to normative prescription where his version of the good life becomes equated with community.

Third, in doing this he commits exactly the same error as those such as Tonnies, Durkheim, Redfield and Frankenberg, all of whom encapsulate notions of the good life at the community end of the *gemeinschaft-gesellschaft* dichotomy and see the dark moments of the future at the opposite pole of society (see pp. 18–24). Stein does not see that community as tradition, communion as sentiment and society as rationality are interacting and vying for supremacy in a cyclical or spiral process of social change.

Finally, Stein does not attempt to establish a model of community and consequently is forced into accepting everything that has been described as such from a small village to a major metropolis. Urbanisation is used inconsistently, first as a community (e.g. Chicago) and then as one of the processes bringing the community into 'eclipse'. As Martindale clearly pointed out, 'If the city is a community and if urbanisation represents the extension of patterns typical of a city, urbanisation ought more logically to represent a peculiar kind of community formation rather than community destruction' (1964: 66). Stein blurs the distinction between localised communities (as social systems), empirical descriptions of them and general definitions or models of community.

Even with these problems, however, Stein does succeed in showing how community studies as a method can contribute to our sociological knowledge of macro-social processes and this in turn had some impact on the theoretical orientation of later community studies.

Plowman, Minchinton and Stacey and Local Social Status

Using data from 21 British community studies Plowman *et al.* attempt to clarify and develop the concept of status. They argue that there is 'evidence for the existence both of systems of local social status and of forms of local social status not constituting systems ... [and they] ... are concerned with the way these two situations are connected' (1962: 161). The authors use Weber's distinction between class and status and discuss their material under the headings of traditional status systems in England, non-traditional status in England, social status in Wales and social status in English urban working-class localities.

They argue that there is 'clear evidence from both Gosforth and Banbury' that 'where people meet regularly, it is possible for social status to be organised in a system, in the sense of an organised whole in which people would have places and behave accordingly' (1962: 164). Such status systems consist of discrete levels rather than continua but the boundaries are not necessarily sharp and may be blurred by 'frontier groups' or buffer zones (see also Wild, 1974: 35). Social mixing, however, rarely spreads over more than a limited range of the status hierarchy. It is not necessary for all the inhabitants to recognise all the levels for there may be differences between, for example, the farming and village population or between different types of localities. The varying status levels tend to exhibit different styles of life including such matters as 'manners, attitudes, beliefs, expectations, patterns of child-rearing, relations between sexes, patterns of visiting, range of travel and kind of work and degree of responsibility' (1962: 166). This type of status system is relational or interactional in that its core is centred on a customary pattern of social relationships. Newcomers are initially evaluated on their objective attributes, such as, where they live and what job they do until they are either absorbed or rejected. Plowman *et al.* use Weber's notion of traditional legitimacy—a belief in things as they have always existed—to describe this sort of status system. Further, they argue that such traditional status systems are characterised by 'total status', that is, 'the tendency for individuals to have similar status in different spheres of activity'. Aspects of total status are clearly seen in Banbury, Gosforth and also Bradstow. Concerning the last I wrote:

> It is clear that where traditional stratification has been maintained in a particular locality, elites tend to converge and a total status outlook is prevalent. Total status is as noticeable in conflicts, where most controversies run along status lines, as it is in coop-

eration, where projects are organised within status groups. The people of Bradstow still conceive of most relationships in terms of a total status. It is a system based on traditional legitimacy and a conservative mentality. (1974: 205).

It is important to point out that the term traditional does not refer to the age of a status system but rather to the claim for legitimacy. Those involved in a system established for only one or two generations may well claim legitimacy on the basis of tradition.

'Everyone in a locality need not belong to a local system ... [and] ... the exclusion of large numbers might lead to another system' (1962: 171). The authors categorise status outside local systems by the term non-traditional. In Banbury, for example, there are many levels of status outside the local system, most of which remain unorganised as a set or a whole. Status in non-traditional situations tends to be largely attributional depending on the distribution of objective characteristics and 'seems to involve uncertainty about status boundaries and resentment at status rejection' (1962: 187). Status in one sphere does not necessarily carry over into another although, as occurred in Banbury, it is quite possible for both traditional and non-traditional status to coexist in the same locality (Bell and Newby, 1971: 202; Newby 1977: 325).

Plowman *et al.* discuss the relationship between traditional and non-traditional status and conclude that 'the trend seems to be entirely away from local systems towards non-traditional status' (1962: 193). The process of change, however, is uneven and depends on many factors such as immigration to a locality, workroles in the area, size, time and so forth. Bradstow, for example, succeeded in maintaining a high level of traditional status by having the ability and power to maintain closure and autonomy and thereby encapsulate many non-traditional elements. Pearson's material on Johnsonville, however, illustrates a different view whereby 'the pattern of local voluntary association participation and political influence prior to the turn of the nineteenth century and, to a lesser extent, on through to the depression years, is reminiscent of what has been described as a "total status situation"' (1980: 82) but 'as township became suburb, and residents encountered a change in population size and the scale of local activities, more formal attributes of status grew in importance by virtue of the fact that the traditional interaction system proved to be increasingly inoperable' (1980: 136–7).

In their section on status in working-class localities Plowman *et al.* isolate the respectable, the ordinary and the roughs as major status levels. 'Respectability is in part a style of life involving appropriate standards of behaviour' (1962: 178), such as high standards of housekeeping, appropriate style of house, furnishing and garden, a steady job and income, and so forth. 'Respectability is thus a claim to status' (1962: 178). Many do not claim respectability and are freer in manners, speech and sociability. These people form the bulk of the ordinary working class. The roughs are 'people who do not conform to minimum standards and are rejected by respectable and ordinary alike' (1962: 180). The no-hopers of Bradstow (1974: 55–7) are a good example. The old, stable working-class areas show some signs of total status in that the population is stable, work is within the locality and the extended family remains a core institution but the new working class housing estates are more clearly centred on non-traditional status. Bryson's and Thompson's *An Australian Newtown* is full of examples of non-traditional status divisions and demonstrates the separation of the respectable and the ordinary (1972: 22).

This ambitious attempt at systematic inter-community comparison centring on the concept of status helps to extend some of the limiting aspects of individual studies. The approach draws attention to the way different localities are related, the effect of immigration and emigration on social status, the relationship of social status to national and local history, the dependence of attitudes to status on background experiences, the relationship between class and status and the specification of types of social status. Plowman *et al.* remain closer to the data than does Stein and consequently their conclusions are more circumspect. It is perhaps for this reason that their insights have not only contributed to the development of such concepts as status, but they have also been integrated into such future community studies as Bradstow and Johnsonville.

Wild and 'Localities, Social Relationships and the Rural-urban Continuum'

In this paper (1975) and a later development of it (1978a: 75–89) I compared five Australian locality studies—Oeser's and Emery's *Mallee Town* (1954); Bryson's and Thompson's *An Australian Newtown* (1972); Brennan's *New Community* (1973); Oxley's *Mateship in Local Organisation* (1974); and Wild's *Bradstow* (1974)—in an attempt to find out what they could tell us about the relationship between social stratification and the rural-urban continuum in Australia. As I have already discussed all but Brennan's study of the Green Valley housing estate in Sydney earlier in this book, the reader will be aware that these five studies range from a small town of 500 people centred on farming, to a city housing estate of over 25 000. It is this rural-urban difference along with patterns of status, class and party with which I am concerned.

It would be easy to follow the points of view of such supporters of the rural-urban continuum as Redfield, Frankenberg, Schnore and others discussed in Chapter 2 and place Mallee Town towards the rural pole because it is a small settlement based on farming; Kandos, Rylstone and Bradstow might be placed somewhere in the middle because they share both farming and industrial enterprises, are bigger and more densely settled; and Newtown and Green Valley would be placed towards the urban end because they represent some of the latest developments in large-scale city settlement patterns whose inhabitants mostly depend on the industrial process. But as I also noted in Chapter 2, this approach has come under powerful criticism from such writers as Gans (1968) and Pahl (1968) who consider rural and urban to be neither explanatory variables nor sociological categories. They consider that relationships of both types could be found in the same localities and that differences in ways of life could be more adequately explained by class, lifecycle variations and the confrontation between the local and the national.

What does the evidence from the five locality-based studies, done in rural, semi-rural and urban parts of Australia, contribute to this debate? To what extent does the rural or urban nature of these settlement types affect the quality and type of social relationships? Is the dichotomous model useful in comparative analysis for explaining ways of life in modern Australia, or has it outlived its value? Do we need to look elsewhere for more heuristic models to explain our increasingly complex patterns of relationships? It is to these questions I shall now turn.

Before I discuss the Australian data, there is a problem concerning comparative analysis that requires elucidation. This is that the individual studies concern different theoretical issues, so the data they present are not always strictly comparable and, further, they were researched and written at different times. The Mallee Town study, for example, was started in the late 1940s and published in 1954, whereas the others were researched in the middle and late 1960s and published in the early 1970s. If, however, we accept Lupri's (1965: 57–76; 1968: 298–300) conservative position that rural and urban differences are gradually diminishing, then we should expect Mallee Town to be more rural in character in the earlier period than it is today.

I shall discuss the three areas of social stratification — family, neighbourhood and voluntary association interaction — and the systems of political power. The comparisons assume knowledge of the discussions of the studies in Chapter 6.

The housing estates obviously have a smaller range of status groups represented than the small towns but within that range some patterns of social stratification are similar. Kandos, for example, with its strong working-class orientation, shows such similarities with Newtown as the role of the local councillors as internal caretakers (Bryson and Thompson, 1972: 264; Oxley 1974: 73), analogous patterns of leadership (Bryson and Thompson 1972: 194, 204; Oxley, 1974: 123, 141, 150, 187), and strong egalitarian participation among men in such clubs as the R.S.L. (Bryson and Thompson, 1972: 185; Oxley, 1974: 78, 110; Brennan, 1973: 176). Bradstow and Mallee Town, with their well-established relations of deference and dominance, diverge from this pattern, as is indicated by the intense status cleavages and the lack of working-class egalitarian participation. Just as there is no single urban way of life, so there is no single rural way of life. The point is not whether the locality is rural or urban, large or small, that determines basic social relationships; rather it is the type of stratification system that has developed that is crucial.

It has often been assumed that people in small towns are more friendly, more neighbourly, and participate more in a common way of life than those in large urban centres (Redfield, 1974; Frankenberg, 1966: 285–87). The small town studies do not concentrate on this issue but they all indicate that there are few, if any, close relations between status groups. Among the workers, however, Oeser and Emery (1954: 27–28) and Oxley (personal communication) note close-knit family networks and extensive neighbouring. In Bradstow some workers' families, especially those who have been in the area for several generations, have wide, intimate networks, but others see their friends as closer than their relatives (Wild, 1974: 55).

Neighbouring and social participation are central issues in the estate studies. Both show a high rate of neighbourliness, friendliness and interaction with kin, especially among those who have been on the estates for more than two years. In Newtown only 2 per cent said they had no contact with neighbours, whereas 41 per cent had very close contact with considerable help (Bryson and Thompson, 1972: 119). Even among the 'problem families' in Green Valley, over half had daily contact with neighbours and most said they would turn to neighbours for help rather than to a social agency (Brennan, 1973: 142).

In Newtown almost 90 per cent of families were in regular contact with kin apart from their own offspring; over a third had kin living in close proximity, and in 5 per cent of these cases the household unit was an extended family (Bryson and Thompson, 1972: 113). Help from relatives did not diminish when deserted wives moved to Green Valley, and good relations with neighbours showed an increase of 30 per cent over that at their previous address (Brennan, 1973: 157–59). Some research in an inner-Sydney suburb has indicated that, as in Bethnal Green, intimate family networks are widespread, and neighbouring activities are intense and extensive (Gillen: n.d.).

It is impossible to compare rates of neighbouring because of the lack of data in the small town studies, but given the available evidence it seems reasonable to suggest that similar patterns of family and neighbouring relationships occur throughout the working class in both rural and urban settings.

Membership in voluntary associations is often used as an index of social participation. In Newtown 28.7 per cent of all adults belong to a formal organisation (Bryson and Thompson, 1972: 170). In Green Valley 27 per cent of those earning less than $40 per week belong, compared with 55 per cent of those earning over $70 (Brennan, 1973: 121). Around 28 per cent is a common figure for working-class areas and can be regarded as high for new housing estates where family life cycle stage inhibits external activities, and where many working-class people prefer neighbourhood participation rather than the middle-class preference for formal associations. Green Valley's 55 per cent for the wealthier group is exceptionally high, and is higher than that found in some small towns (Wild, 1974: 95). In Bradstow 46.6 per cent of the workers and 30 per cent of the no-hopers belong to one or more association (Wild, 1974: 75). In Kandos and Rylstone 15 per cent of the unskilled and semi-skilled, and 36 per cent of the skilled miners and clerical workers belong (Oxley, 1974: 124). In Mallee Town the equivalent figure is approximately 30 per cent for the manual workers (Oeser and Emery, 1954: 34). Further, Bryson and Thompson (1972: 200, 213), Brennan (1973: 120), Oeser and Emery (1954: 34–37), Oxley (1974: 141) and Wild (1974: 76) all mention that higher status people, especially those who are middle class, have higher rates of membership and are more likely to be office-holders and leaders.

The figures for Mallee Town, Kandos and Rylstone, and the estates are similar, whereas those for Bradstow are higher—but Bradstow ranks highly on formal participation even in international terms. The main reason for this is the predominantly middle- and upper middle-class nature of the town. High rates of formal participation, however, do not make Bradstow a 'participating community' as each status group has its own cluster of associations and some groups prevent others from joining their clubs (Wild, 1974: 20, 43, 99). Similarities and differences in rates and types of participation in formal organisations are not determined by the rural or urban nature of the locality, rather they depend on the type and development of the local system of social stratification.

In the analyses of local systems of political power some central differences emerge. In Newtown the middle stratum plays a caretaking role over the workers and holds most positions of leadership and authority. In Kandos and Rylstone almost all reputed influentials and those most active in projects were also from the higher strata and were 'greater joiners, office bearers, and general leaders' (Oxley, 1974: 141). All but three respondents, however, said there was no local ruling group.

In Bradstow 88 per cent thought that 'a small group runs the town' and 69 per cent of them located power in one family (Wild, 1974: 191). The bosses group runs everyday affairs but the Grange-ites have sufficient power to obtain their desires on what they regarded as important issues. In Mallee Town the graziers act as a political elite, as is evidenced by their control over positions of authority and the activities of the Labor Party (Oeser and Emery, 1954: 32).

In Kandos, Rylstone, Newtown and probably Green Valley, local political influence is more equitably shared and is not covert, although it remains concentrated among the higher strata. In Bradstow and Mallee Town political influence is more concentrated within special groups and covert political activities are often pursued. The proposition here, then, is that where local populations display marked social inequalities, and these are emphasised in relationships and ideologies, then the power structure is likely to be more elitist and less visible.

Many people in modern industrial societies have a choice as to the job they do and the place they live. Choice has been extended through technological advance as people have gained greater control over the physical environment. The availability of choice and the choices made are closely related to the roles people play, and one of the most important influences on, and determining factor of, roles is the system of social stratification. The type and quality of social relationships and their variation from locality to locality are not determined by whether a place is rural or urban, or whether it is small or large, rather they are determined more by patterns of social stratification, their historical development, and associated ideologies.

Kandos, for example, is largely the result of a national-level economic decision to establish mines, quarries and a factory. This initial process of industrialisation was quickly followed by increased bureaucratisation and urbanisation. Workers were attracted from larger towns and cities. This emphasises a point made by Pahl concerning the confrontation of local and national forces (Pahl, 1968: 286). Kandos is characterised more by national than by local forces. Its workers' egalitarianism, which is based on such criteria as 'the self-assurance of workers resulting from strong and effective unionisation, the hunger for membership of licensed clubs, an economic based in mining and heavy industry, and belief in the Australian Legend (of mateship)' (Oxley, 1974: 207), is very much, if not wholly, the result of national rather than local forces, and many of these criteria could equally be applied to some of the workers on the housing estates.

Bradstow, however — with its 'concern [for] such things as conservatism, supposed "aristocratic" Englishness, and a desire for genteel conventions that manifest themselves in styles of life, political views, a compulsive interest in gardening, such pastimes as golf and horse riding, and an extensive interest in the arts and education' (Wild, 1974: 31) — is more localised in its characteristics. An analysis of increasing bureaucratisation since Bradstow's first settlement shows how these developments were absorbed into a traditional status structure rather than changing or destroying it. Successful attempts to keep out industry and further development attest to the strength of local forces.

This raises a further question concerning the relation of local populations to wider political structures. The housing estates are firmly under the control of the respective State Housing Commissions. People in Green Valley and Newtown have little say in decisions taken by the Commissions which affect their lives. Similarly, in Kandos and Rylstone few people have any influence at State and national levels. Their prosperity depends on economic management and union activity in Sydney; for example, a five-week strike originated in a factory elsewhere, but the Kandos workers went out on strike.

In Bradstow several high-status people have influential connections at both State and national levels and such networks can be used to local advantage. Influential connections with wider political structures can help to maintain local autonomy and stem the influence of wider level forces.

All the studies emphasise the predominantly *Gesellschaft* nature of social relationships. Oxley (1974: 206) and Thompson (1971: 25) stress the *Gesellschaft* relations that are exhibited in the notion of 'community participation'.

In Bradstow and Mallee Town there is little 'sense of belonging

[that] comes from relationships that are ends in themselves and that have developed in situations of prolonged social contact or consanguinity' (Thompson, 1971: 25). What the five studies describe in part are not groups of people who feel a sense of belonging through emotional solidarity, but rather several localised social systems with varying degrees of inter-relatedness among the social institutions present in the particular places (see Stacey, 1969: 134–47). These social institutions are common to the whole of Australian society. As Oeser and Emery noted several years ago, 'The predominant cultural forms in the rural society are basically similar to those existing in the urban society' (154: 227).

The earlier speculative proposition can now be extended. Where local populations display marked social inequalities and these are emphasised in social relations and ideologies, then the political power structure is likely to be more elitist, less visible and more able to maintain some degree of local autonomy against the influence of wider forces. Conversely, in local populations where there are few inequalities, and even these are deprecated in relationships and ideologies, then the political power structure is likely to be more pluralistic, more visible and less able to maintain local autonomy.

Such a proposition, which concerns the basic social structure of localised social systems, can be tested by examining the relationships between social stratification, community closure and power. Closure can be attempted by any group in the stratification system but the criteria used for exclusion or inclusion purposes will depend on the group's position in the system. Parkin has pointed out 'that techniques of inclusion and exclusion can properly be conceived of as an aspect of the distribution of power' (1974: 4), which ties them closely to the three dimensions of stratification. The success or failure of community closure therefore depends on power, and the criteria selected for exclusion or inclusion may represent class, status or party phenomena. Hence the ability to effect closure depends on the type of stratification arrangement.

An example may help to clarify this point. In the mining town of Broken Hill the working class have successfully effected closure through such criteria as the production of essential resources (which provides them with a highly disruptive potential), the restriction of jobs to those locally born, the high prestige and reward for those working below the surface and so forth. Their economic, or class power, base which has been consolidated through the unions and their control of the Barrier Industrial Council, has given them sufficient monopolisation of social and political interests to ensure a high degree of closure and local autonomy. Similarly in Bradstow, the upper-status groups, through both economic and social criteria, have monopolised crucial political interests, ideologically dominated the townspeople, and effected a high degree of closure and autonomy. In contrast, groups in Kandos and Green Valley have not been able to monopolise their interests and effect closure, and therefore have a low level of local autonomy. The main reason for this is their weak position in the stratification system. That is, they hold insufficient power to monopolise local interests, they have a lack of influence and control in vertical relationships with State and national forces, and as Parkin comments, 'it is the contrast bctwccn productively marginal groups that underlies those analyses of the current situation in terms of a radical cleavage within the working class — between those able to effect social closure and the new "pauper class" unable to exert industrial leverage' (1974: 12).

It is clear that the connecting link between stratification and closure is the concept of power which is, perhaps, the most central and difficult concept in sociology. The structure of power provides the foundations of the stratification system and the processes of power describe the operations of closure.

As is well known, the pluralists concentrated their analysis of power on *actual* behaviour, decision-making, issues and overt conflict. The elitists emphasised *potential* power in their analysis of non-decision-making, potential issues and covert conflict. Others utilised both approaches. Lukes has suggested a further view of power, which:

> allows for consideration of the many ways in which *potential issues* are kept out of politics ... This potential, however, may never in fact be actualised. What one may have here is a *latent conflict*, which consists in a contradiction between the interests of those exercising power and the real *interests* of those they exclude. These latter may not express or even be conscious of their interests ... (1974: 24–25).

As an illustration, Lukes takes Crenson's analysis concerning why the issue of air pollution was not raised as early or effectively in some cities as it was in others (Crenson, 1971). He shows through subjective understanding (Weber's *Verstehen*) that it was in the real interests of the workers not to be poisoned 'even where they may not even articulate this preference' (Lukes, 1974: 45). It was the company towns with a strong party organisation that acted against the real interests of their workers by refusing to even consider air pollution control and hence they were exercising power over their workers' life chances.

This conceptual framework of power not only provides a model for research purposes but it also acts as a baseline for comparative analysis. For example, the Green Valley study does not refer to power in any of the above senses. Oxley's analysis of Kandos operates largely within a pluralist conception. Mallee Town, Newtown and Bradstow include data that refer to both pluralist and elitist orientations. Further, in the discussion of some of the caretakers' activities in Newtown, and in the analysis of the manipulation of the political agenda and the examination of air pollution in Bradstow, there is an incipient movement towards the concept of power detailed by Lukes.

In practice, however, there are some difficulties with Lukes' concept of real interests (see Bradshaw, 1976: 121–32). For Lukes, interests are what people would want and prefer if they were free and *autonomous* to make the choice. The difficulty is how do you determine the difference between real interests and just preferences, and what constitutes autonomy? I cannot envisage a situation where any actor is liberated from all structural conditions, and therefore able to identify correctly what his or her real interests would be in the best of all possible worlds. Consequently, this schema must accept an observer's assessment of interests, otherwise the category includes an infinite range of wants and preferences, and any act that prevents the obtaining of these desires becomes an act of power. There is a case here for arguing for a narrower view of interests. Lukes places the emphasis on the interests of the dominated at the expense of the dominators. It is more valuable to concentrate on the dominators' interests and potentialities for power, and the communal actions through which the dominators determine the life chances of the dominated. From this point of view we arrive at a modified Weberian definition of power where it represents the chance or probability of individuals or a collectivity realising their interests in a communal action that determines the life chances of other individuals and collectivities, even against the possibility of their resistance.

The interrelationships between social stratification, community closure and power provide a broad theoretical framework that allows a thorough description, analysis and explanation of the basic social structural arrangements in localised social systems. In conclusion to their examination of stratification and power in Suffolk, Bell and Newby comment:

> For too long community studies have been the last refuge of abstracted empiricism. Their lack of theoretical relevance has been quite rightly deplored. Yet this need not continue ... there are a body of theoretical concepts that can be used to analyse rural

areas. Power is both the central and most difficult [and therefore 'contested'] of all sociological and political concepts ... an understanding of its operation and very definition can be furthered by studying rural areas through community studies. Indeed because of the 'localness' of many, if not most political decisions in rural areas the mechanisms through which power operates are more, rather than less, open to empirical investigation. For these reasons alone community studies will retain their usefulness. (1976b: 48)

The rural-urban continuum may be of value, as Schnore suggests, for correlating such demographic and ecological data as the size, density and age of settlement patterns but, as he admits elsewhere, social structures and social relationships are much more complex (1966, 1967). In my view the rural-urban continuum has ceased to have much relevance for the explanation of social processes and relationships in Australia. It is ravaged by marked discontinuities and is not sufficient to explain, or even classify, the range of similarities and differences established by the five studies. A new model is required.

For comparative purposes the crucial criteria in locality-based studies are the range and interrelatedness of social institutions (Stacey, 1969); the types and intensities of networks of relationships (Barnes, 1954: 39–58; Bott, 1957; Mitchell, 1969; J.I. Martin, 1970: 301–39); the varying impact of local and national forces (Pahl, 1968; Geertz, 1965); and levels of closure and local autonomy (Weber, 1968; Neuwirth, 1969: 148–63; Parkin, 1974). The single most powerful variable affecting such criteria is the system of social stratification centred on power. I have suggested elsewhere (Wild, 1978a: 16–24) that class, status and party, when integrated with the concept of community closure through the concept of power, could be used to examine the varying structural patterns and ideologies in different localities. If the differing patterns of social stratification can be detailed through time—in terms of the range and connection between social institutions, the types and intensities of relational networks, the confrontation between local and national forces, and levels of closure and autonomy—then this is the beginning of a model for a classification of locality-based studies and, more importantly, for an explanation of social processes through changing social relationships.

Conclusions

The three comparative studies discussed in this chapter have each, in their own way and with varying degrees of success, attempted to extend data and generalisations from community studies towards the consideration of theoretical issues and concepts that are central to sociology as a whole. I mentioned in the Introduction that community studies must become more securely attached to the central theoretical concerns of sociology and one way to do this is through such comparative analyses. A further important contribution of comparative discussions is that the insights generated have been applied in later community studies which provides them with a firmer theoretical focus, and thereby, removes them from the realm of abstracted empiricism or sheer description and moves them closer to core problem areas of the discipline. Systematic inter-community comparisons are fraught with all sorts of dangers and it is perhaps for this reason that more have not been attempted. I have already commented on some of the difficulties — the studies were done at different times, some used team research and others just the single researcher, all contain some degree of subjective interpretation, many are written from varying theoretical perspectives some of which are never made explicit, the substantive issues and problems addressed are enormously variable and so forth — but just because the comparative exercise is difficult is no reason for abandoning it. Even with these problems those few attempts which have been made have proved exceedingly worthwhile, especially in helping to extend community studies beyond the image of the idiosyncratic or unique community, but without destroying the in-depth insights of the community study approach. In the next chapter I consider how community as a type of relationship (as embodied in the models of community formation and community, communion and society) can take community studies beyond analyses of specific localised social systems.

8 Beyond community studies

With two of the models of community outlined in Chapter 2, community formation and closure and community, communion and society, it is possible to extend community studies beyond the traditional approaches of studying community as an object in itself (Hillery, 1968) or as a localised social system (Stacey, 1969), to an examination of more specific patterns of social relationships that contain some elements of community either as structure or as ideology. Such an approach brings community studies closer to central sociological problems in that it escapes from an overwhelming concern with locality and object and examines community as a type of relationship and a social process along with, and in terms of, its connections to such other relationships and processes as power, rationality, ethnicity, class, status and so forth.

In this chapter I attempt to demonstrate the usefulness of community from this perspective in examination of the three areas of local-level politics, Italian immigrants and communes. The first concerns the relationship between local government and resident action politics, the second discusses Italian immigrants in Griffith, and in Sydney, and those who have returned to re-settle in Italy, and the third is about the counter-culture movement and the growth and decline of communes. These are examples to illustrate perspectives on community rather than exhaustive analyses in their own right, but in my view they exemplify how community, as both theory and method, can be used to provide us with a fuller understanding of social structure, ideology and social change.

Local-level Politics

Local Government
Local government is one of a number of institutions that deliver local services but it holds a special position because it is the third level of government, has a representative base, and a multi-

functional charter emphasising development (McPhail, 1978: 105). Along with other forms of administration, local government has become increasingly bureaucratised this century and shows a growing dependence on rational-legal structures (such as the expert who has the requisite knowledge to solve specialist problems) at the expense of traditional relationships. Although some people have argued that local government is not especially important because of its limited powers and means (see Parker, 1978) there is a case for arguing that its importance has increased as it has become bigger and more complex. Local government finance has increased since it was alloted a fixed (1.5 per cent) share of personal income tax collections and it now spends over $2000 million per year. International and national conferences have contributed both to the understanding and prestige of local government (McPhail, 1978: 113). Management courses established at colleges of advanced education for local government administrators and funded scholarships have added to increasing expertise and professionalism. The possibility of a national training school is being investigated. In other words, the development of local government reflects a wider process of change in our society, that is, the increasing rationalisation of many areas of social life. Local government is a true *societal* structure in that its relationships with its constituents are based on rational-legal contracts with individuals and its total operation is based on the calculative accounting principles of the capitalist economic system. Both necessitate a complex form of bureaucratic administration. Such rationalised systems of social organisation are inherently conservative because administrative action is limited to what is in conformity with rules (Weber, 1947: 392). It is almost impossible for such organisations to create new values, and therefore social change, for they primarily function as a means to the furtherance of existing values.

As well as being bureaucratic local government also tends to be elitist in that it represents only a narrow range of interests. In Bradstow (Wild, 1974) of 9 male, middle-aged aldermen, 7 were small businessmen, 1 was a professional and the other was a car salesman. Eight of the 9 were members of the Liberal Party. Of the 26 mayors of the town since incorporation, 22 owned their own businesses, 3 were professionals and 1 was an employee. Similarly the Melbourne city council, once referred to by *The Age* (18 August 1970) as one of the city's more exclusive clubs, is predominantly male with 55 per cent drawn from the commercial and business sector and 45 per cent from the professions, particularly law and architecture (Kilmartin and Thorns, 1978: 29). There is no escaping the fact that the typical local government councillor is male, middle-aged, middle class and conservative in outlook. This composition of councils affects the policies pursued in the allocation of resources and services and determines the image of local government in the eyes of the public, that is, as guardians of the *status quo* rather than agents of social change. Formalised local politics, therefore, because of the nature of councillors and the formal bureaucratic system within which they operate, tends to maintain the *status quo*, and thereby reinforces, rather than reduces, social inequalities.

The rationalisation of administration and the cornering of local political power by sectional interests has produced a system 'which legally allows, and in practice places a premium upon, electoral tactics or manipulations designed to give disproportionate representation to those best equipped with money, inside information, experience, manpower, and organisation to win' (Loveday, 1972: 141). Once in command biases within the system are mobilised to maintain control. In Bradstow, the mayor and town clerk formulated the agenda. Such controversial issues as complaints concerning air pollution from the brickworks, the poor quality of fire-fighting equipment and the possible amalgamation of councils were never allowed on the agenda. As the council was elitist and represented only business interests such matters were never raised from the floor. One of the most insidious uses of power is that which prevents matters of public importance coming into the political arena for debate. There are, of course, many more spectacular cases of the abuse of power. Considerable corruption was revealed in North Sydney in 1969 and in Liverpool in 1953 and 1961. Leichhardt Council was dismissed in 1953 and Bankstown Council in 1963 over charges of bribery concerning building and development applications. In 1973 Randwick Council was dismissed over corruption in flat development. In 1980 the Melbourne City Council was sacked by the State government.

The power and authority of local government determines the distribution of many resources and services in localities. It is the level of government closest to the grass roots. However, increasing bureaucratisation and the narrow range of interests represented have removed the operations of local government from the gaze and participation of its constituents. Formal local politics and administration were seen as being too secretive, too legalistic, too dependent on experts, too remote, too inflexible in its application of rules and regulations, too defensive in facing criticism, too inaccessible to those without contacts and too intent on pushing its own interests. This situation gave rise to various forms of protest.

Resident Action Politics

Max Weber pointed out many years ago that inherent in the process of rationalisation was an irrational protest against its impersonalisation, against the 'iron cage' of life created by its rules and regulations, a protest based on appeals to tradition or to sentiment, that is, to community or communion. In the boom times of the 1960s and early 70s, when consumption and status-oriented behaviour were emphasised at the expense of production and class action, we saw many such protest movements at the wider national and international levels (Wild, 1978a: 174). There were commune movements, demands for women's rights, marches for Aboriginal land rights and other black claims, the flowering of all types of ethnic associations, pensioner power and a recognition of the voting strength of the aged, new youth sub-cultures, and so forth. At the neighbourhood level we witnessed the rapid growth of resident associations, and later, action groups demanding a greater say in local matters affecting their own lives.

The bases of the new local politics were in two spheres. One centred on community. Now community, as I have mentioned, is a social order developed on the basis of natural interdependence through traditional relationships (see pp. 35–6). Resident action politics which are centred on community emphasise the maintenance of tradition, and development only within the guidelines of tradition. Community as given evokes traditionalism as a supreme value which may or may not coincide with such rational interests as the preservation or advancement of property investments. I lived in the municipality of Leichhardt, a predominantly working-class, inner-Sydney suburb into which were moving young professionals of the middle class. In the late 1960s the middle class established such groups as the Glebe Society and the Annandale Association to preserve the special character of their districts and to ensure that any development was in harmony with tradition. Although initially apolitical these groups became the centres of protest against proposed freeways, shopping centres, car parks and flat building and suggested more attention should be given to parks, trees and welfare facilities. The Annandale Association combined with the council to establish a large-scale tree planting programme and to prevent the demolition of several old buildings. Academics in the Glebe Society brought sufficient pressure to bear to have the proposed freeway placed in a tunnel underneath Glebe. There were, however, several conflicts with the Labor machine controlling the Leichhardt council and these resulted in a fiercely contested election in 1971 when several members of the resident groups were elected as aldermen. The new open council encouraged resident participation in its new planning scheme for the municipality but despite enormous encouragement, long-term involvement remained restricted to a small group of middle-class professionals. At the next election in 1974 the old Labor machine was returned to office and the new plans were ignored.

There are several reasons for this series of events. First, the middle class who became involved, in order to realise their conception of community, became disillusioned with the slow and complex rational-legal mechanisms with which they had to cope in order to have any chance of getting the new planning scheme off the ground. Further, wide-scale resident participation was a wieldy process in itself. The traditions of community were gradually worn down by the rational-legalisms of society. Second, they met firm opposition from two major sections of the municipality: the working class who just did not want new trees planted where they had cut them down 30 years previously (Wild, 1976: 108); and the Italians who were more concerned with their narrower networks of extended families and the wider network of a dispersed Italian community. Third, the mid-1970s recession was beginning to bite and such people as architects who had supported the resident groups with their expertise were now in danger of losing their jobs and could no longer afford time and effort for involvement. The status behaviour associated with community gave way under the economic pressure of the rational market to behaviour which was more concerned with class interests. Finally, the Labor machine, caught unawares in 1971, was in 1974 much more efficient at getting out the vote.

The second major basis of the new local politics was communion. Communion concerns feeling or sentiment and is carried by emotion (see pp. 35–6). Grass roots radical politics as witnessed in the conflict-oriented squatting groups have their basis in a form of communion. The Victoria Street squatters in Sydney shared a faith: a commitment to a radical re-distribution of wealth and resources throughout society. In this case it was expressed as housing for the poor before hotels and offices. The majority of the working-class residents of the area happily sold out to move to more modern housing, even though it was on the outskirts of the city. The majority of tenants were also satisfied with their new accommodation. It was a small group of residents who shared a strong re-distributive ideology, along with a group of committed squatters, who held similar ideas, who gave rise to the conflict. For a short period they maintained their solidarity through the emotional and tension-laden atmosphere of the siege situation. However, as in all communion-based movements, the sentiment generated by experience subsided and became routinised into a small squatting community which in turn eventually disbanded.

What may begin as community-based resident action may develop a form of communion and from there return to society. The history of the slum clearance movement by the Victorian Housing Commission is an example. The initial demolition of houses was carried out without much local opposition but gradually resident action groups were established. At the beginning their aims were to prevent demolition in order to preserve traditional community but this experience generated communion which led to such contestatory actions as squatting and the articulation of a redistributive philosophy. Eventually widespread public opposition was sufficient to make the Commission abandon the clearance (Hargreaves, n.d.; Sandercock, 1976). This campaign 'raised serious doubts about the social justice of a public housing policy that is selectively applied to residents of generally low status, against their will' and it 'achieved for residents a voice in the planning process and raised questions of political power or powerlessness, of social justice and human rights' (Kilmartin and Thorns, 1978: 139). It is, of course, very easy to over-emphasise the ability of action groups to innovate and the role of bureaucracies as a form of rational control. The internal politics of bureaucracies, external pressures from governments, and rising costs through inflation all affect decisions taken. The postponement of demolition or of the building of a freeway is often temporary. In the intervening period bureaucracies re-establish control and the energy generated by communion subsides. Like a machine, bureaucracy is the most rational system of harnessing energies to the fulfilment of specified tasks, and in the long-term tends to win.

The green ban movement is a useful example of the development from community to communion-based local politics. The first green ban arose from a dispute between the upper-middle-class residents of Sydney's fashionable Hunters Hill (the first municipality to be classified as an historic area by the New South Wales chapter of the National Trust of Australia) and the developers A.V. Jennings who wanted to build on Kelly's Bush. This area of some eight hectares was one of the last remaining pieces of natural bushland on the Parramatta River and was extensively used by children and adult residents for recreation. In 1968 Jennings presented the Hunters Hill Council with a plan to build 3 eight-storey highrises and more than 40 two-storey townhouses on the site. The Hunters Hill Trust led the opposition and the council rejected the proposal. Jennings changed their plans, lobbied the State Planning Authority (S.P.A.) and submitted to the council a proposal to build 57 town houses and no highrises. After a bitter discussion the council approved the modified plan. According to one of the resident activists, 'There were lots of rumours about why the council changed its mind. The one we gave the most weight to said the minister for local government had informed the council that it would not stop any further light industrial development' (Roddewig, 1978: 6). The councillors did not want any new industry in their quiet residential enclave.

Thirteen women who were strongly opposed to the Jennings plan formed 'The Battlers for Kelly's Bush' group and avidly publicised and lobbied for their cause. They wrote to local government, the State premier, the leader of the opposition, Sir Garfield Barwick and to Prince Philip, the Duke of Edinburgh. The only compromise was to build 25 single-family houses on the site. A National Trust employee suggested to the group that they get the trade unions on-side. They wrote to several unions who brought the matter to the notice of the Trades and Labour Council, the principal avenue of inter-union cooperation. The Council expressed its total opposition to the development and lobbied the minister for local government.

Meanwhile, the Battlers for Kelly's Bush were approached by the Builders' Labourers' Federation (B.L.F.), a union they had not contacted because of its communist leaders Joe Owens, Bob Pringle and Jack Mundey. The Battlers accepted the offer of help, the B.L.F. banned any construction work at Kelly's Bush and 'two months later the entire Sydney Trades and Labour Council resolved that all affiliated trade unions should refuse to work at the site' (Roddewig, 1978: 10). Mundey coined the term 'green ban' and received the lion's share of publicity. He is a trendy charismatic radical who 'can quickly spellbind an audience of any political persuasion with his eminently reasonable, commonsense arguments' (Roddewig, 1978: 12) and shows his concern for the nature of society in the long-term (Sandercock, 1976: 207). Kelly's Bush was saved and this experience led Mundey, as the charismatic leader, and his followers into a series of communion-based green bans across the city, and later interstate. They espoused ideas of the redistribution of wealth and power and argued that the green bans 'demonstrate a refusal any longer to concede that the rich and powerful and entrenched interests have any unchallengeable right to make all the decisions . . . responsibility cannot be left to those whose obsession is with profits amassed by exploitation' (Thomas, 1973: 131). Some conservationists saw the movement as an 'awakening . . . dedicated to protecting their way of life from developers' (Reilly, 1978: v). Communion was generated and maintained for a period with mass meetings, more green bans and songs. The following two verses and chorus are from a song sung to the tune of 'Waltzing Matilda':

Once a jolly resident living in his bungalow
Found he was threatened by redevelopment;
And he cried as he watched his city slowly crumbling,
'Who'll come a green ban defending with me?'

Chorus:
'Green ban defending, green ban defending,
Who'll come a green ban defending with me?'
And he cried as he watched his city slowly crumbling,
'Who'll come a green ban defending with me?'

Down came developers to profit from their residents,
Up jumped the people to fight for their homes;
And they sang when the B.L.'s started up their green bans,
'We'll come a green ban defending with you!'

Chorus: etc.   (Roddewig, 1978: viii.)

Eventually, routinisation set in. A panel of experts was established to review requests for bans and a gradual bureaucratisation of the movement began. In an attempt to maintain momentum Mundey applied bans in support of such wide-ranging social issues as feminist studies in philosophy at Sydney University. The Master Builders' Association applied to the Australian Industrial Court to have the B.L.F. deregistered as a union for 'industrial confrontation'. The union was deregistered and another faction led by Norm Gallagher ousted Mundey and formed a new branch of the union in 1974. The mid-1970s was a time of increasing unemployment and the underlying issue in the union was 'jobs or green bans'. The workers said they 'would rather eat than preserve old buildings' (Newsweek, May 5, 1975: 34) and Mundey lost his power base.

The movement did have some long-term effects although the possibilities for change were gradually whittled away by bureaucratic routinisation and the desire of State governments and bureaucracies to maintain their power and authority over local government and regional groups. The New South Wales government finally admitted that its planning and environment laws needed a major overhaul. The State Planning and Environment Commission (S.P.E.C.) was created in 1974 and its first task was an investigation into land use planning. The first stage of the study, the Green Book, recommended sweeping changes including the strengthening

of local decision-making, more attention to environmental considerations, greater concern with the social and economic consequences of planning and public involvement at all stages of the planning process. A series of 85 meetings to discuss these matters were
held across New South Wales and over 281 written submissions
were considered (Minister for Planning and Environment, 1975: 6).
On this basis a Blue Book was issued which retreated from the
earlier bold proposals for regional planning. It was now suggested
that instead of independent regional planning authorities, only regional offices of the central bureaucracy would be created. It repeated the desire for more public participation but added, 'If there
are objections or unacceptable conditions, the minister will make
the final decision' (1975: 24). Finally, for the preservation of historic buildings yet another body would be established, the Historic
Buildings and Sites Advisory Committee. The Blue Book was
circulated for public discussion and debate and eventually the final
report, the White Book, was published.

The White Book back-pedalled even further. Regional planning
bodies were now to be advisory only. There was to be no devolu-
tion of important development or planning responsibilities to regional bodies or local councils. In fact further bureaucratic restrictions were imposed by insisting that local councils ensure that their
statutory land use plans conformed with the planning directives of
S.P.E.C. Further, the White Book rejected the proposal of the
Green and Blue Books that full third-party rights of appeal be
granted to objectors to development applications, which was a
fundamental objective of the green ban movement. Central government and bureaucracy were reluctant to part with any power or
authority.

On this basis the New South Wales government drafted the Environmental Planning Bill, 1976. As Roddewig concludes, 'the bill
failed to create a strong regional planning framework or to vest
local councils with more power than that needed to certify that local plans met State and regional directives. Because of these fail-
ures, many of the basic grievances of the green ban movement
were not resolved' (1978: 117). The communion generated by the
green bans was now truly routinised into the rational-legal
framework of society without substantially affecting the power of
government, bureaucracy and the developers.

The story of the green ban movement is typical of much other
grass roots political activity in that the achievements gained are
not so great as often thought. First, in some localities it has resulted in a further entrenchment of the sectional interests of local
government. Some councils have furthered the bureaucratic

approach by establishing resident liaison committees which advise rather than decide. The resident members of such committees are often treated as market research phenomena, and the whole process diffuses conflict and minimises differences of opinion through routine bureaucratic operations, whereas decision-making power is preserved in the hands of a few councillors.

Second, the most identifiable achievements concern specific issues, such as direct decision-making participation on committees with some authority or such particular neighbourhood action as adventure playgrounds and tree planting. Most achievements distinctly favour the interests of conservative, community-based, middle-class activists. Those best able to organise and shout the loudest have gained most and there has been no attempt to weight the interests of different groups within localities in terms of some notion of social justice.

Third, the radical communion-based action groups have certainly not achieved their primary aim of re-distributing wealth and resources, neither do they appear to be, as some commentators have argued (Mullins, 1977; Kilmartin and Thorns, 1978: 129–40), a new social base instituting structural change in Australian society. Rather they have succeeded in such restricted issues as Kelly's Bush and the Moreton Bay fig trees near the Opera House, partially succeeded in others such as the postponement of the Brisbane freeway and slum clearance in Melbourne, and failed altogether as with many of the large building site bans.

Most citizen political activity is conservative rather than radical. The great majority of groups are concerned with either preventing something from happening or ensuring that development follows customary patterns. Many resident action groups have found themselves faced with enormous rational-legal barriers when they have attempted to put some of their ideas into practice. As a consequence of such problems, along with more difficult economic times in the mid- and late-1970s, most groups have restricted their activities to narrow issues and when these were either won or lost they disbanded. Essentially the best organised with the most expert advice, that is, those most bureaucratically oriented, benefited most, and in the process they often created antagonism between other classes and ethnic groups in their localities (Wild, 1973, 1976). In almost all cases those unable to organise — the poor, the old, the ethnic under-class, the struggling single-parent families, the Aborigines, and the alienated jobless youth — those who spend most of their time just surviving in a hostile environment, have been excluded from the benefits of citizen participation movements. In some cases the lower classes have lost ground. In the absence of decisive government action for re-distribution, and given the political and economic strength and organising ability of the middle and upper classes to protect their immediate environment, then the only place for polluting industries, low-cost housing and other undesirable development is alongside equally undesirable existing developments, where they will further increase the problems already suffered by the lower classes (Sandercock, 1976: 210, Wild, 1970a: 29).

If the achievements gained have been small and the lessons learned disappointing, often painful and always time consuming, what does citizen participation through grass roots politics offer? There are some benefits. A keen force of active residents at the local level helps to ensure that local government authorities concern themselves with public accountability; with some consideration for other people's lives. Resident representation on committees creates more channels of communication, and consequently reassures people by keeping them informed of policies and decisions through consultation. There is a potential for creating more flexible structures at the local level, which in turn would allow a wider representation and the participation of groups with differing values and interests. Local government should be able to fulfil its duties in a way that relates to tradition and sentiment as well as to rational-legal rules and regulations. The difficulty with this is that there is an inherent conflict of rights. To resolve this conflict the moral rights of people must have a place within society's rational-legal framework and only governments and politicians can do this.

Even if all this happened, which of course it does not, the organised middle class would still extract the greatest benefits. The only avenue for instituting such changes is through more rules and regulations. In policy-making and administration, local government along with the other tiers of government, has become bigger, more complex, more formally bureaucratic and more dependent on experts. As this process of rationalisation will continue, the middle class, as they are largely the result of bureaucratisation themselves, are the ones with the abilities to cope, question and thereby benefit. It is important for local government to be able to relate to those who do not have these abilities, which is the majority of the working class and certainly the ethnic and deprived under-class. Local government bureaucrats and councillors need to be concerned not with enhancing their own values and interests, not just with providing services for the affluent majority, not just with the checks and demands of a myriad middle-class action groups, but most importantly with the welfare and needs of the poor in Australian society (Henderson, 1975).

I once said something along those lines to an alderman and he replied, 'Well, let them come along and participate. They should come along, put their point of view and fight for what they want.' The problem with this is that participation is not a substitute for formal government (Sandercock, 1978: 117), it has not been successful in altering important policies, and that whereas the middle class may be happy because they can get their trees and adventure playgrounds from the local council, the poor know that they cannot get jobs, improved housing or better education from the same source. Grass roots politics do not provide such things, therefore why participate? Sharing in decisions may aid the human dignity of a few but it is certainly no cure for an unjust system. Although local government can and should help the have-nots the real issues lie elsewhere. The problems and aspirations of the poor can only be furthered through the power interests of the State.

Matters of improved employment, housing, education and health for the poor concern policies that must be re-distributive and are therefore deeply political. In Australia large property owners have been able to use the political institutions of the State to prevent incursions on their property rights by legislation which has attempted in a small way to re-distribute resources. Most Australian States, for example, have long histories of rejecting planning bills (Sandercock, 1976: 216) and in several cases political institutions have been used to support activities in land speculation. Grass roots politics may sometimes be able to bring such issues to public notice, but generally local politics concerning such major and crucial matters are unlikely to succeed unless they are tied to national level political policies which are redistributive. If this does not occur then we can only expect 'a succession of briefly spluttering popular local action groups that if successful will ... direct resources to themselves but *away* from others who either have not or cannot mobilise' (Bell and Newby, 1976).

Conclusions
My conclusions concerning the ability of grass roots politics to institute significant social change, or for that matter, the likelihood of developing a more equal society in Australia, are pessimistic. There are two main reasons. The first concerns class. The entrenched class interests of the upper class, centred on property ownership, and of the middle class, based on expertise, are not likely to be easily changed. Further, the vast majority of the working class have, through such rational-legal mechanisms as arbitration, conciliation and wage indexation, been incorporated into the capitalist system (Wild, 1978a: 59–65). Australian workers are not fighting to overthrow or even radically change the system, rather

they want a bigger share of the capitalist cake. As the great majority of Australians accept the present capitalist system as about the best possible, there is unlikely to be any major force for radical change.

The second reason concerns bureaucracy. Wherever people seek to increase their freedom or impose equality by making life more predictable, the structures they create take on a life of their own and come to limit that freedom and equality. Now egalitarianism may be interpreted at two levels. First, there is the distributive equality of political, economic and social rights. Second, there is the relational equality of people which derives from their intrinsic personal human worth. At the distributive level little has been achieved in terms of the re-distribution of wealth and power — these remain concentrated in the hands of a minority, who thereby deny the equality of opportunity to become unequal (Wild, 1978a: 43–5, 180). At the relational level the movement has been away from intrinsic human equality towards the impersonality and detachment of the contract as demanded by rationalisation. Australian egalitarianism, as a description of social rights and conditions, never existed; as a meaningful ideology about personal relationships it is virtually dead. Movements centred on communion or community periodically resurrect matters of sentiment, equality and tradition but as we have seen most are short-lived outbursts against the imperatives of rationalisation. The cause is the final paradox of bureaucracy. Rules and regulations are formulated to impose equal conditions and treatment, and the rules give rise to bureaucrats who create a complex hierarchy of authoritative levels. Their formal domination of others, and the impersonality of their office and their work, undermines the original idea of equality, adds new distributive inequalities and destroys intrinsic human equality in personal relationships.

The development of democratic government and the growth of advanced capitalism necessarily depends on the further advance of bureaucratic organisation. Consequently, any idea 'that some form of democracy can destroy the domination of men over other men' (Weber quoted in Mommsen, 1959: 392) is utopian. Those who look to the transcendence of human conflict through political activity, who seek to attain an end to 'the domination of man by man' are turning their backs on reality just as much as those who drop out of modern life into some form of mystical retreat. Those who wish to maintain 'the domination of man by man' are in a stronger position by the very nature of politics. In the last analysis politics involves struggles for power and there is never any final conclusion to such struggles.

Although class interests and bureaucratic domination will continue to determine the broad nature of Australian society it remains possible to implement policies of re-distributive social justice to achieve a more equal, just and participatory society within this framework. There are at least two avenues that can be followed to achieve these aims.

First, more and constant public pressure from the grass roots upwards is necessary to ensure public accountability for policies and decisions, to restrain the tendency inherent in bureaucracies to exceed their function as an administrative instrument and to argue for some re-distribution of wealth and resources, especially to the poor.

Second, we require politicians with special qualities to formulate and implement policies to ensure social justice and to control the excesses of bureaucracies, politicians who have long-term notions of the sort of society they wish to create. Our contemporary social order requires, but lacks, politicians who have both passion and perspective. They need what Weber called 'passion in the sense of matter-of-factness.' They require an ability to balance devotion to a cause with an awareness, firstly, of the tension between means and ends, and secondly of the paradox of consequences. Neither radicals nor conservatives exhibit this awareness; both think it possible for modern man to escape from the 'iron cage'. The radicals who are looking forward to their utopian society fail to see that the means which have to be used to reach their goal inevitably bring about a state of affairs which is discrepant from their stated end, whereas the conservatives who are looking to a reversion to a previous age fail to see the often tragic consequences of their abiding concern with an inequitable established order and individual self-interest. As I look around Australia from the grass roots upwards I see few politicians with the passion and perspective to create a more just society.

The challenge to local government, and to all grass roots politics, is to help produce a fairer and more just society in Australia through incorporating meaningful public participation in existing structures, and by producing politicians who have the passion to fight for a cause and the practical, down-to-earth knowledge of the means by which it could be obtained, as well as the insight into the paradoxical nature of social change in modern societies.

Italian Immigrants

Two recent studies of Italian immigrants have centred their attention on emigrants from the Treviso area of the Veneto region of northern Italy and provide useful examples for a discussion of the relationship between immigrant groups and the concept of community (Thompson, 1980; Huber, 1977).

Since 1947 approximately 365 000 Italians have come to settle permanently in Australia. Of these some 90 000 (24.7 per cent) have left again, most to return to Italy. Thompson's book *Australia through Italian Eyes* describes the aims, hopes and experiences of some Italians who emigrated to Australia and subsequently returned to Italy to re-settle during the period 1960 to 1970. This book is an attempt to explain why these people left Australia. It is a study based on 116 interviews with people who returned to live in the provinces of L'Aquila in the Abruzzi region of southern Italy and Treviso in the northern region of the Veneto. These areas were selected for their sustained high levels of emigration.

The respondents were asked about their origins, the reasons for their return, employment in Australia, living conditions and social security arrangements in Australia and Italy, personal and family relationships, discrimination and their experiences of re-settlement in Italy. Most of the material is presented in an extremely clear, readable and well-written style with a liberal use of quotations which give the reader a vivid picture of how these people felt about the circumstances in which they found themselves. An example at random is a man from Bazzano (L'Aquila) who had been in Australia from 1955 to 1966, between the ages of 26 and 36. He said:

> I worked for eleven years cane farming. For seven or eight months at a time we would work from 4 a.m. to dark five days a week. It was a hard job. At first when I was young it did not matter that it was hard. But in the last years it became a bit too much. You can do it for four or five years; I did it longer. I used to alternate between sugar cane, tobacco and work in the bush. The cane cutting wrecked my back, and I had to come back [to Italy]. I had had a hernia operation too, and I could not continue with very hard work. Because I couldn't speak [English] really well I wasn't able to go and find light permanent work. (1980: 84–5)

Other parts of the book, however, are at times confusing. There is a tendency, which is common to many survey studies, to constantly refer to the numbers of people who said this or believed that but without establishing a general pattern from the plethora of facts. One of the reasons for this is that the facts are supposed to speak for themselves without being interpreted with reference to a theoretical model. The methodology, the demographic influence and the final message that Australians should fully accept and integrate future settlers into a multi-cultural society indicate the dependence on a functionalist-equilibrium model of society. Such a view pays scant attention to the inevitability of conflicting interests and values and the struggles for power and domination which are built in to the social structure of capitalist societies.

Thompson however, treats her data with the utmost care and fairness and is well aware of its limitations, most of which stem from the survey approach. She found a tendency to state only acceptable reasons for returning, such as family obligations and a reluctance to admit to failure or difficulties in Australia (1980: 48). Many claimed that their initial accommodation in Australia was satisfactory because they did not want to criticise relatives with whom they stayed. One man, for example, 'who did not complain about initial hardship joined his sister, brother-in-law and their child who were living in a garage at Guildford, N.S.W. About the only facility was a small ring stove for cooking on which they heated water for washing' (1980: 102). Some people exaggerated the amount of social activity they had had in Australia and were picked up on this by their spouses or children. One 'householder and his wife said that they had visited other homes and friends had visited them. "Who?" asked Maurizio, their eleven-year-old son. "We used to see friends every week", they replied. "Once a year!" Maurizio suggested' (1980: 154).

Social difficulties experienced in Australia were a major factor in the decision to return. Many felt they did the hardest type of work in Australia. Almost all were unanimous in their condemnation of Australia's system of social security. They felt especially bitter that after working perhaps most of their life in Australia they were debarred from taking their pension back to Italy whereas British immigrants were able to do this. The chapter on discrimination is the most revealing, largely through an historical discussion of Australian-Italian relationships in the late nineteenth and early twentieth centuries. Thompson concludes that the origins of anti-Italian feeling are in the labour market but takes the analysis no further (1980: 173).

Thompson also concludes that the return to Italy 'seemed to have been predetermined ... Like the swallows, these emigrants had travelled along migratory routes established by relatives and *paesani* (persons from the same village), routes which led to Australia and back to Italy again' (1980: 227). Most emigrated along chain migration patterns whereby *paesani* lived in the same locality in Australia. The long hours of hard work, which were necessary for economic progress in Australia, led to reduced opportunities for socialising and, at the same time, made Australians suspicious. Hostility and discrimination heightened the isolation of the Italians who, in response, opted out of direct competition with Australians by working for Italian companies and living separately. Family, health, employment, discrimination and social security all contributed to the decision to return and one family's return and successful re-settlement precipitated others as the news quickly spread. Despite their economic achievements in Australia, however, the profits of migration were largely consumed in re-settlement. Many were happy to be back home and those who were not could not afford to leave again.

Although Thompson takes her data at face value explaining the return in terms of some of this and some of that within functionalist-positivist assumptions, there is another scenario that shouts from these pages. If community represents tradition, communion the emotion or sentiment of belonging and society rational-legal individualism, then all the Italians interviewed either opted for community and communion and rejected society or wished to use society in an attempt to make their community and communions more secure. There are examples of this general process in each chapter. Most regarded emigration 'as a temporary period of hard labour overseas, the returns from which would enable them to enjoy a higher standard of living back in Italy' (1980: 36). Most claimed they returned for family reasons. 'The young migrant looks some 35 years ahead and sees himself abandoned by his Australian children to an old people's home. On the other hand, if he returns to Italy, old age within his *paese*, (community of origin), where he can continue to be a useful and respected member of the community, will be as satisfactory as old age can be' (1980: 49,131). The 'emotional feelings of *paesi* and *paesani*' were enormously strong and 'their memories of socially satisfying ways of living which they had once known were reinforced by letters from relatives' (1980: 62).

Many expressed an 'emotional attachment to their house in Italy' (1980: 117). According to one man 'he and his family could live on "natural products" from their farm' whereas 'in Australia they had been prevented from keeping poultry and rabbits' (1980: 117). The Australian nuclear family 'seemed to the Italians to have insulated themselves within their small houses and gardens from which they seemed to wish to shut out the rest of the world' (1980: 138). Many complained that Australian families do not gather or share their houses with elderly dependents and that the loneliness and isolation they felt was demoralising. One man said 'it was hard to get used to seeing no-one walking around the streets at night ... I used to walk round and round my small garden like a caged dog with no-one to talk to' (1980: 153). Many referred to the better 'air' in Italy meaning the social climate and their emotional reactions to the people amongst whom they lived (1980: 175).

Associated with the emphasis on close family relationships is the clear differentiation made between male and female roles. According to one man, in Australia 'the woman wants to take control and she has the support of Queen Elizabeth' (1980: 191). For many of those interviewed, 'The Australian family seemed to be morally decadent, a laissez faire institution, within which men had ceased to exercise their traditional authority and women and children had acquired more freedom than was good for them' (1980: 191). In one case when a man raised his hand to his son, the son called the police. According to the respondent, 'The son's action was a terrible blow to the father, and Australian law defended the son, not the father! The government should compel children to respect their parents. In Australia, there are many children who break away from their families' (1980: 192). This is a good example of the change from traditional authority associated with community to the rational-legal authority of society. 'For the Italians, one basic value which settlement in Australia threatened was that of traditional family morality' (1980: 200), perhaps the cornerstone of Italian ethics. As one man who returned to Celano in 1968 commented, 'for community, friendship and moral values, it is better here [Italy] where you can have things that are yours'. His wife added, 'In Australia there is just work ... people in Italy are more expansive and happier' (1980: 211). Another man succinctly put the case for community and communion and against society when he said, 'I am happier because there is everything here: my mother, my home and my language — I am able to express myself' (1980: 222).

Those who returned to Italy chose tradition and sentiment, that is community and communion centred on custom, locality, kinship, morals and feelings through experience. They rejected the impersonality and individualism of rational society. Those who remain in Australia must inevitably accept the rational-legal society and along with this the rationalisation of their traditional values and their life.

Huber's work on the Trevisani in Griffith clearly shows the impact of the processes of rationalisation, community formation and community closure on the lives of these immigrants but the data is not interpreted from this perspective. *From Pasta to Pavlova* is in three parts. Part one examines the main features of traditional Treviso society and details changes occurring after the Second

World War. Before 1939, the extended family, dominated by the eldest male with the eldest wife in charge of the daughters-in-law and the kitchen, was a core institution characterised by tension, gossip and a rigid code of behaviour. Male and female roles were strictly separated and the church had an all-embracing hold on life. The drudgery and hard work of everyday life was lightened by festivals, ritual occasions and evening gatherings emphasising 'intimate association' (1977: 27). Seasonal migration to Germany and Switzerland was an accepted means of subsidising the family economy. A smaller number emigrated overseas, some intending to return, others planning to settle permanently in their new country. Post-war Treviso was characterised by high unemployment, an exodus from the land and a shortage of food. More education was available, more girls went out to work, the nuclear family began to take over from the extended family, the influence of the church declined and male-female roles were less segregated. Assisted passages, available work with high wages and the changing nature of traditional life made emigration overseas, and the possibility of an early return trip, easier than before the war.

Huber uses documentary evidence and in-depth interview data to support her arguments. The former provides a rather dull and dry text but the latter brings things to life, as is indicated in the following extract from the biography of a Treviso woman who lives in Sydney.

Apart from working on the land, my father was employed at an ammunition factory nearby. Then the factory was shifted because there was so much bombardment during the war, and he lost his job. Although we grew all our food, we had to pay the landlord 30 000 lire a month and give him half the produce. Money was very short. I didn't have a pair of shoes until I was 14. At 12 I was sent to look after the station-master's children each afternoon till nine in the evening. I also milked the cows and washed the dishes there. At 14 I went into service full-time ... At 16 I was sent to Venice and was a maid in an admiral's household. There were no days off, no regular hours, and just two weeks a year holiday ... All the money went home to help pay the rent. When I was 17 my aunt and I left for France, where I had a job as a cook in a convent ... My mother told me that a woman should delay marriage for as long as possible because living with a mother-in-law is hell. She'd lived like a slave with hers for 16 years ... My parents-in-law were not happy when Paolo wanted to marry me because my family was very, very poor, but he didn't mind, so we became engaged when I returned from France at 21.

Two years later, in 1956, Paolo left Italy as an assisted migrant to Australia. He paid for my passage when I followed him to Sydney in 1958. We were married three days later. (1977: 41–2)

Part two examines the historical and contemporary situation of Trevisani immigrants who settled in Griffith, the centre of the Murrumbidgee Irrigation Area (M.I.A.). In 1921 there were 33 Italians in the M.I.A. This number increased to 747 in 1933, 1889 in 1947 and 4185 in 1954 (1977: 57). In Griffith approximately 50 per cent were from the Treviso region. The typical pattern of settlement was for a father, or father and son, to emigrate and work as labourers on a farm. They saved for fares and brought out the rest of the family. They leased land to grow vegetables, work which was labour intensive and not liked by Australians. The profits were saved and most bought farms. The profits from the farm were used to buy another farm in the name of the eldest son as M.I.A. legislation did not allow any individual to own more than one farm. In this way sons were set up with a farm early in their career. By the early 1960s, however, farm prices were too high for newcomers and they moved into such jobs as waiters, bricklayers and carpenters. Many relatives and *paesani* arrived through chain migration and lived on farms close to each other in nuclear family units.

Griffith is well known for its club life and the Italians started their clubs as early as the mid 1930s. Huber sees them as an adaptation of the *trattoria* or *osteria* providing first, opportunities for males to get together, second, a place for family gatherings, and third, they were a 'media for partial assimilation' (1977: 113). The last was given great impetus by Al Grassby who used the clubs to initiate and establish relationships with Australians and other ethnic groups and who was responsible for 'the emergence of a new *campanilismo*' [a sentimental attachment to home] (1977: 119).

The Trevisani in Griffith then, became commercial farmers, established their sons on the land, moved into nuclear families, mixed with the relatives of their choice, used formal clubs as social centres, and educated their children. This has gradually resulted in such changing values as women not now being expected to work in the fields and a move to modern specialised farming methods that 'are not compatible with traditional Italian values that accept intensive family labour' (1977: 127). Huber mistakenly sees all this as fostering a '*gemeinschaft*-type community' (1977: 127).

Trevisani in Sydney, however, Huber found, were in a totally different situation and this is the subject of Part three. Most were post-war immigrants who lived in the major cities because the jobs were there. In Griffith Huber met and stayed with many families and through participant observation she was able to develop an overall view of their situation. Such an approach was impossible in Sydney and she concentrated on eight families, all of them recent immigrants with young children. Consequently her comments cannot be generalised to all Trevisani, or all Italians, in Sydney. The writer isolates five stages in the post-war city settlement. The male emigrated and worked on the cane fields or as an unskilled labourer to save money; in two or three years 'either the fiancée followed him to Sydney or he returned briefly to Treviso, married and came back' (1977: 141); a house was bought and paid off within about five years and a further few years savings financed the trip home with the possible aim of re-settlement; the return trip of some six to twelve months was a time of conspicuous consumption to impress *paesani* but disillusionment with traditional ways gradually set in; finally they returned to Australia and started afresh with the aim of permanent settlement. Some brief biographies indicate why the males left Italy in the first place; the main reasons were to escape parental domination, to earn money and return with prestige and to avoid conscription. These accounts also describe, albeit indirectly, how rural peasants became urban labourers.

Huber vacillates between seeing the Sydney Trevisani as lonely and isolated—only three of the eight families have relatives in Sydney (1977: 160, 209) and none belong to clubs (1977: 171)—and viewing them in terms of close networks of *paesani*, workmates and neighbours, where sometimes all three 'role-sets overlapped' and created 'a consciousness of kind' (1977: 171). This problem is partly one of slippage between the selected eight families (who are especially atypical, given their stage in the life cycle with men working long hours to buy a house and the women tied to young children) and the activities of Trevisani, and Italians generally, throughout Sydney.

Huber's insights into the problems the families had accord with Thompson's evidence. They had difficulties with reading and writing (both English and Italian) and the English language, with employers and such bureaucracies as banks and government departments, and with naturalisation and what it meant. They encountered little discrimination because they worked with and for Italians and lived in such Italian districts as Leichhardt, (Sydney).

In a postscript the writer mentions that two of the families remained in Italy to re-settle and she visited them in Treviso. One inherited land and the other bought land and built a house. At the time of the visit in 1974 one of the males was 'working in a tile factory earning about half of what he earned in Australia' as well as working on his parents' farm 'often till ten at night' (1977: 200). They like Italy because they 'feel at home' but they do not like the long, hard working hours, the political situation and inflation. They often speak about returning to Australia but will probably remain in Italy because of traditional ties and the expense of re-emigration.

Huber explains these situations with the vague functionalist statement that 'the varying economic conditions in Australia at the time of the migrations led to different sequences in the process and attitudes to permanent residence in Griffith and Sydney. Furthermore, the environment in Griffith favoured adaptation and reconstruction of traditional institutions. This was not so in Sydney' (1977: 207). The impression the reader is left with is that everything affects everything else in a complex way and it all comes out in the wash in the way the data emerges. The facts are expected to speak for themselves without being interpreted with reference to a theoretical model. The description and analysis in this study, as in Thompson's, depends on an implicit functionalist-equilibrium model of society. This approach largely ignores the inevitability of conflicting interests and values and the struggles for power and domination which are part of the social structure of capitalist societies.

As with much localised anthropological-style research, the bulk of the data, and certainly the best and richest material, concerns the hopes and experiences of individuals and families struggling to achieve a satisfying life for themselves and their children. Such situations can be described, as they are here, from the viewpoint of the subjects' perceptions and the observations of the researcher. The interaction of such variables as traditional values, job opportunities, industrialisation, government policies, land-tenure systems, education and so forth, are seen to be affecting, or perhaps determining, the outcome. The problem here is that no broader pattern of why things happen this way is feasible from this multi-factorial perspective. A Marxist arguing from a macro-sociological level may suggest, for example, that all immigrants, to advanced capitalist societies, are serving the interests of capital by filling jobs which the local 'aristocracy of labour' would not do and by forming a 'reserve army of labour' which would be easily dismissed in an economic downturn. Such a view might go even further and suggest that immigrants help to divide the working class and suffer from false consciousness because they tend not to unionise and are not aware of their true or real interests (see Collins, 1975: 126). This position is, of course, vulgar Marxism, but it makes clear that although in this case a general pattern is established, this determinist view pays little attention to the intricacies and richness of the data. In other words the theory is imposed and Trevisani in Griffith and Sydney are brought together under the same theoretical umbrella.

In my view the data in this study suggests a different perspective — one that takes into account the two-way relationship between theory and data. In her explication of Weber's view of community Neuwirth (1969) isolated four characteristics: community formation, community closure, associational relationships and harmonious and conflictual relations. These processes can be clearly identified in the Griffith material. Community formation begins through the competition for interests. The Trevisani, through chain migration and family solidarity, attempted to corner the vegetable and horticultural farms close to Griffith. Processes of exclusion constitute communal action and the Trevisani excluded such others as the Calabresi and took pride in their northern heritage which became a focus of positive identification for community members. It is exactly these processes of competition and exclusion that enable communities to be formed. In the Griffith case this was further emphasised by Australian xenophobia which contributed towards closer relationships among Italians (1077: 97).

Once communal relationships have been formed, people attempt to maintain this situation by monopolising their advantages and the Trevisani did this through the process of farm purchasing. This is called community closure and in this case economic closure was pursued through the monopolisation of farming opportunities.

Associative relationships are closely related to closure as they enable communities to consolidate their interests. The Trevisani accomplished this through their clubs which were initially formed for themselves and only later when secure, were opened up by Grassby as a way of establishing contacts between different ethnic groups. In a classic pattern communal interests were delegated to officers of the associations and the clubs began to enforce and change community norms by setting standards and wielding sanctions. One Italian club official recalled how, 'The Calabresi used to come and often started fights. One day I called in their head, a fellow called Joe, and said to him, "Why do your boys always pick fights? It makes it tough for the rest of the members". Joe slapped the table with the palm of his hand and said, "O.K. Peter, from now on there'll be no more fights!" Sure enough, there was no trouble after that' (1977: 99–100).

This interpretation of the role of associative relationships generated through formal clubs in an attempt to consolidate interests within ethnic groups is supported by Martin's study *Community and Identity: Refugee Groups in Adelaide* (1972). This book is a history of formal group organisation attempting to examine the changing structure and functions of ethnic associations in 14 Eastern European minority groups in Adelaide from 1948 to approximately 1967. Martin points out that common ethnic origin is a basis of network connections that work similarly to kinship networks 'except that they may act as the basis of more formal groups such as ethnic churches or community associations' (1972: 132). Her research revealed considerable evidence of a close relationship between ethnic networks and formal organisations and she concludes 'associations often appeared to have developed as a formalisation of network ties' (1972: 132).

Martin does not specifically discuss community formation in terms of competition for interests and attempts at closure but her final conclusion concerning community organisations among the 14 ethnic minorities clearly demonstrates the importance of power, tradition and positive location in the host society, and therefore, indirectly, she demonstrates the processes of community formation and closure. She writes:

> The effective stimulus to group organisation ... comes, for one thing, from the positive value attached to the opportunities for self-expression, gaining *recognition* and exercising *influence* provided by *ethnic associations* and to the role of informal networks in channelling *resources from the wider society* to the individual immigrant. Above all, this stimulus represents the positive concern to maintain group—and hence individual—identity, to keep alive 'long and profound' *traditions* or, less self-consciously, simply to preserve continuity between past and present, and so safeguard the individual's sense of personal location in time. (1972: 133; emphasis added)

Finally there are processes of consensus and conflict. Compliance to community norms does not necessarily rest on voluntary consent. Because this study is based on a functionalist-equilibrium perspective there is little data on conflict and power relations, nevertheless from several passages it emerges that there are differences between the more successful Trevisani who have formed companies and work bigger farms and those who have remained as a family farming unit, between the farmers and the non-farmers and between the political elite and the rest. Those with more power are more influential in establishing and maintaining community norms and values.

The Trevisani in Griffith, most of whom arrived with the notion of permanent settlement, were, from the start, involved in the process of community formation. First, economic (farms), second, social (clubs) and third, political (Grassby) closure provided them with substantial control over their own affairs and a positive focus of identification. Over time, however, routinisation sets in and children marry outside the community, Australian xenophobia declines, especially in times of affluence and stability, politicians preach consensus and cooperation between ethnic groups and so forth. One of Huber's informants expressed it well when she said, 'We wouldn't dream of leaving Griffith. This is our home, and we have a good life, but in the old days when things were harder people stuck together a lot more than now' (1977: 127). This does not represent a return to *gemeinschaft* as suggested by Huber, rather, it indicates the ability of rational association centred on capitalism to incorporate, encompass and gradually change notions of tradition and sentiment.

The situation in Sydney was different and Huber's descriptions of the experiences of the young post-war immigrants accord with Thompson's account provided by those who had decided to resettle in Italy. Community formation was a much more formidable task in a large metropolis and a substantial level of community closure could not be effected. Those who returned to Italy to resettle, as those in Thompson's sample, did so for reasons of tradition and sentiment, that is, community and communion. 'Here we feel at home', was a common answer to the question, 'Why did you return?', and it expresses an inner sense of emotional well being and 'peace of mind' centred on custom (1977: 196). Those who returned to settle again in Australia were attracted by the greater freedom and independence, less gossip, a closer relationship with the spouse and better opportunities for their children that a more rational society offers. One respondent indicated clearly how rational ways were destroying traditional relationships when she remarked:

> We don't speak to my husband's cousin and his wife any more. They had a grocery shop in Leichhardt and were offended because I didn't buy everything there. But I said to him, 'This isn't Treviso. I have money every week and don't need credit and then pay at the end of the season. If I see something cheaper in another shop I buy it. Why should I buy it from you?' So we haven't spoken for a long time, even though they're godparents to one of the children'. (1977: 161)

The relationships between community, communion and society and the development of community formation and closure provide us with some valuable insights into this material on Italian immigrants at a more general level of explanation than the multi-factorial functional-positivism Huber and Thompson prefer. Furthermore, this viewpoint retains the data, and their relationship to the concepts, in a central position, and is, therefore, not as rarified or as determinist as a macro-structural Marxist account.

Communes and the Counter-Culture

Utopian movements of many types, and at different times in history, have striven to achieve that emotionally charged sense of belonging I have called communion. Rosabeth Kanter in her book *Commitment and Community*, which remains one of the best sociological analyses of utopian movements and settlements, described the basis of the utopian tradition when she wrote:

> Utopia is the imaginary society in which humankind's deepest yearnings, noblest dreams, and highest aspirations come to fulfilment, where all physical, social and spiritual forces work together, in harmony, to permit the attainment of everything people find necessary and desirable ... Underlying the vision of utopia is the assumption that harmony, cooperation, and mutuality of interests are natural to human existence, rather than conflict, competition and exploitation, which arise only in imperfect societies ... Utopia, then, represents an ideal of the good, to contrast with the evils and ills of existing societies. (1972: 1)

Kanter isolates waves of utopian movements in America in the 1840s and the 1960s–70s and suggests that these stem from a desire to live according to religious values which reject the sinfulness of the established order; or a desire to reform the economic and political ills of capitalism; or a desire to develop the psychological growth of the individual by establishing close and meaningful relationships and rejecting the impersonality and alienation of the wider society. Religious themes were prominent before 1840, the economic and political issues were prominent post-1840, and the psycho-social matters were in the 1960s. In each period, however, all three are represented and have much in common, especially the rejection of the established order and the possibility of perfection through social change.

Similar processes can be identified in Australia. Religious utopian movements have existed since the beginning of substantial European settlement. Secular groups protesting about the ravages of the depression flourished in the 1890s. Unemployed and unskilled workers formed communes along the Murray River and demanded land to provide subsistence. After some initial opposition the State governments provided aid (Cock, 1979: 15). Most of these settlements were gradually disbanded as prosperity increased. The utopian movements and settlements of the late 1960s and early 1970s largely centred on opposition to the affluence of the post-war period; the impersonality generated by the increasing role of the State, especially bureaucratisation; and the psycho-social desire to find oneself and to be able to relate meaningfully to others. Many were short-lived experiments; others, unstable through the lack of property, rapid membership turnover, and poor leadership and organisation, disbanded with the onset of the late 1970s recession. A small number established themselves permanently, almost all as *private* land cooperatives.

Some commentators on the Australian scene had great expectations for the counter-culture movement. According to Turner it is capable of 'a transformation of values akin to that of the Renaissance and Reformation' (1978: 112). Connell hopes that the movement constitutes a break with capitalism and that this cleavage should 'be occupied in a more general movement towards socialism' (1977: 189). For Altman the counter-culture has attempted to 'transcend' capitalism and he suggests that it represents 'a direction that Western society may well have to follow' (1977: 463). Peter Cock, a participant in, and observer of, the movement, became disillusioned with many of the attempts to establish new lifestyles, nevertheless he still believes that 'the alternative community movement . . . may well be an old dream that can now be reborn on a new basis, without many of the limitations of the past' (1979: 255). An examination of the available data, however, does not support such optimism. Before I discuss the Australian counter-culture scene, some clarification of basic terms is required.

Counter-culture is a general term used to describe the social movement common to most Western societies in the mid 1960s and 1970s which consisted of young people believing in, and acting out, opposition to the dominant values of their society. It is 'an alternate set of values and beliefs and a set of alternative institutions and behaviour patterns' (Altman, 1977: 450) unified in opposition to the established order. A commune 'consists of a group of people, of three or more persons in size, drawn from more than one family or kinship group, who have voluntarily come together for some purpose or other, shared or otherwise, in the pursuit of which they seek to share certain aspects of their lives together, and who are characterised by a certain consciousness of themselves as a group' (Rigby, 1974: 3; see also Abrams and McCulloch, 1976: 45). Finally, a cooperative refers to a number of families living together or in close proximity with clearly defined, limited and often legally enforceable sharing arrangements.

The counter-culture movement emerged from mid-twentieth century capitalist society. It centred on youth as a distinct form of identity. The middle-class youth of the mid-1960s had experienced post-war stability and affluence, the rapid expansion of higher education which created a prolonged period between adolescence and working adulthood, and the general encroachment of the State and bureaucracy into most spheres of life. These people came almost wholly from middle-class backgrounds, were not yet fully integrated into the system through occupation and marriage and had sufficient freedom and time to question the established order. All of this arose, as I have suggested elsewhere, (Wild, 1978a: 174–5) from the substantial economic growth and stability since 1945 and which led to a rise of status-oriented behaviour emphasising consumption at the expense of class action and a concern with production.

As with many other cultural phenomena the Australian counter-culture movement was modelled on the United States' version. 'Modern communications, travel and affluence all contributed to the replication of many of the features of the American counter-culture in Australia' (Altman, 1977: 455). Similar underground newspapers, journals and records, sexual liberation movements, a concern with the occult, macrobiotic food, alternative medicine, Indian herbs, clothes and jewellery and so forth were all quickly established. But perhaps the most central movement was back to the land to develop self-sufficient communes and a new lifestyle free from established constraints. This occurred in all States but the heaviest concentration of communes is on the north coast of New South Wales around Nimbin and Byron Bay, a region I shall examine in more detail shortly. Many of these people shared a powerful utopian vision and a communion of belonging. They saw themselves at the forefront of a movement for alternative lifestyles and believed that small groups can work together to build the future and change the established order. Many shared the faith that in re-making the self, they automatically re-made society. But as we shall see social change is not quite so simple.

It is extremely difficult to obtain exact figures for such a diffuse and fluctuating movement as the counter-culture, nevertheless, the research carried out by Lindbad (1976) and Cock (1979) provides some approximate details. The former estimates that 1 per cent of the Australian population was involved in the alternative society movement but that only 3 in 10 made a reasonable success of the attempt. Approximately 95 per cent of the 1 per cent are middle-class people from the five capital cities, most of whom have had some association with a university or college. Over 95 per cent are within the age range 17 to 45 years but 75 per cent are between the ages of 23 to 35 years. According to Cock, Australia now has 'about 600' substantial communes and cooperatives which follow counter-culture ideology and practices. 'Overall those who were, are, or sought to be involved in alternative living efforts comprised at least 100 000 people' (1979: 50). However, those actually living in an alternative settlement 'would be less than half this number' (1979: 50).

Robert Houriet (1973) speculates that the average commune lasts no more than four months and the vast majority do not operate for more than one year. Virtually all commentators on communes have referred to the difficulties inherent in trying to maintain this type of social organisation for any substantial period. Kanter attempts to explain this problem by examining the components of utopian communes which might account for their differential durability. For Kanter the basic organisational problems of all communes are:

> How to get the work done, but without coercion. How to ensure that decisions are made, but to everyone's satisfaction. How to build close, fulfilling relationships, but without exclusiveness. How to choose and socialise new members. How to include a degree of autonomy, individual uniqueness and even deviance. How to ensure agreement and shared perception around community functioning and values. (1972: 64)

The resolution of these problems, according to Kanter, lies in commitment. 'The problem of securing total and complete commitment is central' (1972: 65). Because communes deliberately set themselves apart from the wider society they have far greater needs for the almost total commitment and concentration of members' loyalties and devotion than those of groups operating within the many support systems of the established order. Simmel's comments on secret societies can be equally applied to communes. He wrote, 'The secret society claims the whole individual to a greater extent, connects its members in more of their totality, and mutually obligates them more closely than does an open society of identical content' (1964: 366). The capacity for the continued existence of a utopian commune then, depends on the presence or absence of ways of maintaining a high level of commitment. Kanter explores processes whereby commitment is maintained and attempts to explain the success or lack of success of communal ventures in terms of the presence or absence of these processes.

There are two difficulties with this view. First, it assumes that a successful commune is one that lasts. This ignores the fact that communal experiences are often self-terminating in that they have a therapeutic value for some people for a limited period of time after which members return to the established order. Second, it pays little attention to social change and unintended consequences. Processes introduced to maintain a high level of commitment often develop into structures of order and control. In other words, processes are routinised into patterns of action which eventually take on some elements of tradition. As Peter Cock found out from his association with many communes, structure and organisation were necessary for group survival, 'for the development of a sense of continuity, and to maintain the link between the past and the present' (1979: 235). He found the need for rituals and rules to stabilise 'fluctuating feelings' which can easily destroy group boundaries. Further, he comments, 'as rules become accepted and part of unconscious behaviour, they were harder to challenge' consequently the commune's energy 'could be more easily directed to its living' (1979: 235–6). It is in such a way that the emotionally charged, but precarious, communion which provides the initial commitment is gradually routinised into traditions of community. I shall discuss this process with respect to the start and development of what is probably Australia's largest and best-known communal venture, Tuntable Falls, at Nimbin in northern New South Wales.

In May 1973 the tiny village of Nimbin in northern New South Wales was invaded by over 10 000 people for the ten day Aquarius Festival. This 'happening' was organised by the Australian Union of Students (A.U.S.) who had become dissatisfied with earlier festivals which centred on rock music. The aim of the Nimbin gathering was 'for a total cultural experience through the lifestyle of participation' (*Nimbin Good Times*, April, 1973). A.U.S. appointed John Allen and Graeme Dunstan as Festival coordinators and they adopted the pseudonyms Kaptian Kulcha and Superfest — somewhat indicative of charismatic gurus personifying the new age and attempting to establish a following through some form of mystical communion. The coordinators, with several others, went to Nimbin several weeks before the Festival to establish liaison with the residents and to organise facilities. They systematically won over Nimbin's church leaders, policemen, publican, shire officials and newspaper editor before launching a public meeting. At the meeting Allen stressed anti-city sentiments and sugggested that Nimbin would become famous and benefit financially. As a depressed dairying region the offer was too good to refuse and the public gathering accepted the Festival by 180 votes to 5.

People from all over Australia, New Zealand and several other countries flocked to Nimbin for the Aquarius Festival which became 'the first obvious expression of a national alternatives movement' (Cock, 1979: 47). For the participants it represented 'a prophetic vision of the world we wish to live in. It will be an experience to creative living' (*Grass Roots Express*, 1, 1972). Through the experience of the Festival many remained in the area to establish alternative lifestyles in communal living. Small communes were established across the countryside but conditions were poor. Farmhouses were overcrowded, some had no electricity or water, and there was a high rate of mobility with people arriving, demanding a crash-pad, and leaving again, usually to visit Sydney. Many who had squatted after the Festival were eventually evicted and they returned to the city. Those who remained had to cope with 'hangers-on who appeared to drain the energy of those who are making serious attempts at establishing something lasting' (*National Times*, July, 1973). The successful ones were those who could afford to buy land and houses and impose restrictions on access but the price of land was rapidly escalating, thus excluding those without substantial financial resources. It was in this context that Tuntable Falls Coordination Cooperative Limited was established.

The name embedded a basic principle that 'cooperation replaces competition and coordination replaces organisation' (*Nimbin Times*, 12 May, 1973). The unofficial aims were to 'live in harmony with nature and with ourselves with love and understanding. To be free from pollution of air, food, bodies and mind. To create a socicty on these grounds for the betterment of other societies and the world'. (*Nimbin Cooperative Newsletter*, January, 1974). The official aims as in the registered document of the Cooperative were:

> to help set up and coordinate a new community of persons living and working together on common property in a total creation environment of discovering, learning and perfecting modes of living, works of art, forms of communication, methods of awareness, and skills of cultivation, craft and construction.

These enterprising communards found a property of approximately 400 hectares for sale at the head of the Tuntable Falls valley, some five kilometres north-east of Nimbin. The cost was $104 000 which was raised by the sale of $200 shares. By December 1973 the cooperative had $45 000 in the bank, an offer of a $20 000 loan at low interest and a promise of $3000. This was sufficient to allow official occupation of two-thirds of the property in late December.

The Cooperative began with a set of rules which gradually expanded both in numbers and capacity. The initial basic rule was the constitution of a governing body called the general assembly which consisted of seven coordinators who were elected annually. Owning one share gives a family access to the total property and territorial rights are left up to the discretion of those living there because no-one can own a specific piece of land and no subdivisions are permitted. Since habitation other formal and informal rules have developed. General assemblies worked out policies on common facilities, allowable animals, education, the use of timber resources, communication with outsiders, food and its production and the process of decision-making. Development started and the 'White House', one of the original buildings, became the centre of operations.

In February 1974 there were 306 members, most of whom lived in the major cities and spent holidays on the property. By the end of 1974 there were 502 full shareholders and in 1976 this had increased to 652 with 160 of these resident on the land. As the Cooperative evolved its policies, rules became rigid in an attempt to maintain its boundaries. The telephone was to be used only for Cooperative business and incoming private calls; no individual was allowed to contact outside authorities without the prior permission of a general meeting or of three coordinators, no soap was permitted in the creek, no dogs or cats were to be kept, no motor vehicles were allowed on the property, and so forth. The Cooperative gradually became more formal, organised and specialised — in other words, patterns of relationships were becoming more routinised and rationalised. Several dispersed settlements established their own particular lifestyle and calls were made to sectionalise the property to allow each group its own expression. One group established a private shop selling homemade bread, others sold garden produce, still others sold their craft work in nearby towns. Some, attempting to establish a 'social credit' system, began printing their own cardboard coins. Many developed deep interests in various forms of mysticism. The area became known for its powerful magic and its mysterious rocks. Rituals were developed as the communards attempted to establish their own traditions. Such processes are illustrated by the christening of Softly Sigh, nine months after his conception under the full moon of the Aquarius Festival. The christening took the form of a mystical and ritualistic procession from the White House to a valley on the property where the stream widened into a large pool.

Accompanying the division of labour and variations in lifestyles came increased internal conflict. Disputes occurred over the education of young children born in the Cooperative and eventually a minimal type of schooling was established. There was considerable tension between those who wanted to organise and get things done and those who just wanted to let things happen spontaneously. Antagonism grew between those members who spent their time in the cities promoting the Cooperative's ideals and selling shares and those who worked the land. It was easier to sell shares than to settle the land. External conflict also became problematic. Police raids in 1976 resulted in 42 arrests for drugs. The media was constantly seeking new stories. Local residents began to see their own lifestyle threatened with the growing impact of those seeking a different way of life. Visitors became such a problem that at one stage they were all asked to leave until a visitors' camping area was established. More recently, in September 1979, the conservation issue exploded with the Terania Creek rain forest logging dispute when communards lay in front of bulldozers and drove bolts into trees. This conflict has brought Cooperative members into the arena of business and politics — the very world they were trying to escape.

Such difficulties as these will continue to be solved by more centralised organisation, that is, with more rules and regulations. Now the Cooperative has established itself as a relatively secure and stable arrangement, it can be expected that any future problems will be solved by more, rather than fewer, formal procedures. The communion of the Aquarius Festival has been slowly routinised into both some traditions of community and some rational-legal relationships of society in this idyllic region of New South Wales.

The counter-culture began with young people reacting against their disillusion with bureaucratic authority, impersonality and capitalist greed. They went in search of the good life. Kanter is right when she remarks that the search was 'primarily a white middle-class utopian vision, pursued mostly by those unfulfilled by affluence who turn to their emotions for salvation' (1972: 226). But emotions are precarious and unstable and do not form a solid basis for a stable and long-term alternative lifestyle. Further, part of this search involved the attempt 'to find oneself', to establish one's own personal autonomy. This pursuit of personal autonomy fought against the desires of some for building viable alternative lifestyles and even a new society. As Cock found, 'when these people struck trouble in their alternative community ventures, their survival culture of providing for themselves took precedence over their involvement in the community. They took actions which in essence were merely an extension of individualistic capitalism' (1979: 136). This is part of the process described by Lasch (1980) in his analysis of 'the culture of narcissism'. Here the counter-culture is seen as an extreme example of 'the culture of competitive individualism':

> which in its decadence has carried the logic of individualism to the extreme of a war against all, the pursuit of happiness to the dead end of a narcissistic preoccupation with the self. Strategies of narcissistic survival now present themselves as emancipation from the repressive conditions of the past, thus giving rise to a 'cultural revolution' that reproduces the worst features of the collapsing civilisation it claims to criticise. (1980: xv)

Those who did succeed in establishing stable alternative lifestyles did so through organisation and in the process built up their own traditions and formulated their own systems of rules and regulations. In contradiction to the claims made for the counter-culture by those sociologists mentioned above, the movement has done little to change either Australian society or capitalism. As Kanter concludes, 'They may provide an intensely participatory group in which power is equitably shared, but they do not affect the power structure of the surrounding society' (1972: 225). In fact, they often become enmeshed in the localised political issues of the established order. Internally they may become totally cooperative but this does nothing to change the unequal allocation of, and access to, resources in Australian society. They may develop intense loving relationships in a small group, but this does not rid Australian society of conflict, racism, sexism, ageism and so forth. They contribute to, and affect, popular culture but not the political and economic structures. Even their contributions to popular culture were easily and quickly co-opted by consumer capitalism, especially in such areas as clothes, music, organic foods, therapy sessions and so forth. In other words, capitalism encompasses the movement and as Abrams' and McCulloch's (1976) study of British communes indicates, most tend either to disintegrate or become as authoritarian and as mystified as the societies from which they are trying to escape. Rather than creating a break with capitalism, as Connell (1977: 189) suggested, the history and structure of these movements emphasises the flexible and incorporating nature of capitalism.

The aim of many in the counter-culture to build a new society from the grass roots has not been, and is not likely to be realised. 'There are no answers in the experience of utopian communities of the past or present to the problem of building large and complex structures out of very small ones — especially when the small ones may need their distinctiveness and identity in order to survive' (Kanter, 1972: 229). An increase in scale brings an increase in complexity and more rules and regulations must be introduced to maintain some level of social stability and order. For the needs of large-scale administration and organisation some form of bureaucracy 'is completely indispensable' (Weber, 1947: 337) — hence the impossibility of creating a new society from the counter-culture.

According to Weber the growth of formal rationality through the increasing application of knowledge and the rules of logic to the economic process is accompanied by two other phenomena. First, there is the replacement of religious or mystical norms by abstract rational-legal imperatives. Second, there is increasing disenchantment with the world as impersonality spreads. But as religion, magic and mysticism are squeezed out, the main form of protest arising from disenchantment becomes utopian outbursts against the imperatives of rationalisation — these outbursts are often themselves of a mystical or religious nature. In other words, here is a movement from *society* emphasising the individual and rational-legal authority to *communion* centring on powerful emotional feelings and charismatic authority. Communion, however, is dynamic, unstable and unpredictable and soon becomes routinised into either *community* emphasising given or set ways of behaviour, and therefore, traditional authority, or *society* with its contractual relationships between individuals.

The tension-filled relationships between community, communion and society create complex processes of social change. This is a cyclical or spiral view of change where the differential interaction of the three provides a range of explanatory typologies. In these terms an ideal-typical summary of the argument presented is as follows: the increasing rational demands of society, emphasising impersonality, create reactions which centre on the emotional experience of communion and result in a drop-out movement into communes and mystical cults. As the division of labour develops and children are socialised the sentiments of communion are routinised into traditional patterns of settled community. As the community grows and creates more complex forms of social organisation, buys or sells more land, distributes its produce in the marketplace, takes part in political issues and loses its young generation through outward migration, the ties of rational-legal society take over, often in a more pervasive way than previously. Social change then can be conceived partly as developmental and partly as cyclical. Some social forms of antiquity form the basis for later developments, and therefore lie along a unique linear sequence. Others are repeated again, albeit at different levels of development.

9 Conclusion

In this book I attempt to draw together the major theoretical views on community and the empirical investigations of the anthropological style of community studies. I try to show how this relationship between theory and substantive data was mediated by the methodological pluralism characteristic of community research, especially emphasising the background of the projects and what the sociologists actually did during fieldwork. This discussion leads to several conclusions concerning the limitations and potentialities of community studies.

The traditional community study of a particular localised social system will continue to be researched and published first, because 'they present in an easily accessible and readable way descriptions and analyses of the very stuff of sociology, the social organisation of human beings' (Bell and Newby, 1971: 250). Second, because they provide a valuable methodological approach for the empirical investigation of a specific sociological problem within the confines of a locality. Third, because they offer perhaps unique opportunities for examining the impact of externally induced changes on the social structure of localised social systems. In each of these areas community studies can be improved upon by the better use of historical material, the wider application of different methods of gathering data, the detailed description of the 'natural history' of the project and, above all, by addressing themselves to more of the debates and issues that are central to sociology as a whole. Future community studies need to pay much closer attention to the complex, dynamic and tension-filled relationships between sociological theory and theorising, methods of data collection and the description and analysis of substantive data.

There are many things that community studies cannot and should not be expected to do. They are unable to provide a comprehensive picture of the class structure of a complex, advanced capitalist society but what they can do is show how such a class structure constrains people's behaviour and beliefs in specific social situations. Community studies cannot describe the status system of a nation but they can provide insights into how status is established, maintained and transformed in one, or several, localised parts of that nation. Community research can never determine whether or not a large-scale ruling class or power elite exists but it can describe the mechanisms through which power operates and how and why political decisions are made within the context of localised social systems. Indeed significant theoretical advances concerning power have been developed from the community studies tradition (see Bachrach and Baratz, 1970; Lukes, 1974). Community studies have a potential to contribute even more than they have so far to sociology by relating their projects and their findings to the core theoretical issues of the subject, especially those concerning such matters as class, capitalism, rationality, bureaucracy and power. But at the same time the limitations imposed by the localised context must be recognised. This is both the strength and the weakness of community studies.

If traditional community studies are restricted in the generalisability of their findings because of their orientation to the localised social system—the sociology of community is not constrained in the same way. The concept of community where locality is not necessarily a central element, as in the models of community formation and closure and community, communion and society, allows the community sociologist to pursue interesting sociological problems across a broader canvas than does the localised social system. The discussions of resident action politics, Italian immigrants and communes in Chapter 8 all indicate how such models of community enable the sociologist to investigate areas of central concern to sociology as a whole, free from the restrictions of a specific locality. The distribution of power between government and residents, the relationship of immigration to the desire to belong and the demands of rationality and the expressions of community in the counter-culture movement all tell us something about broad social structures and processes that are affecting society as a whole and their relationship to community. In this way the concept of community is brought back towards the centre of the sociological stage.

A further area of potential development for community studies is in comparative analysis. Those few examples available of this difficult task have all created new insights and contributed to the specification of new concepts and models which in turn are available for empirical application in later studies. With more theoretically directed studies becoming available comparative community analysis may well become a most fruitful exercise.

Community studies has a solid future. The more traditional type of studies of localised social systems will become more theoretically relevant to the central issues of the subject nevertheless, the best will always present a balance between community as object and community as method. The true community sociologist must first be able to describe, understand and analyse the community under observation, and second, establish generalisations from the basis of the interrelationship between empirical data and theoretical propositions. Pure method studies will increase but become narrower as their problems for investigation come from increasingly specialised sections of sociology. Models of community will be further refined which will continue to bring the concept back to its rightful place in sociological theory along with such others as power and class. With such developments comparative analysis will become relatively easier and richer. The time has come, indeed it is long overdue, for community sociologists to tackle some of the big theoretical questions of sociology using their undoubted expertise in fieldwork and data gathering. To do this successfully community sociologists must move outside their specialties and engage themselves in wider theoretical debate. This in itself would be a valuable move against the increasing tendency towards fragmentation and theoretical and methodological exclusivism in sociology. It would also make community studies more theoretically relevant, for as Elias concludes:

> The significance of community research as a sociological speciality is not impaired—it is rather enhanced if one becomes aware that communities cannot be adequately studied as isolated units and that this type of enquiry, in order to be fully productive, needs to take into account the structure of the wider social field and its changes. The structure of the wider social field in turn is illuminated . . . through the study of communities. (1974: xxxix)

Bibliography

Abrams, P. and McCulloch, A. (1976): *Communes, Sociology and Society*, Cambridge University Press, Cambridge.

Albrow, M. (1970): *Bureaucracy*, Macmillan, London.

Altman, D. (1977): 'The Counter-Culture: Nostalgia or Prophesy', in A.F. Davies, and S. Encel, (eds): *Australian Society*, 3rd edn, edn, Cheshire, Melbourne.

Andreski, S. (1971): *Herbert Spencer*, Nelson, London.

Arensberg, K. and Kimball, S. (1940): *Family and Community in Ireland*, Harvard University Press, Cambridge, Mass. (2nd edn, 1968).

Arensberg, K. and Kimball, S. (1967): *Community and Culture*, Harcourt Brace and World, New York.

Avila, M. (1969): *Tradition and Growth*, Chicago University Press, Chicago.

Bachrach, P. and Baratz, M.S. (1970): *Power and Poverty: Theory and Practice*, Oxford University Press, New York.

Baldamus, W. (1972): 'The Role of Discoveries in Social Science', in T. Shanin, (ed): *The Rules of the Game*, Tavistock, London.

Baldamus, W. (1976): *The Structure of Sociological Inference*, Martin Robertson, London.

Barnes, J. (1954): 'Class and Committees in a Norwegian Island Parish', *Human Relations*, Vol. 7, No. 1.

Barnes, J. (1970): 'Some Ethical Problems in Modern Fieldwork', in W.J. Filstead, (ed): *Qualitative Methodology*, Markham, Chicago.

Barnes, J. (1968): 'Networks and Political Process', in M. Swartz (ed): *Local-Level Politics*, Aldine, Chicago.

Barnes, J. (1979): *Who Should Know What?* Penguin, London.

Becker, H. (1964): 'Problems in the Publication of Field Studies', in A. Vidich, *et al.* (eds) *Reflections on Community Studies*, Wiley, New York.

Becker, H. (1970): 'Problems of Inference and Proof in Participant

Observation' in W.J. Filstead, (ed.), *Qualitative Methodology*, Markham, Chicago.

Becker, H. and Greer, B. (1970): 'Participant Observation and Interviewing: A Comparison', in W.J. Filstead, (ed) *Qualitative Methodology*, Markham, Chicago.

Bell, C. (1969): 'A Note on Participant Observation', *Sociology*, 3, 417–8.

Bell, C. (1977): 'Reflections on the Banbury Restudy', in C. Bell, and H. Newby, (eds): *Doing Sociological Research*, Allen and Unwin, London.

Bell, C. and Encel, S. (eds) (1978): *Inside the Whale: Ten Personal Accounts of Social Research*, Pergamon Press, Sydney.

Bell, C. and Newby, H. (1971): *Community Studies*, Allen and Unwin, London.

Bell, C. and Newby, H. (1976a): 'Community, Communion, Class and Community Action', in D. Herbert and R. Johnson, (eds): *Social Areas in Cities*, Wiley, London.

Bell, C. and Newby, H. (1976b): 'Community Power in Rural Areas'. Unpublished paper delivered at the 47th ANZAAS conference, Hobart, May.

Bell, C. and Newby H. (1977): *Doing Sociological Research*, Allen and Unwin, London.

Bendix, R. (1960): *Max Weber*, Doubleday Anchor, New York.

Berger, B. (1960): *Working Class Suburb*, University of California Press, Los Angeles.

Bott, E. (1957): *Family and Social Network*, Tavistock, London.

Bottomore, I.B. (1975): *Marxist Sociology*, Macmillan, London.

Bradshaw, A. (1976): 'Debate with Lukes', *Sociology*, 10, 121–32.

Brennan, T. (1973): *New Community*, Angus and Robertson, Sydney.

Brown, R. (1963): *Explanation in Social Science*, Routledge and Kegan Paul, London.

Bryson, L. and Thompson, F. (1972): *An Australian Newtown*, Penguin, Ringwood.

Bryson, L. and Thompson, F. (1978): 'Reflections on an Australian Newtown' in C. Bell, and S. Encel, (eds): *Inside the Whale*, Pergamon Press, Sydney.

Castells, M. (1976): 'Is there an Urban Sociology?', in C.G. Pickvance, (ed) *Urban Sociology: Critical Essays*, Tavistock, London.

Chinoy, E. (1950): 'Research in Class Structure', *Canadian Journal of Economics and Political Science*, 16, 259—60.

Cock, P. (1979): *Alternative Australia: Communities for the Future?'* Quartet Books, Melbourne.

Collins, J. (1975): 'The Political Economy of Post-War Immigration', in E.L. Wheelwright, and K. Buckley, (eds): *Essays in the Political Economy of Australian Capitalism*, Vol. 1, Australia and New Zealand Book Company, Sydney.

Connell, R.W., (1977): *Ruling Class, Ruling Culture*, Cambridge University Press, Cambridge.

Crenson, M. (1971): *The Unpolitics of Air Pollution*, John Hopkins University Press, Baltimore.

Dahrendorf, R. (1968): 'On the Origin of Inequality Among Men', in Dahrendorf, R. *Essays in the Theory of Society*, Stanford University Press, Stanford.

Duncan, O.D. (1957): 'Community Size and the Rural-Urban Continuum', in P.K. Hatt, and A.J. Reiss, (eds) *Cities and Society*, Free Press, Glencoe.

Durkheim, E. (1960): *The Division of Labour in Society*, Free Press, Glencoe.

Elias, N. (1974): 'Towards a Theory of Communities', Foreword to C. Bell, and H. Newby, *The Sociology of Community*, Cass, London.

Erickson, K. (1970): 'A Comment on Disguised Observation in Sociology', in W.J. Filstead, (ed): *Qualitative Methodology*, Markham, Chicago.

Frankenberg, R. (1957): *Village on the Border*, Cohen and West, London.

Frankenberg, R. (1966): *Communities in Britain*, Penguin, London.

Frankenberg, R. (1976): 'In the Production of their Lives, Men (?) ... Sex and Gender in British Community Studies', in D. Barker, and S. Allen, (eds) *Sexual Divisions and Society*, Tavistock, London.

Gans, H. (1962): *The Urban Villagers*, Free Press, New York.

Gans, H. (1967): *The Levittowners*, Allen Lane, London.

Gans, H. (1968): 'Urbanism and Suburbanism as Ways of Life', in R.E. Pahl, (ed): *Readings in Urban Sociology*, Pergamon Press, Oxford.

Garfinkel, H. (1967): *Studies in Ethnomethodology*, Prentice Hall, Englewood Cliffs, N.J.

Geertz, C. (1965): *The Social History of an Indonesian Town*, MIT Press, Cambridge, Mass.

Giddens, A. (1971): *Capitalism and Modern Social Theory*, Cambridge University Press, Cambridge.

Giddens, A. (1973): *The Class Structure of the Advanced Societies*, Hutchinson, London.

Giddens, A. (1974): *Positivism and Sociology*, Heinemann, London.

Gillen, K. (n.d.): 'Gossip Networks in the Rocks Area of Sydney', an unpublished paper read in the Department of Anthropology, University of Sydney.

Ginsberg, M. (1934): *Sociology*, Butterworth, London.

Glass, R. (1966): 'Conflict in Cities', in R. Glass, (ed), *Conflict in Society*, Churchill, London.

Goldthorpe, J. Lockwood, D., Bechhofer, F. and Platt J. (1969): *The Affluent Worker in the Class Structure*, Cambridge University Press, Cambridge.

Gouldner, A. (1976): *Enter Plato*, Routledge and Kegan Paul, London.

Gouldner, A. (1980): *The Two Marxisms: Contradictions and Anomalies in the Development of Theory*, Macmillan, New York.

Gusfield, J.R. (1975): *Community: a Critical Response*, Blackwell, Oxford.

Hammond, P. (ed) (1964): *Sociologists at Work*, Basic Books, New York.

Handlin, O. (1942): 'Review of the Social Life of a Modern Community', *New England Quarterly*, 15, 555—6.

Hargreaves, K. (n.d.): *This House not for Sale*, Centre for Urban Research and Action, Melbourne.

Havinghurst, R.J. and Jansen, A.J. (1965): 'Community Research', *Current Sociology*, 15, 2.

Henderson, R.F. (1975): *First Main Report of the Australian Government Commission of Inquiry in Poverty*, Vol. 1, Australian Government Printing Service, Canberra.

Hillery, G.A. (1955): 'Definitions of Community; Areas of Agreement', *Rural Sociology*, 20.

Hillery, G.A. (1963): 'Villages, Cities and Total Institutions' *American Sociological Review*, 28.

Hillery, G.A. (1968): *Communal Organisations*, Chicago University Press, Chicago.

Houriet, R. (1973): *Getting Back Together*, Abacus Books, London.

Huber, R. (1977): *From Pasta to Pavlova*, Queensland University Press, St. Lucia.

Jupp, J. (1966): *Arrivals and Departures*, Cheshire-Lansdowne, Melbourne.

Kanter, R. (1972): *Commitment and Community*, Harvard University Press, Cambridge.

Kilmartin, L. and Thorns, D. (1978): *Cities Unlimited*, Allen and Unwin, Sydney.

Kreigler, R. (1980): *Working for the Company*, Oxford University Press, Melbourne.

Lasch, C. (1980): *The Culture of Narcissism*, Abacus Books, London.

Lewis, O. (1951): *Life in a Mexican Village: Tepoztlan Restudied*, University of Illinois Press, Urbana.

Lewis, O. (1953): 'Controls and Experiments in Fieldwork', in A.L. Kroeber *et al.* (eds), *Anthropology Today*, Chicago University Press, Chicago.

Lewis, O. (1964): *Children of Sanchez*, Penguin, London.

Lindblad, J. (1976): 'Where the Drop-outs are', *The Bulletin*, 27 March and 3 April.

Lipset, S. and Bendix, R. (1951): 'Social Status and Social Structure', *British Journal of Sociology*, 2, 241–44.

Littlejohn, J. (1963): *Westrigg: The Sociology of a Cheviot Parish*, Routledge and Kegan Paul, London.

Loveday, P. (1972): 'Citizen Participation and Urban Planning', in R.S. Parker, and P.M. Troy, (eds) *The Politics of Urban Growth*, Australian National University Press, Canberra.

Lukes, S. (1974): *Power: A Radical View*, Macmillan, London.

Lupri, E. (1975): 'Industrialisierung and Strukturwandlugen in der Familie: Ein interkultureller Vergleich', *Sociologia Ruralis* 5, 1.

Lupri, E. (1968): 'Introduction to the Discussion on the Rural-Urban Continuum', in R.E. Pahl, (ed): *Readings in Urban Sociology*, Pergamon Press, Oxford.

Lynd, R. and Lynd, H. (1929): *Middletown*, Harcourt Brace, New York.

Lynd, R. and Lynd, H. (1937): *Middletown in Transition*, Harcourt Brace, New York.

McGee, T.G. (1971): *The Urbanisation Process in the Third World*, Bell and Sons, London.

McPhail, I. (1978): 'Local Government', in P.N. Troy, (ed), *Federal Power in Australian Cities*, Hale and Iremonger, Sydney.

Maine, H. (1861): *Ancient Law*, London.

Mallet, S. (1963): *La Nouvelle Classe Ouvrière*, Paris editions du Seuil, Paris.

Martin, J.I. (1970): 'Suburbia: Community and Network', in A.F. Davies, and S. Encel, (eds): *Australian Society*, 2nd edn, Cheshire, Melbourne.

Martin, J.I. (1972): *Community and Identity: Refugee Groups in Adelaide*, Australian National University Press, Canberra.

Martindale, D. (1958): 'Introduction', in M. Weber, *The City*, Free Press, New York.

Martindale, D. (1964): 'The Formation and Destruction of Communities', in G.K. Zollschan, and W. Hirsch, (eds): *Explorations in Social Change*, Routledge and Kegan Paul, London.

Marx, K. and Engels, F. (1965): *The German Ideology*, London.

Merton, R.K. (1942): 'Review of Social Life of a Modern Community', *Survey Graphic*, 31, 438.

Mills, C.W. (1942): 'Review of the Social Life of a Modern Community', *American Sociological Review*, 7, 264–5.

Mills, C.W. (1963): 'The Social Life of a Modern Community' in I. Horowitz, (ed): *Power, Politics and People*, Oxford University Press, New York.

Mitchell, J.C. (ed) (1969): *Social Networks in Urban Situations*, Manchester University Press, Manchester.

Mommsen, W.J. (1959): *Max Weber und die deutsche Politik, 1890 –1920*, J.C.B. Mohr, Tubingen.

Mullins, P. (1977): 'The Social Base, Stake and Urban Effects of a Brisbane Urban Social Movement' *Australia and New Zealand Journal of Sociology*, 13, 1, 29–35.

Neuwirth, G. (1969): 'A Weberian Outline of a Theory of Community', *British Journal of Sociology*, 20, 2, 148–63.

Newby, H. (1977): *The Deferential Worker*, Allen Lane, London.

Newby, H. (1980): 'Rural Sociology', *Current Sociology*, 28, 1.

Newby, H., Bell, C., Rose, D. & Saunders, P. 1978, *Property, Paternalism and Power*, Hutchinson, London.

Nisbet, R. (1966): *The Sociological Tradition*, Heinemann, London.

Oeser, O.A. and Emery, F. (1954): *Social Structure and Personality in a Rural Community*, Routledge and Kegan Paul, London.

Ossowski, S. (1963): *Class Structure in the Social Consciousness*, Routledge and Kegan Paul, London.

Oxley, H.G. (1973): *Mateship in Local Organisation*, Queensland University Press, St. Lucia (Revised edition 1978).

Pahl, R.E. (1968): 'The Rural-Urban Continuum', in R.E. Pahl, (ed): *Readings in Urban Sociology*, Pergamon Press, Oxford.

Pahl, R.E. (1975): 'Review of Power, Persistence and Change', *New Society*, 20 March, 1975.

Parker, R.S. (1978): *Government of New South Wales*, University of Queensland Press, St. Lucia.

Parkin, F. (1974): 'Strategies of Social Closure in Class Formation', in F. Parkin, (ed): *The Social Analysis of Class Structure*, Tavistock, London.

Parsons, T. (1959): 'The Principal Structures of Community', in C.J. Friedrich, (ed): *Community*, Liberal Arts Press, New York.

Pearson, D. (1980): *Johnsonville: Continuity and Change in a New Zealand Township*, Allen and Unwin, Sydney.

Pfautz, H.W. and Duncan, O.D. (1950): 'A Critical Evaluation of Warner's Work in Stratification', *American Sociological Review*, 15, 210–11.

Pickvance, C.G. (ed) (1976): *Urban Sociology: Critical Essays*, Tavistock, London.

Plowman, D., Minchinton, W. and Stacey, M. (1962): 'Local Social Status in England and Wales', *Sociological Review*, 10, 2.

Redfield, R. (1941): *The Folk Culture of Yucatan*, Chicago University Press, Chicago.

Redfield, R. (1947): 'The Folk Society', *American Journal of Sociology*, 52, 3, 293–308.

Rees, A. (1950): *Life in the Welsh Countryside*, University of Wales Press, Cardiff.

Rees, A. (1973): *Celtic Heritage: ancient tradition in Ireland and Wales*, Thames and Hudson, London.

Reilly, K. (1978): 'Foreword', in R. Roddewig, *Green Bans*, Hale and Iremonger, Sydney, 1978.

Rex, J. (1978): 'Threatening Theories', *Transaction*, March/April, 1978, 46–9.

Richmond, A.H. (1969): 'Sociology of migration in industrial and post-industrial societies', in J.A. Jackson, (ed): *Migration*, Cambridge University Press, Cambridge.

Riesman, D. (1957): 'The Suburban Dislocation', *The Annals*, 314, Fall, 123–46. Reprinted in D. Riesman, *Abundance For What?*, Doubleday, New York.

Rigby, A. (1974): *Communes in Britain*, Routledge and Kegan Paul, London.

Roddewig, R. (1978): *Green Bans*, Hale and Iremonger, Sydney.

Roth, J. (1970): 'Comments on Secret Observation', in W.J. Filstead, (ed): *Qualitative Methodology*, Markham, Chicago.

Runciman, W.G. (1966): *Relative Deprivation and Social Justice*, Routledge and Kegan Paul, London.

Sandercock, L. (1976): *Cities for Sale*, Melbourne University Press, Melbourne.

Sandercock, L. (1978): 'Citizen Participation: the New Conservatism', in P.N. Troy, (ed): *Federal Power in Australia's Cities*, Hale and Iremonger, Sydney.

Schmalenbach, H. (1961): 'The Sociological Category of Communion', in T. Parsons, (ed): *Theories of Society*, Free Press, New York, Vol. 1.

Schnore, L.F. (1966): 'The Rural-Urban Variable', *Rural Sociology*, 31.

Schnore, L.F. (1967): 'Community', in N. Smelser, (ed): *Sociology*, Wiley, New York.

Schutz, A. (1967): *The Phenomenology of the Social World*, Northwestern University Press, Evanston, Illinois.

Simmel, G. (1964): *The Sociology of Georg Simmel*, Free Press, New York.

Simpson, R.L. (1965): 'Sociology of the Community: Current Status and Prospects', *Rural Sociology*, 30, 3, 127–49.

Spectorsky, A. (1955): *The Exurbanites*, Lippincott, Philadelphia.

Spencer, H. (1896): *The Principles of Sociology*, London.

Stacey, M. (1960): *Tradition and Change: a Study of Banbury*, Oxford University Press, Oxford.

Stacey, M. (1969): 'The Myth of Community Studies', *British Journal of Sociology*, 20, 2, 134—47.

Stacey, M., Batsone, E., Bell, C. and Mucott, A. (1975): *Power, Persistence and Change: a Second Study of Banbury*, Routledge and Kegan Paul, London.

Stein, M. (1964): *The Eclipse of Community*, Harper Torch, New York.

Thernstrom, S. (1964): *Poverty and Progress: Social Mobility in a Nineteenth Century City*, Harvard University Press, Cambridge, Mass.

Thomas, P. (1973): *Taming the Concrete Jungle*, Builders Labourers Federation, Sydney.

Thompson, E.P. (1978): *The Poverty of Theory*, Merlin Press, London.

Thompson, F. (1971): 'Suburban Living and the Concept of Community', *Australian and New Zealand Journal of Sociology*, 7, 2, October.

Thompson, S.L. (1980): *Australia Through Italian Eyes*, Oxford University Press, Melbourne.

Tonnies, F. (1957): *Community and Association*, Routledge and Kegan Paul, London.

Turner, I. (1978): 'The Bastards from the Bush' in E.L. Wheelwright, and K. Buckley, (eds): *Essays in the Political Economy of Australian Capitalism*, Vol. 3, Australia and New Zealand Book Company, Sydney.

Turner, R. (ed) (1974): *Ethnomethodology*, Penguin, London.

Vidich, A.J. (1970): 'Participant Observation and the Collection and Interpretation of Data', in W.J. Filstead, (ed): *Qualitative Methodology*, Markham, Chicago.

Vidich, A.J. and Bensman, J. (1958): 'Comment on Freedom and Responsibility in Research', *Human Organisation*, 17.

Vidich, A.J. and Bensman, J. (1960): *Small Town in Mass Society*, Doubleday Anchor, New York.

Vidich, A.J. and Bensman, J. (1964): 'The Springdale Case', in A.J. Vidich, *et al.* (eds): *Reflections on Community Studies*, Wiley, New York.

Vidich, A. Bensman, J. and Stein, M. (eds) (1964): *Reflections on Community Studies*, Wiley, New York.

Walker, A. (1945): *Coaltown: A Social Survey of Cessnock*, Melbourne University Press, Melbourne.

Warner, W.L. (1941): *The Social Life of a Modern Community*, Yale University Press, New Haven.

Warner, W.L. (1952): *Structure of American Life*, Edinburgh University Press, Edinburgh.

Warren, R.L. (1963): *The Community in America*, Rand McNally, Chicago.

Weber, M. (1964): *Grundriss der Sozialokonomik*, 1 Abeilung, Tubingen.

Weber, M. (1947): *The Theory of Social and Economic Organisation*, Free Press, New York.

Weber, M. (1948): *From Max Weber*, C.W. Mills and H.H. Gerth (eds), Routledge and Kegan Paul, London.

Weber, M. (1968): *Economy and Society*, Roth, G. and Wittich, G. (eds), Bedminster Press, New York.

Whyte, W.F. (1955): *Street Corner Society*, Revised edition, University of Chicago Press, Chicago.

Wild, R.A. (1972): 'Class and Community', *Nation*, 13 May, 22–3.

Wild, R.A. (1973): 'The Problems of Neighbourhood' in E. Hipsley, (ed), *Family Health*, Inger Rice Foundation, Canberra.

Wild, R.A. (1974): *Bradstow: A study of Status, Class and Power in a Small Australian Town*, Angus and Robertson, Sydney. (Revised edition 1978.)

Wild, R.A. (1976): 'A Treatise on Trees', Australian Quarterly, December, 102–12.

Wild, R.A. (1978a): *Social Stratification in Australia*, Allen and Unwin, Sydney.

Wild, R.A. (1978b): 'The Background to Bradstow: Reflections and Reactions' in C. Bell, and S. Encel, (eds): *Inside the Whale*, Pergamon Press, Sydney.

Wild, R.A. (1979a): 'Politics at the Grass Roots' in *Future Questions in Australian Politics*, Meredith Memorial Lectures, La Trobe University, 1979.

Wild, R.A. (1979b): 'Community: Locality, Tradition or Sentiment?', *Inaugural Lecture*, La Trobe University, 1979.

Williams, R. (1976): *Keywords*, Fontana, London.

Williams, W.M. (1956): *The Sociology of an English Village: Gosforth*, Routledge and Kegan Paul, London.

Willmott, P. and Young, M. (1957): *Family and Kinship in East London*, Routledge and Kegan Paul, London.

Willmott, P. and Young, M. (1960): *Family and Class in a London Suburb*, Routledge and Kegan Paul, London.

Winkelmann, J. (1952): *Legitimität und Legalität in Max Weber's Herrschaftssoziologie*, J.C.B. Mohr, Tubingen.

Zubrzycki, J. (1960): *Immigrants in Australia*, Melbourne Unversity Press, Melbourne.

Subject Index

Author Index

QUEEN MARY
COLLEGE
LIBRARY

WITHDRAWN
FROM STOCK
QMUL LIBRARY